WOMEN PLAYWRIGHTS

The Best Plays
of 2000

SMITH AND KRAUS PUBLISHERS
Contemporary Playwrights / Full-Length Play Anthologies

Humana Festival '93: The Complete Plays

Humana Festival '94: The Complete Plays

Humana Festival '95: The Complete Plays

Humana Festival '96: The Complete Plays

Humana Festival '97: The Complete Plays

Humana Festival '98: The Complete Plays

Humana Festival '99: The Complete Plays

Humana Festival 2000: The Complete Plays

Humana Festival 2001: The Complete Plays

Humana Festival: 20 One-Acts Plays 1976–1996

New Dramatists 2000: The Best Plays by the Graduating Class

New Dramatists 2001: The Best Plays by the Graduating Class

New Playwrights: The Best Plays of 1998

New Playwrights: The Best Plays of 1999

New Playwrights: The Best Plays of 2000

Women Playwrights: The Best Plays of 1992

Women Playwrights: The Best Plays of 1993

Women Playwrights: The Best Plays of 1994

Women Playwrights: The Best Plays of 1995

Women Playwrights: The Best Plays of 1996

Women Playwrights: The Best Plays of 1997

Women Playwrights: The Best Plays of 1998

Women Playwrights: The Best Plays of 1999

If you require prepublication information about forthcoming Smith and Kraus books, you may receive our semiannual catalogue, free of charge, by sending your name and address to *Smith and Kraus Catalogue, PO Box 127, Lyme, NH 03768.* Or call us at (800) 895-4331, fax (603) 643-1831. www.SmithKraus.com.

WOMEN PLAYWRIGHTS

The Best Plays of 2000

Edited by D.L. Lepidus

CONTEMPORARY PLAYWRIGHTS
SERIES

SK
A Smith and Kraus Book

A Smith and Kraus Book
Published by Smith and Kraus, Inc.
177 Lyme Road, Hanover, NH 03755
www.SmithKraus.com

CAUTION: Professionals and amateurs are hereby warned that the plays represented in this book are subject to a royalty. They are fully protected under the copyright laws of the United States of America, and of all countries covered by the International Copyright Union (including the Dominion of Canada and the rest of the British Commonwealth), and of all countries covered by the Pan-American Copyright Convention and the Universal Copyright Convention, and of all countries with which the United States has reciprocal copyright relations. All rights, including professional, amateur, motion picture, recitation, lecturing, public reading, radio broadcasting, television, video or sound taping, all other forms of mechanical or electronic reproductions such as CD-ROM and CD-I, information storage and retrieval systems and photocopying, and the rights of translation into foreign languages, are strictly reserved. Particular emphasis is laid upon the question of public readings, permission for which must be secured from each author's agent. For information concerning rights, refer to information on play title pages.

First Edition: November 2002
10 9 8 7 6 5 4 3 2 1
Manufactured in the United States of America

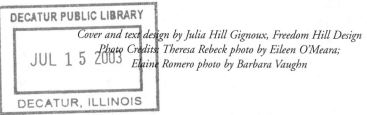

Cover and text design by Julia Hill Gignoux, Freedom Hill Design
Photo Credits: Theresa Rebeck photo by Eileen O'Meara;
Elaine Romero photo by Barbara Vaughn

The Library of Congress Cataloging-In-Publication Data
Women playwrights : the best plays of 2000 / edited by D.L. Lepidus
p. cm. — (Contemporary playwrights series)
ISBN 1-57525-248-1
1. American drama—women authors. 2. American drama—20th century. 3. Women—drama.
I. Smith, Marisa. II. Series: Contemporary playwrights series.
PS628.W6W668   1994
812'.540809287—dc20
94-10071
CIP

CONTENTS

FOREWORD

When I started going to the theater in New York, covering plays on behalf of newspapers, publishers, and so forth, there weren't a lot of plays by women being produced. Consequently, there weren't many successful female playwrights. Why write for a theater that doesn't want you? All that started to change by the late 1970s, with the arrival on the scene of the likes of Tina Howe, Wendy Wasserstein, Marsha Norman, and Shirley Lauro, and with the inception of Julia Miles' inestimably valuable Women's Project. I am told that in the last few years the number of produced plays by women has declined in relation to plays by men. If this is true, this may only be some sort of temporary bump in the road, because some of the best American playwrights happen to be female.

So, then the question becomes, "What do you mean by *best?*" We've used that adjective in the title of this anthology, after all. Has there been some quantitative/qualitative search going on for what may — by anybody's standards — be considered the "best" plays? Of course not. The plays in this book are, in fact, my favorites among the hundreds of plays I saw or read, which had a production in 2000, to which Smith and Kraus were able to get publishing rights. Play selection, whether for production or, in this case, publication is — let's face it — completely subjective, sort of like judging Olympic figure skating.

I have chosen the plays in this book because I think they represent well the incredible quality and variety of new playwriting by women. Some of the playwrights herein have been produced in New York City, some not. Are the New York City plays, such as *Landlocked* (Off Off Broadway) and *The Butterfly Collection* (Off Broadway) better plays than, say, *Full Bloom* or *¡Curanderas! Serpents of the Clouds?* Who's to say?

Allow me to honestly define what we in truth mean by *good,* in relation to plays, novels, movies, and so on. A play is *good* to the degree that it is useful and informative to *me* (or *you*), to the degree that it effectively portrays some aspect of our world of interest to *us*.

In my informed yet humble opinion, the plays in this book are *damn* good, worthy of publication by Smith and Kraus but even more importantly, worthy of your time, those of you who care about enjoying and indeed nurturing the abundant garden that is the American theater.

D. L. Lepidus

INTRODUCTION

Writers over the ages, regardless of gender, have written of what they know and what they imagine. Being human, they write of the human condition. In the tenth century, Hrotswitha of Gandersheim, arguably the first European and first female dramatist after the decline of the Roman Empire, wrote of passion and repentance. Since then, women and men have written plays on every topic imaginable. We continue to enjoy plays of passion and repentance as well as plays of loss, discovery, friendship, and the struggle for identity, such as those in this volume.

These plays tell the stories that help us understand what it is to be human and to live in our society. Our humanity destines us to have much in common, but because society's view of women differs from that of men, women and men also experience society in ways that are unique to their gender. This variety of experience not only inspires the stories writers tell but shapes the very structure and language of their plays. To seek honestly, the fullest understanding of what it is to be human in our society, we must embrace the stories of women and men. Listening to the stories of both enriches our understanding of life and inspires our imaginations as well.

While the general population is nearly balanced between women and men, the stories told by women playwrights make up 16 percent of the plays presented on American stages today. The excuses for this imbalance are myriad and often boil down to a perceived lack of good plays by women and to audience disinterest. Not only is this insulting to all of us as audience members, but it reflects a simple ignorance of the vibrant works of women playwrights. As the literary manager at Women's Project and Productions, I read hundreds of plays each year by women playwrights, of which many are ready or nearly ready for production. The Women's Project and other theater organizations around the country work with talented women playwrights on daily basis and are excellent sources of information about the wide array of plays by women, striving to be part of the solution to the current inequity.

In these pages are great stories by seven of today's many talented women playwrights. They are the tip of the iceberg of contemporary women's writing. Read them, enjoy them, share them, produce them: Just as our society's gender composition is balanced between women and men, so must society's narrative be balanced between stories by women and men.

Great stories speak to all of us because they are great stories. Celebrate the variety of excellent stories that contribute to our understanding of ourselves as humans and as a society. I hope they inspire you as they have me.

Karen Keagle
Literary Manager,
Women's Project and Productions

Full Bloom

By Suzanne Bradbeer

To my parents Clive and Wilma Bradbeer,
who always encouraged me to do what I love,
and who every now and then slipped me a few bucks
when I needed it most.

And to the New Harmony Project.

PRODUCTION INFORMATION

Workshopped at the New Harmony Project
New Harmony, Indiana

Under the leadership of:
ARTISTIC DIRECTOR: James Houghton
EXECUTIVE DIRECTOR: Jeffrey Sparks
CREATIVE TEAM: JV Mercanti, Janet Allen, Joseph Rosswog, Kelli Giddish, Jan Lucas, Judith Hawking, Tim Grimm and Dave Briggs.

World Premiere (July 2000)
Barrington Stage Company

ARTISTIC DIRECTOR: Julianne Boyd
DIRECTOR: Mary B. Robinson
SET DESIGN: Sarah Lambert
SOUND: Bruce Ellman
LIGHTING: Victor En Yu Tan
COSTUMES: Mattie Ullrich
PRODUCTION STAGE MANAGER: Renee Lutz

CAST:
PHOEBE HARRIS. . . . . Kelli Giddish
JANE HARRIS . . . . Christine Farrell
CRYSTAL DAWN. . . . . Gordana Rashovich
JIM GIANNINI . . . . Gerard O'Brien
JESSE WILLIAMS . . . . Michael Benjamin Washington

Already deep in pre-production during the Barrington run was
Hudson Stage Company

PRODUCERS: Dan Foster, Olivia Sklar and Denise Bessette
DIRECTOR: Dan Foster
SET DESIGN: Victor Whitehurst
LIGHTING: Andrew Gmoser
COSTUMES: Myra Oney
ORIGINAL MUSIC: Sid Cherry
PRODUCTION STAGE MANAGER: Ann Revelt

CAST:

PHOEBE HARRIS . . . . Christina Lynne Smith
JANE HARRIS . . . . Denise Bessette
CRYSTAL DAWN . . . . Catherine Campbell
JIM GIANNINI . . . . Christopher Innvar
JESSE WILLIAMS . . . . Gregory Marlow

ABOUT THE AUTHOR

Full Bloom was workshopped at the New Harmony Project and had its world premiere at Barrington Stage Company in Great Barrington, MA (Summer 2000). This was quickly followed by productions at Hudson Stage Co., Westchester; Main Street Theater in Houston; Bloomington Playwrights Project in Bloomington, IN as well as readings by the Women's Project, New York City, the BoarsHead Theater in Lansing, MI and Dreamcatcher Repertory in Bloomfield, NJ. *Full Bloom* won first prize at the Dayton Playhouse FutureFest, received an honorable mention from the Jane Chambers Award, was a finalist for the 2000 Humana Festival at Actors Theater of Louisville, KY and was named Best New Play of the 2000 season by Jeffrey Borak of the *Berkshire Eagle*.

Suzanne's first play, *Will o' the Wisp*, was produced in New York by Six Figures Theater Company. Six Figures also produced her plays *Lone Star Grace* and *Rita Faye Pruitte*. *Lone Star Grace* was just produced at the Stamford Center for the Arts Fringe Festival. Suzanne collaborated with Linda Ames Key and area high school students on *Fringe High* for the 1999 New York International Fringe Festival. One-acts *Bethlehem* and *McIntyre's* produced at Vital Theatre Co., and The Drilling Company, respectively.

As a dramaturg, Suzanne had the enormous privilege of working with Jim Houghton and Arthur Miller on Signature Theater Company's production of *The American Clock*. Suzanne is a member of the Dramatists Guild and the Playwright's Unit at EST. She is a writer/member of Six Figures Theater Company and the Blue Collar Theater Co., and is a recipient of playwriting fellowships from the New York Foundation for the Arts and the Berrilla Kerr Foundation. Suzanne is a graduate of Augustana College.

INTRODUCTORY STATEMENT

I think the play speaks for itself; I hope so anyway because I'm always kind of unsatisfied with my own comments on it. Let me just say that a large part of the impulse for writing *Full Bloom* was my observations and experiences living in a culture that too often seems to value form over substance, and I wondered and wanted to explore in dramatic form how this might affect a young girl who is coming of age — with all the hope and confusion, potential and impressionability that that implies.

CHARACTERS
PHOEBE HARRIS: 16 years old
JANE HARRIS: Her mother, late 40s
CRYSTAL DAWN: Their friend and neighbor, an actress. Originally from
    Texas; early 40s
JIM GIANNINI: Crystal's husband. A fireman, early 40s
JESSE WILLIAMS: Just moved to New York from Minnesota. African-
    American; 16

TIME AND PLACE
Early September 1999, beginning of the school year. In and around the Harris'
West Village Brownstone, New York City.

PRODUCTION NOTES
Some things to keep in mind, perhaps obvious, but I have found them worth
saying: Phoebe may seem deceptively casual at times — she is not. She should
charm us into listening, but her journey gets dark; please craft with care. Crystal is funny and her humor is a vital engine to the piece. Jane loves her daughter. Also the production should be fluid, it should move; try not to get bogged
down in the transitions between the monologues and scenes.

If this play is enjoying a nice life, it is in large part due to some wonderful people who have been its champions. These are my knights: Mark St.
Germain, Julianne Boyd, Cass Morgan, Sloane Shelton, Janet Blake, Jeffrey
Borak, Mary Robinson, Denise Bessette, and Theresa Rebeck. Also: Gay Isaacs,
the dear friend and wonderful actress who first brought Crystal so vibrantly
to life; Rob Skolits, who was willing to hear countless versions, some sections
over and over and over . . .; Jim Houghton for bringing me to New Harmony
and lifting the play into wider notice; Janet Allen, who embodies the best of
theatrical collaboration; the Dayton Playhouse for their astonishing commit-
ment to new plays; Sarah Brockus for writing all kinds of people to tell them
about it; Anne Gwynn, who looks out for me like a sister and for getting me
in the cheaper housing that has afforded me the extra time to write(!); the New
York Foundation for the Arts and the Berrilla Kerr Foundation, whose gen-
erous grants eased my life considerably in 2000; Chris Campbell, who has lent
her talents to the very first readings of two of my plays; Linda Ames Key, director extraordinaire, whose amazing theatrical eloquence continues to inspire
me; and finally, the Six Figures Theater Company, who has given me an artistic home for the last seven years.

FULL BLOOM

ACT ONE

PHOEBE'S LIGHT

Lights up on Phoebe Harris, sixteen years old. She speaks to the audience.

PHOEBE: There's this painting at the Museum of Modern Art, it's called *Onement I*. It's by this guy, Barnett Newman, I'd never really noticed him before, but I can't stop thinking about this painting he did. First of all it's not that big, maybe two by three, something like that. And it's not that striking — you know, when you think of some of the stuff that's there: Picasso's *Demoiselles*, for instance; or *Starry Night*. The one or two Frida Kahlo's that they show. This Newman, it's not like those, it's not a "look at me" kind of painting. So I don't know why I keep . . . OK. It's maroonish, reddish-maroonish mostly. Rust colored. And it's got this vivid — not bright exactly — but this vivid orange line down the center of it. About an inch wide. But the rust color, it's like it's taking over, while that orange line is getting thinner and thinner. It's like the orange line is being swallowed up. Right in front of you almost.

    I just got back from Italy about a week ago. My name's Phoebe, by the way, Phoebe Harris. Phoebe Louise Harris. I went with my best friend, Steffani Sabatini and her parents. We stayed the whole summer, traveling around. I was very lucky to get to go; I'm sixteen years old, and I just spent the summer in Italy. With one of my best friends. Without my parents. Now I'm back. My Mom's just inside, in our apartment. It's a pretty good bet she's looking in the mirror. My Dad's with his . . . with, Emma.

    Anyway, you should really look for that painting sometime. At the Museum of Modern Art, the Barnett Newman, third floor. You could go there a million times and never notice it.

    I've been thinking about that crazy painting for days.
(Lights shift.)

SCENE ONE

As lights start to fade on Phoebe, they come up on Jane in the living room of the Harris apartment, on a small, quiet block in the West Village, New York City. The Harrises occupy the first two floors in the building. There is a small 'bar' at one end of the room, used mainly by Crystal, who lives in the apartment above. Jane Harris is downstage, staring at herself in a fourth wall 'mirror.' We hear the sound of someone gently kicking the front door.

CRYSTAL: *(Offstage.)* Hey — hey! Jane! *(Pause, kicking.)* Janey — hey Jane! Yoohoo! Phoebe!? *(Kicks at door a little harder. Jane has not moved.)* Good Lord. Jane Harris! *(Sound of something dropping.)* Shit. Jaaane!!!
(Jane is roused, opens the door to Crystal, who enters, laden down with grocery bags, bottles, etc. She is wearing some cute sexy outfit.)
CRYSTAL: Let me in, let me in, my arms are breaking. Can you pick up that bag there? Lucky it wasn't the rum. How're you doing honey, you look great, let me look at you.
JANE: Hi.
CRYSTAL: Hey I booked that big ol' horror movie — *huge* budget — did you get that bag? How're you doing honey?
JANE: Just fine.
CRYSTAL: I thought my arms were about to break, were you working?
JANE: No. *(Has turned away, Crystal hesitates, then takes supplies to the 'bar' and to the 'kitchen,' upstage left. She bustles around making a drink.)*
CRYSTAL: It's a fun part — I play some scream queen's *mother*, and I get swallowed alive by this Giant Moth. Did you forget about our Tuesday night special?
JANE: No.
CRYSTAL: The Moth is called Merv, Merv the Giant Moth — can I talk you into a Mai Tai tonight?
JANE: Wine's fine.
CRYSTAL: Where's Phoebe, is she here?
JANE: All these questions. No.
CRYSTAL: I still haven't seen her.
JANE: She's having dinner with Richard.
CRYSTAL: Already? Can't he let her settle in first?
JANE: —
CRYSTAL: Uh-oh — is that a bad question?

JANE: No, no, I'm sorry. But she's been back a week, it's time they saw each other.

CRYSTAL: I still can't believe he just moved out of the house while she was *gone*. As sensitive as she is.

JANE: *(Opening the wine.)* I asked him to leave.

CRYSTAL: He forced you to ask him, the weenie.

JANE: Is there enough ice for you there, I forgot to check.

CRYSTAL: Plenty. What about the little zippety-doo-dah?

JANE: What about her?

CRYSTAL: Is she having dinner with them too?

JANE: I guess. I didn't ask.

CRYSTAL: You *didn't* ask!? Jesus, we are so different.

JANE: *(Holding the wine bottle, pouring herself a drink.)* Did you say you brought wine?

CRYSTAL: It's right there on the side-thingy — Oh you have it! *(Stumbles on a box.)* Yikes, what the hell is this — *(There is a knock at the door.)* Oh my God it's Merv-The-Man-Eating-Moth. Run everyone, run for your lives!!

(We hear Jim, offstage, singing something goofy, like "Windy." The next few lines overlap.)

JIM: "Who's tripping down the streets of the city,"

CRYSTAL: Jimmy!! *(Runs to open the door to Jim.)*

JIM: "waving at everybody she sees — "

CRYSTAL: Look at him. Would you look at him? Hey Sweetheart, I thought you'd've left already so I didn't come up.

JIM: Yeah, forgot the pasta though. *(To Jane.)* I'm making Nonna's Bolognese for the guys tonight. Is Phoebe around?

JANE: She's with Richard.

CRYSTAL: His Nonna who hates me.

JIM: Here we go. She doesn't hate you.

CRYSTAL: From the moment she met me she hated me.

JIM: She just had to get used to you. Didn't school start today?

JANE: Sure did.

CRYSTAL: It's been twenty-two years and she's still not used to me.

JIM: If we had stayed in Pittsburgh she'd see you more often, and then she'd like you. She'd love you.

CRYSTAL: See!? She doesn't like me!

JIM: She's just not very affectionate.

CRYSTAL: His *Italian Grandmother* is not very affectionate.

JIM: Honey, I've gotta go.

CRYSTAL: Anyway, he's making his "Nonna's" spaghetti sauce, he's making.

JIM: *(With a wink to Jane.)* Bolognese.

CRYSTAL: Frankly, I don't find it that special, I mean it's *fine*, there's nothing wrong with it per se — you've had it Jane, what do you think?

JANE: Is it going to be quiet at the station tonight Jim?

JIM: Hope so, there a big game on.

CRYSTAL: Everyone ignores me.

JIM: Tell Phoebe we can't wait to see her.

PHOEBE: *(Has entered from the French window, she's been on the balcony/fire escape.)* Pirates are playing the Mets tonight.

JIM: There's the kid!!

JANE: Phoebe!

CRYSTAL: Phoebe Honey, we thought you were out!! *(Rushes to give her a great big bear hug.)*

JANE: What's going on?

CRYSTAL: Sweetie, it's been way too long, how does that happen? Good Lord. Jim — look at her, would you look at this *beauty!*' We've missed you terribly sweetheart — oh, look at you!! Look at her Jane! You have grown, have you grown? What was it, the Italian wine, the men, the sun? It was a boy, right? You had a little romance.

PHOEBE: No . . .

JANE: I thought you were with your father.

CRYSTAL: You've grown so much, somehow. You look like a model, she's stunning, Jane, look at her. She could be a model, I swear to God. Ah honey, did you have a great time?

JIM: You look great, hon.

JANE: I thought you were going to have dinner with your father, how long have you been outside? Did he drop you off?

PHOEBE: Yeah — no. I walked.

JANE: You walked?

PHOEBE: *(To Jim.)* I met a man in Pescara named after Roberto Clemente.

JIM: You're kidding!

JANE: Who?

CRYSTAL: Jim's hero.

PHOEBE: Mine too!

JANE: Of course.

PHOEBE: He's my hero too.

JANE: I know that.

CRYSTAL: All I know is, the man was built like a Greek God.

JIM: Did you talk to him?

PHOEBE: Yeah, he was introducing himself to someone in this café where I was; anyway I just wanted to tell you that.

JANE: You were talking to strange men?

PHOEBE: *(To her mother.)* He was really nice.

JANE: Where were the Sabatini's?

PHOEBE: In the hotel. *(To Jim.)* He always introduces himself like that, with his full name: Roberto Clemente Carolini. He had this American pen pal who wrote all these letters about the Pirates. It's almost like he saw the games himself. We talked about the '71 Series and he got tears in his eyes, we were both practically crying! He's lived in Italy his entire life and the only other person he's ever talked to about Roberto was this pen pal. And then me.

CRYSTAL: In English?

PHOEBE: English, Italian, sign language.

JANE: That's very nice.

JIM: You knock me out, I swear to God.

PHOEBE: It was so neat.

JIM: I wish I didn't have to go to work, we could watch the game.

CRYSTAL: Jimmy —

JIM: OK Ladies, I'm late. Babe *(A quick smooch to Crystal.)* Jane, keep everyone in line. Phebes — tomorrow, OK? I want to hear all about Italy, the whole trip.

PHOEBE: OK. That was the best part though.

JANE: What!? Oh come on.

CRYSTAL: You tell everyone what I told you, Jimmy.

JIM: You bet. *(He's almost out the door.)*

CRYSTAL: I mean it. Tell them they've got to be extra careful.

JIM: Honey, we are always extra careful.

CRYSTAL: Jimmy —

PHOEBE: Careful about what?

CRYSTAL: I read his cards last night.

JIM: Without me there.

CRYSTAL: I can do it without you if I have to —

JIM: I'm out the door.

CRYSTAL: The cards were unusually —

JIM: Why did I stop by?

CRYSTAL: — someone in his environment is in danger — look at him, he doesn't take me seriously.

JIM: I will honey, I'll be extra careful.

CRYSTAL: There's just something in his aura, it scared me. I'm not usually nervous about his work, y'all know that; I usually think of it like he's going to the office —

JIM: I promise.

CRYSTAL: And you'll tell the guys? Make sure you tell Ernesto and Steve.

JIM: I'll tell them. I'm late.

CRYSTAL: All right, Jimmy.

JIM: Goodnight!

CRYSTAL: *(Rushes up to him at the door.)* I love you sweetheart.

JIM: I know. *(Winks at Phoebe.)*

CRYSTAL: You're a crumb, though.

JIM: I love you too, Babe. I love this face. Hey, tell Jane about your big idea, she'll talk some sense into you. *(He exits.)*

CRYSTAL: He adores me.

JANE: Uh-huh. What idea?

CRYSTAL: You'd think after all these years of doing what he does — and yet every now and then I still go cold all over when he leaves.

PHOEBE: Was the danger in the cards definitely work related?

CRYSTAL: That's true maybe it's me, maybe I'm in danger — I'm in his aura. I *am* his aura.

(Phoebe is going back to the window.)

JANE: Where are you going?

PHOEBE: Back outside.

CRYSTAL: Or someone we know . . . Jane — let me read your cards tonight.

JANE: Absolutely not, Phoebe where are you going?

PHOEBE: Just outside. On the balcony.

JANE: Wait, wait a minute. Why are you back so early, I thought you were spending the rest of the evening with your father?

PHOEBE: *(Gently.)* It's OK Mom, we just changed our minds. That's all. *(She exits.)*

JANE: They changed their minds. What does that mean? She's going to drive me crazy.

(End of scene. Lights shift, Phoebe has gone to her balcony.)

PHOEBE: I can see the moon from here. She just came up over that building. Did you know that Phoebe was one of the names of the Goddess of the Moon in Classical mythology? Artemis is the more common name, but not as nice, in my opinion. Dad says that's where my name came from. Mom says I was named for Phoebe Caulfield from *The Catcher in the Rye*, but Dad *insists* there was this incredible Harvest Moon the night I was conceived. And then Mom says maybe so, but she was reading and re-reading *The Catcher in the Rye* all the time she was pregnant with me. So finally Dad says, "ah-hah!," Phoebe Caulfield was probably named after the Goddess of the Moon too. When my parents were in love they used to enjoy that kind of argument.

Either way, I've always loved the moon. I'll even go out looking for her, if she's not in sight. We read *Romeo and Juliet* in school last year and I was surprised and kind of mad that Juliet called the moon unreliable — "inconstant," she called it. I tried to start a discussion about that in class, but it didn't really go over. Juliet seemed to be saying that since the moon is never in the same place from one night to the next that that means the moon is "inconstant." I think she just liked hearing the sound of her own voice.

Juliet was very beautiful. Romeo couldn't talk to her for five seconds without going on and on about how beautiful she was. The thing is, five seconds earlier he was gong on and on about someone else.

But I think the moon is very constant. She's always there. Not in the same place all the time, and you can't always see her, but she's always there somewhere. And tonight she's right above that building. Just a little sliver on her way across the great big sky.

(Lights shift.)

SCENE TWO

Jesse Williams jogs by, sees Phoebe, pauses, jogging in place. Phoebe doesn't seem to notice. He calls out.

JESSE: "But soft, what light through yonder window breaks"? *(No reaction from Phoebe.)* "If music be the food of love, play on!" *(No reaction.)* "Once more into the breach, dear friends, once more . . ." Hi up there! *(Phoebe looks at him.)* You're still here!

PHOEBE: What do you mean?

JESSE: You were there the other night, when I ran by.

PHOEBE: Is that all right with you?

JESSE: Oh yeah, it's fine. I was hoping — I mean — Jesse Williams. We go to the same school.

PHOEBE: Uh-huh.

JESSE: We're in the same English class.

PHOEBE: I know.

JESSE: *Great!*

PHOEBE: —

JESSE: You know who I am then, great.

PHOEBE: I don't know who you are, I just recognize you from class.

JESSE: OK well, yeah, good point but what I meant was, I just didn't want you to think this strange guy was coming up to . . . hold on — Shh, shhh.

PHOEBE: What?

JESSE: ~~*(Whispers.)*~~ Shhhh. ~~Don't~~ move.

PHOEBE: *(Whispers.)* What is it?

JESSE: See that? On that branch there?

PHOEBE: What? A burglar?

JESSE: *(He looks at her.)* A bird.

PHOEBE: Oh. Neat.

JESSE: It's a . . . yeah, it's a redheaded woodpecker! On that lower branch. Right *there.* Wow — see it? With the red — Oh — there it goes, there — it's gone. Did you see it?

(They return, variously, to their normal voices.)

PHOEBE: Kind of.

JESSE: What was it doing in the city? And at night? Wow.

PHOEBE: Where do you come from?

JESSE: Minnesota. I just moved here a couple weeks ago. My Mom's an ornithologist.

PHOEBE: —

JESSE: It's a nice night.

PHOEBE: Uh-huh.

JESSE: And . . . did you see the moon?

PHOEBE: Yeah. I did.

JESSE: I had this idea — it's dumb I know, but I had this idea that you couldn't see the moon that well in the city. I had other preconceptions about New York, too. Like, that people wouldn't be friendly, for instance.

PHOEBE: And now you see how wrong you were. You *can* see the moon. *(Maybe she smiles.)*

JESSE: *(Encouraged.)* I like it here so far! It's a lot different from Minneapolis but you know, Minneapolis is a big city too, pretty big. Not like here of course, nothing's like here. You live here obviously. I mean, in this building.

PHOEBE: I'm not supposed to tell strangers where I live.

JANE: *(Appears at the balcony window.)* Phoebe, shouldn't you come in now?

PHOEBE: Soon.

JANE: Who are you talking to?

PHOEBE: This is Jesse. He's in my English class.

JESSE: Hi Ma'am. Jesse Williams.

JANE: Nice to meet you, Jesse.

JESSE: You too.

JANE: Come in soon Phoebe, it's after ten.

PHOEBE: I am.

(Jane turns back inside.)

JESSE: Was that your Mom?

PHOEBE: I can't tell you, you might figure out where I live.

JESSE: Your name's Phoebe?

PHOEBE: Yeah. I'd better go in now. Not that I live here or anything. I'll see you around.

JESSE: As in Phoebe Caulfield?

PHOEBE: Are you serious!?

JESSE: What do you mean?

PHOEBE: *(As she climbs down from the balcony.)* Wait — wait — wait. You're the first person to ever ask that.

JESSE: "If a body catch a body coming through the rye" — I love that guy.

PHOEBE: Do you think he ever gets out of that asylum? I've been wondering.

JESSE: What are you talking about.

PHOEBE: Holden's in an asylum.

JESSE: It's not an *asylum.*

PHOEBE: Yes it is.

JESSE: No it's not.

PHOEBE: What is it then?

JESSE: It's a, what do you call it. A sanitorium or something. A place to rest. Not an asylum.

PHOEBE: Whatever it is, I hope he gets out.

JESSE: He *does.*

PHOEBE: OK. *(Beat.)* Jesse as in Jesse James?

JESSE: No.

PHOEBE: Jesse Jackson?

JESSE: No.

PHOEBE: Jesse Helms.

JESSE: Yes. No, Jesse as in, there's this Jesse Tree in the Bible, it means "God exists," or something, you'd have to ask my Mom and Dad — but as far as I'm concerned, it's Jesse as in Jesse Owens.

PHOEBE: Oh.

JESSE: You don't know who Jesse Owens was?

PHOEBE: No.

JESSE: Oh man! He was this runner in the 30s, a sprinter! He won four — he was black — it was the '36 Olympics in Berlin, Hitler had been, I'm not sure if he was killing people yet but, you know what he was like, and here comes this *black* guy who wins four gold medals. It was like a personal slap in the face to all the Nazis. Hitler was so mad he left the stadium so he wouldn't have to congratulate a black man. Four gold medals.

PHOEBE: I met someone recently named after my hero.

JESSE: Who?

PHOEBE: Roberto Clemente.

JESSE: Roberto Clemente's your hero?

PHOEBE: Yeah, you know him?

JESSE: Sure. Right fielder for the Pittsburgh Pirates. Number 21. Great hitter.

PHOEBE: Do all guys know that stuff?

JESSE: Yes we do. So listen, would you . . .

PHOEBE: . . . What?

JESSE: Nothing . . .

PHOEBE: I should probably go in now.

JESSE: I should probably get home.

PHOEBE: OK.

JESSE: OK.

PHOEBE: My Mom and stuff.

JESSE: Right.

PHOEBE: Get home safe.

JESSE: Oh yeah.

PHOEBE: I'll see you in class.

JESSE: Right. Yeah. So — yeah. Right.

PHOEBE: Oh there's Jim — my friend Jim — he's my neighbor, and my friend. *(Jim has entered, walking from stage right.)* Hi Jim!

JIM: Hi, hon. *(To Jesse.)* Hey.

PHOEBE: Jesse's in my English class.

JIM: That's great.

JESSE: I guess I'd better go.

PHOEBE: OK.

JESSE: Goodnight.

PHOEBE: 'Night. *(As Jesse leaves, Phoebe calls out to him.)* Hey Jesse, do you promise he gets out?

JESSE: What?

PHOEBE: Do you promise he gets out of that asylum?

JESSE: It's not an asylum, it's a sanitor —

PHOEBE: Sanitorium or something, I know. You promise?

JESSE: I promise.

PHOEBE: OK. *(Jesse bounds off. Jim has sat down next to Phoebe.)* He's nice.

JIM: Seems like it.

PHOEBE: He's from Minneapolis.

JIM: How about that.

PHOEBE: Have you ever heard of Jesse Owens?

JIM: Sure have.

PHOEBE: He won four gold medals against Hitler.

JIM: That's right.

PHOEBE: Do you think he's cute?

JIM: Your friend there?

PHOEBE: Yeah.

JIM: I think he's very cute.

PHOEBE: You do?

JIM: You bet.

PHOEBE: Me too.

JIM: You know, I met Crystal when I was not much older than that? Only a few years older than you. OK Kid. Tell me about Italy. I've been thinking about you all day.

PHOEBE: I already told you the best part.

JIM: Oh, c'mon.

PHOEBE: I did.

JIM: What about the — what about all that art you were so excited to see — the Sistine Chapel?

PHOEBE: It was OK.

JIM: Or that statue you couldn't stop talking about, the David, did you get to see that?

PHOEBE: Yeah . . .

JIM: I get it, you're still thinking about your cute friend there.

PHOEBE: —

JIM: Phebes.

PHOEBE: Why don't you have kids?

JIM: Whoa.

PHOEBE: What?

JIM: That's quite a transition.

PHOEBE: Oh sorry. Um, yeah, I liked the David — I stared at it for at least an hour — you should see it sometime — why don't you have kids?

JIM: We have you, we've always thought of you as our kid.

PHOEBE: I know, me too. But why didn't you have kids of your own? Didn't you want to?

JIM: Sure we did, but we, it didn't work out. Where's this coming from, Phebes?

PHOEBE: I don't know, I've decided not to have kids too and, I was just, I was thinking about it and wondered . . . about you, I realized that I never knew why you didn't have any. It seems like a weird thing not to know. Was it because of Crystal's acting, she didn't have time or something?

JIM: No. Crystal wanted to, very much. Very, very much.

PHOEBE: Really?

JIM: Very much.

PHOEBE: So . . .

JIM: We tried, honey, but she — *we* couldn't, there were medical things, it's kind of complicated. But we have you. And that has made all the difference.

PHOEBE: Oh.

JIM: Hey. Look at me. *(She does.)* What is going on in that head of yours?

PHOEBE: Nothing.

JIM: Nothing?

PHOEBE: Yeah.

JIM: You'll tell me if there is.

PHOEBE: Yeah.

(End of scene; lights shift.)

PHOEBE'S LIGHT

PHOEBE: I saw this guy today, Danny Harris. I used to have this huge crush on him when I was about . . . well starting when I was about twelve, probably.

He's two years older than me, but I was kind of buddies with his younger brother and I'd see him around. We already had the same last name so I kind of assumed that we would get married . . . It was the same way I used to assume that I'd get to Oz or Narnia when I was a kid. Dumb, because he never paid any attention to me. Except this once at school when he called me over to where he and his friends were smoking.

He said he and his friends had been trying to figure out what it was that made me so unbelievably ugly. He said when they figured it out they'd let me know.

When I was a kid I used to put my hand right up to the mirror and wonder if this was the day. I really thought that eventually, when everything was in place, when the time and the magic were right, I would put my hand up to the mirror and I'd pass through the Looking Glass into Wonderland, or Middle Earth, or get somehow to Stable Hill in the last days of Narnia, in time to save the Talking Horses. I thought there was nothing to stop me.

So today Danny Harris sees me sitting here and he comes over and starts talking to me like we're old friends. I guess he doesn't remember about me being a dog because he's flirting like crazy. And then he asks me out.

When I was a kid it never occurred to me to think about what I look like.

Anyway, I told Danny Harris . . . yes.

(*Lights shift.*)

SCENE THREE

Lights brighten on the Harris living room. The remains of cheese and crackers and chips are on the coffee table. There is an empty wine bottle, and the same bottle of rum is on the bar from Tuesday night. Crystal is looking out of 'Phoebe's' window.

JANE: What's she doing?

CRYSTAL: She's just sitting there. Sitting.

JANE: Don't let her see you watching her.

CRYSTAL: She's blossomed in the last, I don't think I had seen her since — between the mini-series, her trip to Italy, and our vacation, I don't think I had seen her since . . . April, could that be right? It's not that she was an ugly duckling before —

JANE: Thank you.

CRYSTAL: It's *not* that she was an ugly duckling, and of course *we've* always thought she was beautiful but she's grown into herself. She looks older than sixteen, I swear to God — she's got a figure! She suddenly looks like a woman and not a girl anymore.

JANE: You're scaring the crap out of me.

CRYSTAL: Jane. Your language.

JANE: I don't want my little girl to look like a woman yet. What's she doing?

CRYSTAL: Sitting. She's still sitting. She's sitting like she's been sitting all night. Looking up at the sky like she does.

JANE: Is she singing?

CRYSTAL: Singing? Singing what?

JANE: Remember how she used to sing to herself when she was little? When she was playing in her room?

CRYSTAL: Yeah, yeah I do. That was the sweetest sound I ever heard.

JANE: I used to walk by her door and just listen, listen to her sing. I don't think I've ever been so happy as in those moments.

CRYSTAL: We've been neighbors a long time, Jane.

JANE: I know.

CRYSTAL: I feel very lucky about that.

JANE: Me too. Don't cry.

CRYSTAL: OK.

JANE: It's nothing to cry about.

CRYSTAL: I just feel so lucky.

JANE: Are you all right?

CRYSTAL: Sure, you know me.

JANE: What's wrong?

CRYSTAL: Nothing, you know me, I get all nostalgic and sentimental at the drop of a hat, it's *horrifying*. It's just, it just seems like yesterday that she was this funny little kid, and Jim and I would baby-sit her and we always looked forward to it. It was never a burden, she was a breath of fresh air into the day. Or we'd all go to Shakespeare in the Park and she always got it, you know? She always had some amazing observation and she appreciated it somehow, even if it was an utter failure, she would try to figure out why. I felt so vital then, it all still seemed possible. *(Beat.)* Jane. Our Lives Are Over.

JANE: For God's sake —

CRYSTAL: I'm sorry, I'm getting us all maudlin here, you hate that.

JANE: Do you think she's unhappy?

CRYSTAL: Phoebe?

JANE: She's been a little odd lately.

CRYSTAL: She's a teenager. They're odd people.

JANE: I know . . .

CRYSTAL: And her parents are separated. If I may be so bold —

JANE: Thank you, that's been pending for a while. This is new, I think.

CRYSTAL: She's always been a little, 'in her own world.'

JANE: I guess.

CRYSTAL: She's not unhappy, she's sixteen. She's *sixteen*, Jane. Oh my God, yesterday she was two and now she's almost thirty.

JANE: She's much more sensitive than I ever was. Or Richard. See if she's singing.

CRYSTAL: Jaaaane —

JANE: *I* can't, she'll notice me, she's like the princess and the pea where I'm concerned.

CRYSTAL: But the window's shut —

JANE: Just go up to it and put your ear against it. Check.

CRYSTAL: Honey —

JANE: I want to hear her singing! She might be singing, and we might be missing it!! Check! Check!

CRYSTAL: I'm checking, I'm checking. Calm down. (*Creeping very carefully over to the window. As she reaches it she meets Phoebe coming in. They all scream.*)

PHOEBE: (*Enters.*) What's going on?

CRYSTAL AND JANE: Nothing.

PHOEBE: (*Bumps into the box.*) Why is this still here?

JANE: Your father was looking through it for some things to, take with him.

PHOEBE: Today?

JANE: No, a couple of days ago I guess. A week, I don't know. Saturday.

PHOEBE: Oh.

JANE: He's not necessarily —

PHOEBE: Right.

JANE: I guess I should put it away.

PHOEBE: If you want. (*She goes down the hall.*)

CRYSTAL: If she goes to her room do you want me to listen at the door, see if she starts singing?

JANE: I guess I should move the box.

CRYSTAL: It looks pretty heavy, I'm sure Jim would help you. What's in it?

JANE: Nothing much — papers, old pictures — the detritus of a marriage.

CRYSTAL: OK, that does it — you're having a Mai Tai — and then you're going to talk to me.

JANE: What are you looking for?

CRYSTAL: The knife. You haven't really talked about this whole —

JANE: Try the kitchen.

CRYSTAL: I guess. Hold that thought. *(She goes to the kitchen.)*

JANE: So what was that business Jim was talking about? The other day?

CRYSTAL: *(Offstage.)* What? What business?

JANE: That business — he said ask Jane about your plans, tell Jane about your big plans — something like that.

CRYSTAL: *(Offstage.)* What made you think of that?

JANE: I don't know.

CRYSTAL: *(Comes back from kitchen with the paring knife, goes to bar to cut some orange slices.)* He's such a troublemaker, I wanted it to be a surprise. I'm going to have my eyes done.

JANE: Oh, for God's sake.

CRYSTAL: Jimmy seems to think he's going to talk me out of it, actually I don't even think he realizes how serious I am, but I've found a doctor, I've made an appointment. September 20.

JANE: That's in a couple of weeks!

CRYSTAL: I made the appointment ages ago. I just didn't tell Jim until recently because I knew how he'd react. I've got a very good doctor, and the money from that God-awful mini-series is going to pay for it. Olé, Sugar.

JANE: Crystal —

CRYSTAL: No scolding.

JANE: You're too young.

CRYSTAL: No disagreeing.

JANE: You already look thirty, practically.

CRYSTAL: I will look thirty, with this body I'll look twenty-five.

JANE: What does Jim say about it?

CRYSTAL: He's upset. He's old-fashioned and I love him for it, but he'll get used to it. He'll get used to a wife who looks twenty-five — I'm sorry. I'm sorry, I'm an idiot! I'm sorry, sweetie. *(Crystal, who has been hovering here and there about the room practically the entire night making drinks, snacking, dancing, etc., comes to rest next to Jane on the sofa, with the drinks.)* I'm sorry. It's not going to last, you know that. It's just a fling.

JANE: You still think so?

CRYSTAL: Yes.

JANE: She's very bright, apparently. Ph.D. in Greek Mythology. Now wait just a minute, that's my husband's field. *(Phoebe has appeared from the hall.)* Today's my twentieth wedding anniversary.

CRYSTAL: I know sweetie, I remember. I actually came over here to cheer you up — am I doing a good job — you can tell me the truth.

JANE: Phoebe's met her. She seems so much more real now that Phoebe has actually met her. *Emma.* I've dreamed about her probably thirty times in the last six months and in almost every dream she looks different. But she usually looks beautiful and she always looks young. I don't mean to get so — Uchhkh.

CRYSTAL: . . . go on.

JANE: No.

CRYSTAL: Come on sweetie, talk to me.

JANE: No, that's enough of that.

CRYSTAL: Jaaane —

JANE: *NO.* I will not right now. I'm sorry. But I will not. Not now, not today. God. *(Beat.)* And you. Getting surgery. See? It's absurd. Everything is so absurd.

CRYSTAL: Yes it is.

JANE: It's absurd.

CRYSTAL: It certainly is.

(Pheobe takes this opportunity to head back outside.)

JANE: Phoebe! I didn't know you were there.

PHOEBE: I wasn't. I was just passing through.

JANE: Are you hungry?

PHOEBE: No thanks.

CRYSTAL: Phoebe, we're getting all maudlin in here sweetie, come cheer us up.

JANE: Tell Crystal she doesn't need a face-lift.

CRYSTAL: Jane!

PHOEBE: Sylvia Plath wrote a poem about somebody's face-lift.

CRYSTAL: Sylvia Plath? I bet that's a real cheerer-upper.

PHOEBE: Why are you getting one?

CRYSTAL: Not *lift* — I'm just getting my eyes done. Probably. Hey, let's pull out that Sylvia Plath poem and have some laughs.

PHOEBE: I'm going back outside. I'll be on the steps.

JANE: Crystal has been saying how beautiful you look, how much you've blossomed —

(Phoebe gives her mother a look, then exits.)

CRYSTAL: Sylvia Plath. Good Lord, Jane.

(End of scene; lights shift.)

PHOEBE: So I told my Dad I'd been going out with this guy, a guy I met at McDonalds. Named Jake. I said his drug problem is pretty much history, and that his time in prison had made him very humble. I explained how he was a really *nice* Republican, and that his gun collection is actually very valuable. And mostly legal in thirty-eight states, just not this one. I also happened to mention that he is thirty-six years old. *That's* when Dad got so upset. Said he was going to ground me and call the police and everything.

"What are you so upset about Daddy? Is it the age thing? Because if you think about it, it's the same difference as the one between you and Emma."

I was sorry I said that though. It was just a joke, the whole thing was just a joke. But I was sorry about the whole thing because it looked a lot like Dad was about to cry.

(Lights shift.)

SCENE FOUR

Jane enters the living room, rushing around, trying to get everything together to go out to a benefit.

JANE: *(Calling out.)* How much time before you leave?

PHOEBE: *(Offstage.)* About ten minutes.

JANE: I'm going to be horribly late, can you run out to the corner and get some aspirin for me?

PHOEBE: *(Entering.)* OK.

JANE: Is that what you're going to wear to the game? That little top?

PHOEBE: Why?

JANE: *(Grabs her purse, pulls out some money.)* It's pretty honey, it's just . . . it's fine. I've got a splitting headache. *(Jane heads off to her room, there is a knock at the door, Phoebe answers it to Jim.)*

JIM: Ready for the game?

PHOEBE: Yeah, I just have to run to the store real quick, get some aspirin for Mom.

JIM: I'm a little early, Crystal said there were a couple of things Jane needed moved. A box?

PHOEBE: It's over here.

JIM: Do you know where it goes?

PHOEBE: I think at the top of the closet. *(Points to the closet, Jim picks up the box as Jane enters.)*

JIM: Looks like this box is going in the closet, is that right?

JANE: Don't worry about it, it's too heavy.

JIM: No, I've got it.

JANE: Phoebe, the aspirin?

PHOEBE: I'm going.

JANE: Put that down, it's too heavy.

JIM: It's not, just tell me where it goes.

JANE: Phoebe! *(To Jim.)* It's too heavy.

JIM: It's not a problem, just tell me —

JANE: Put it down, it doesn't go anywhere, it goes right where it was, put it down!! Phoebe, are you going or not? *(As Phoebe exits.)* I'm sorry, I'm very on edge, I'm going to be late for this damn benefit and I can't find the folder with all the name cards and the annual budget — I was supposed to drop everything off an hour ago —

JIM: Jane —

JANE: I just had it in my hands —

JIM: Jane —

JANE: They need to put it all together for the tables, they need enough time to put everything in the pretty packets, before the guests arrive —

JIM: Sit down for a minute —

JANE: I should have had it all ready yesterday —

JIM: Can I help you look?

JANE: And now I can't *find* anything. I just had it five seconds ago —

JIM: I'm sure they can manage —

JANE: No they can't, they can't manage, I'm the one, I'm the one, it's my job!!

JIM: Sit down.

JANE: I know you talk to Richard.

JIM: Yes I do.

JANE: Crystal doesn't.

JIM: Crystal won't see him.

JANE: Good.

JIM: This hasn't been — he misses Phoebe.

JANE: Poor him.

JIM: She barely talks to him.

JANE: Why should she, she barely talks to me.

JIM: She told him she was seeing some thirty-six-year-old guy.

JANE: I know. She made it up, she wanted to get a reaction. Have you met Emma?

JIM: Yes.

JANE: Do you like her?

JIM: Jane.

JANE: Do you?

JIM: I've only met her a couple of times.

JANE: If anyone's going to lose friends over this it should be him. *He* should lose his friends. He should lose everything he cares deeply about.

JIM: You don't mean that.

JANE: Of course I mean it. I mean it, *I mean it,* God-dammit!!! *(Beat.)* Phoebe's going to be back any minute, I can't let her see me like this.

JIM: Maybe she should, maybe it would help with some of the tension.

JANE: I can't talk to her, not yet. I'm afraid it would all come out, I would vomit up all this bile, and it would hurt her. Her spirit is so delicate right now, Jim, I'm terrified of doing or saying the wrong thing, something damaging. She should love her father, of course she should but I can't seem to — I'm not equipped, I'm just not *equipped* for this . . .

JIM: You are Jane, you're a strong woman. And a good mother.

JANE: Don't platitude me, for God's sake — I'm sorry. I'm sorry! I've become a harridan, no wonder — I'm late, I've got to get going —

JIM: How can I help you?

JANE: You can't. You know? You just can't. *(She's looking for the folder again.)* And I don't care what anyone says — I think your grandmothers' Bolognese is just great, I really do. Delicious.

JIM: Thank you . . .

JANE: *(Sees the folder in the bookcase or somewhere.)* There it is, thank God! Richard's not a bad person.

JIM: —

JANE: Every now and then I feel a glimmer — a glimmer — a *second's* worth of grace, I do. *(As she gets her stuff together.)* It's funny that you two became good friends. It took a while though, it took a few years didn't it? Five or six years I think, to really develop something.

JIM: Yeah, I remember exactly what, Crystal and I, it was after the second miscarriage and Crystal had pulled away from me. One, lousy night I was sitting on the stoop thinking I . . . and Richard came outside and sat with me, all night. We didn't even talk that much but he was there, the whole night.

JANE: I remember that.

JIM: I felt like he had saved our marriage somehow. The both of you, you both did.

JANE: He's not a bad person.

JIM: No.

JANE: I feel sick to my stomach.

PHOEBE: *(Enters.)* Sorry, I had to go to two different delis. *(Jane turns away, to gather herself together. Phoebe puts the aspirin and change on a table.)* Stuff's on the table.

JANE: Thank you.

JIM: Jane?

JANE: I'm fine, you go on now, I've got to get myself out the door.

JIM: Jane?

JANE: Go on, have fun. I've got to get myself out the door.

PHOEBE: *(Has grabbed a jacket or a sweater.)* Bye. Bye, Mom.

JANE: I'll see you when you get back.

(Phoebe and Jim exit, Phoebe looking back at her mother. Jane looks around the room, puts on a wrap, grabs the folder, the aspirin and her purse. She starts for the door, stops, breathing heavily. End of scene.)

PHOEBE'S LIGHT

PHOEBE: There was something about that trip to Italy that I didn't mention, I don't know why. Now it's pretty much the only thing I remember.

I took a lot of walks by myself. Whenever I could, wherever we were. Which wasn't as often as I wanted because the Sabatini's are very conscientious people. I got tired of being around them, and very tired of Steffani. Anyway, near the end of the trip I slipped out of the hotel during our afternoon 'quiet-time.' I was walking along the Via Ricasoli — in Florence — when these guys started following me. I didn't notice them at first because I'd been thinking about the David and Michelangelo. I used to want to be an artist. Mom says it's almost like I go into a trance when I think about stuff like that. So these guys were very close to me before I noticed them, and suddenly they sort of . . . forced me into this side street. Not by touching me, but by just . . . surrounding me. They were so close I couldn't see past them. I thought I was going to get raped or mutilated for sure and I felt like such a jerk for letting them corner me like that. There were four or five of them, talking, gesturing, looking me up and down, I couldn't really, breathe. And then it dawned on me: it was like they were *admiring* me. I almost felt like I should feel *complimented.*

They never touched me. Nothing happened.

I didn't realize I'd thrown up on myself until I got back to the hotel. *(Lights shift.)*

SCENE FIVE

Jesse bounds down the street, sees Phoebe on the steps.

JESSE: "Sweet Phoebe, do not scorn me; do not, Phoebe."
PHOEBE: Hi.
JESSE: "Say that you love me not; but say not so in bitterness." What's up?
PHOEBE: *(Distracted.)* Nothing, I'm just, waiting for someone — Jim — the guy you met.
JESSE: You weren't in class today.
PHOEBE: Yeah, I had a, I went to the — I might have to switch my schedule around. It conflicts with this other class I have to take.
JESSE: Wow.
PHOEBE: It's no big deal.
JESSE: Have you ever had Ms. Henderson? For history?
PHOEBE: No.
JESSE: Maybe you could get in that class, she's great. We were talking about Alfred Nobel and how he invented dynamite. Did you know that?
PHOEBE: No.
JESSE: Alfred Nobel — Alfred *Nobel* was having breakfast one day — checking out the paper and stuff — when he comes across his own obituary —
PHOEBE: Weird.
JESSE: *(In an enthusiastic rush, but Phoebe is looking down the street for Jim.)* Yeah, the paper made this mistake! But because of it Alfred realizes he's going to be remembered mostly for inventing dynamite — that that was his big contribution to the world, you know? So he begins re-thinking his whole life, what he wants his legacy to be. And he starts a trust for this prize, to honor people who try to make the world *better,* and now that's what he's remembered for. The Nobel Peace Prize. Wow. Isn't that *great!?* . . . I don't know, maybe you had to be there.
PHOEBE: No, that's great, it is.

JESSE: Anyway . . . Ms. Henderson, I love that class. You should get in that class.

PHOEBE: You're on my block again.

JESSE: It's my block too.

PHOEBE: Since when?

JESSE: Since I moved here a couple weeks ago. Like I said the other day.

PHOEBE: You didn't tell me you lived on the same block.

JESSE: Near the corner, next to the flower shop.

PHOEBE: We're neighbors, practically.

JESSE: I know. We should probably get married.

PHOEBE: —

JESSE: I'm just kidding! Obviously.

PHOEBE: I know! Seen any birds lately?

JESSE: Yeah, on my way over I saw a pigeon. Do you have a boyfriend?

PHOEBE: No.

JESSE: Interesting.

PHOEBE: But I have a date.

JESSE: With who? When?

PHOEBE: Wednesday.

JESSE: *Wednesday?*

PHOEBE: My Mom thinks I'm doing something else.

JESSE: Wow, New York, the city never sleeps. Is it serious?

PHOEBE: No . . . first date.

JESSE: Someone at school?

PHOEBE: Jesse —

JESSE: I know, I know, none of my business — do you like him?

PHOEBE: I don't know, I guess. I used to have this big crush on him. Along with half the school.

JESSE: Oh OK, he's like that.

PHOEBE: Like what?

JESSE: Like the guy that half the stupid school has a crush on. Like that.

PHOEBE: No, not like that, you don't get it. *(Jesse doesn't seem to know where or how to arrange his body in a natural position all of a sudden.)* It's no big deal.

JESSE: Right, no, I was just thinking — Ms. Henderson gave us a ton of home-work, I should go.

PHOEBE: It's no big deal!

JESSE: I'm already late. *(He starts to leave.)*

PHOEBE: Wait! *(He hesitates, awkward. She holds up some baseball cards.)* I mean . . . look, I found all my old baseball cards, look. *(Jesse is still poised to leave.)* My friend Jim and I, we collected them together. With my Dad.

JESSE: —

PHOEBE: *(Starts flipping through the cards.)* Barry Bonds, Steve Finley, Curt Flood — see? Andy Van Slyke, Bobby Bonilla, Lance Blankenship .. . Here's my Roberto Clemente. It's not in very good shape, I used to carry it around everywhere. I always wanted a rookie Clemente, you know, before he knew how good he would be. Although Jim thinks he always knew. Do you?

JESSE: Maybe.

PHOEBE: But do you think he knew that he'd be *great?*

JESSE: I don't know.

PHOEBE: 'Cause Lance Blankenship probably thought *he'd* be great, too. *(Jesse smiles.)* Did you collect baseball cards?

JESSE: Yeah.

PHOEBE: Who's your best card?

JESSE: I have a Hank Aaron '53, his rookie card the one year he was with the Boston Braves.

PHOEBE: No you don't — are you serous?

JESSE: Yeah, it's very valuable. My Dad gave it to me, it used to be his and I'd always wanted it and he gave it to me on my twelfth birthday. He said I was "old enough to take care of it." If my house ever burned down or something — *that's* what I'd grab first.

PHOEBE: Your rookie Aaron.

JESSE: *(Nods. Beat.)* I'm really late for dinner.

PHOEBE: Do you miss living in a house? You know, a *house?*

JESSE: . . . I miss everything. It's different here.

PHOEBE: What do you mean?

JESSE: I don't know . . .

PHOEBE: I thought you liked it.

JESSE: I do! It's just . . . I don't know. *(He shrugs, vulnerable. She waits.)* People want to judge you all the time, seems like.

PHOEBE: I know.

JESSE: I know.

PHOEBE: . . . when they don't even know you.

JESSE: I know!

PHOEBE: It's . . . exhausting.

JESSE: *(Beat).* Would you want to, not a date or anything, and I don't know where you usually eat lunch, would you want to meet me for lunch sometime? I like talking to you and everything — not a date.

PHOEBE: No, yeah — at school?

JESSE: Yeah why — where else?

PHOEBE: Nowhere. When?

JESSE: Like tomorrow?

PHOEBE: Tomorrow . . .

JESSE: Or Wednesday? Or not, I don't know.

PHOEBE: No, tomorrow. OK.

JESSE: Good.

PHOEBE: —

JESSE: I guess I'd better go for real, dinner and all that.

PHOEBE: OK . . .

JESSE: I'll see ya tomorrow though.

PHOEBE: *(Suddenly.)* I like talking to you too. Sometimes it's like, my head just gets too full of . . . everything — and — you know? Anyway I just, I like talking to you, too.

JESSE: Me too.

> *(Beat. He smiles as he takes his leave with a flourish. Phoebe watches him go, then leans back against her building. Lights shift, time has passed, perhaps a couple of hours. She is waiting, has been waiting. She has now curled up into herself, in a ball, on the steps. Jim enters slowly.)*

PHOEBE: Where've you been?

JIM: I gotta see Crystal, she home, do y'know? She had a job today.

PHOEBE: She's not back yet.

JIM: How do you know, how long have you been out here?

PHOEBE: Since about four.

JIM: Jesus, Phoebe.

PHOEBE: I've been waiting for you.

JIM: Why what's wrong?

PHOEBE: Nothing — I don't know — your eyes are bloodshot.

JIM: Yeah.

PHOEBE: Something happened.

JIM: Just a long day. It's all right. Let's sit outside for a minute or two though.

PHOEBE: OK. You smell like smoke.

JIM: Yeah. How was school?

PHOEBE: Fine.

JIM: That's good.

PHOEBE: I mean, it was OK.

JIM: You're lucky you've always loved school so much, that's a blessing.

PHOEBE: Yeah. Actually I don't love it so much anymore. People are . . . I don't know.

JIM: So, how's Steffani?

PHOEBE: Steffani and her nose job made cheerleader.

JIM: Isn't that something.

PHOEBE: We don't get along so well, I never even see her anymore.

JIM: Good for you.

PHOEBE: What?

JIM: I guess I'll go in.

PHOEBE: I wanted to . . . there was something that, I wanted to talk to you —

JIM: Honey —

PHOEBE: What?

JIM: I've gotta go inside.

PHOEBE: But Jim —

JIM: Long day, you know?

PHOEBE: Can I come up with you?

JANE: *(Comes out on the balcony.)* Phoebe! I thought — Jim, where's Crystal?

JIM: Work.

JANE: If she has a moment when she comes in, could you ask her to stop by? Doesn't matter how late. I already left a message on your machine, but . . . doesn't matter how late.

JIM: Sure.

JANE: What are you guys doing?

PHOEBE: Just hanging out.

JANE: *(Starts back inside, pauses.)* Tell Crystal it doesn't matter how late, OK Jim? Jim?

JIM: Yeah.

(Jane goes back inside.)

JIM: *(Continues.)* I kept telling her it would be all right . . .

PHOEBE: Who?

JIM: This kid, five years old maybe. I yelled to her, "I'll be right there, no, no, stay *there*" — we had the ladder almost to her, and I was telling her it would be all right, to stay where she was but she climbed out on the window sill to try to reach me cause she was so scared, the little thing was so scared and she thought she could reach me . . . but I wasn't close enough yet —

(Phoebe is at a loss.)

JIM: When I left, a block away from the fire some asshole was blowing on his horn, just laying on it because the light five cars ahead of him was *about* to turn green and this guy was anxious to get somewhere.

CRYSTAL: *(Enters from the other end of the street.)* There you are, thank God!! I'm hopeless, I know, but I had such a silly, spooky feeling today —

JIM: Babe —

CRYSTAL: *(Looks in his face.)* Oh my God. What happened, are you all right? Ernesto, Steve, is everyone all right?

JIM: This kid, she lost her balance, the kid lost her balance . . .

CRYSTAL: *(Takes Jim in her arms and holds him.)* My baby, my poor baby, it'll be all right . . . I'm so sorry . . . let's go inside, c'mon . . .

(After a moment or two, she half supports him as they walk inside together. Beat. Phoebe remains on the steps looking out. End of scene.)

PHOEBE'S LIGHT

The emotion she had been trying to suppress the entire last scene threatens to tumble out.

PHOEBE: I found this little, pottery-animal . . . thing I made when I was about . . . I don't know, six? It was in that box of stuff my Dad was looking through. Along with the baseball cards and everything.

I can't figure out what it's supposed to be, a bear, or a . . . it's not a dog. It's got no — it's not a definable creature, really. It's very sweet though, it has personality. And it's got this expression on its face . . . like it's trying to smile, but it's not smiling. Like it's anticipating something from you and has no idea what to expect. It's also got a very thick neck, but I don't think I did that on purpose. *(She holds up the little sculpture.)*

Anyway, it's a very *distinct* creative, whatever it is. I'm sorry you can't really see it. Because it's very sweet. If I hadn't made it, and I saw it somewhere, at someone's house or somewhere, I'd think, "I'm going to like this person, whoever made this." At least, that's what I'd think if that person wasn't me.

OK, I have a question. If you give something to your Dad, if you give him something you made when you were six, something sweet, and distinct . . . don't you think he should take it with him when he goes? *(End of Act One.)*

ACT TWO

PHOEBE'S LIGHT

PHOEBE: I saw this billboard yesterday, just off the Brooklyn-Queens Expressway. It said, "Drive Carefully. We Can Wait." And underneath in smaller type — "Rock of Ages Gravestones, Monuments, and Vaults. "Drive Carefully. We Can Wait."

I was on my way to Bay Ridge with Danny Harris. That's when I saw the billboard. It was our first date, we were going to this party a friend of his was having. He picked me up at the Museum and gave me this big smooch before we started out. That was nice. But then he talked sort of non-stop the whole way and I started getting scared that he was bringing me to this party just to make fun of me, that he still thought I was ugly and he was going to laugh at me again, with all his friends. He didn't though. He seemed very proud the whole night. Very proud. And then we went off to somebody's room.

I didn't really want to have sex with him, but he really did want to, and I, didn't feel like saying no.

Anyway, during the whole thing I was thinking about that billboard. Wondering if it gets old Rock of Ages a lot of gravestone business. *(Lights shift.)*

SCENE ONE

Phoebe crosses to the living room. There are a few changes; a missing chair, etc. Phoebe goes to the box center stage, starts pulling out pictures. It is evening.

JANE: *(Enters the front door.)* Well, hi.
PHOEBE: Hi.
JANE: Watcha doing?
PHOEBE: Nothing. Just looking at stuff.
JANE: Did you have a nice time with your father?
PHOEBE: Fine.
JANE: When did you get back?
PHOEBE: About an hour ago.
JANE: My meeting ran so late. Did you, what did you do?
PHOEBE: Had dinner.

JANE: Where?

PHOEBE: There. At his place.

JANE: You're kidding, did he cook?

PHOEBE: . . . No.

JANE: Oh.

PHOEBE: Emma did.

JANE: Oh. I guess I'll, get to my reading. Book club tomorrow. We're reading *A Farewell To Arms* — re-reading really, since we all read it years ago.
We thought we'd revisit some old favorites this year . . . I never used to
leave it to the last minute like this. Anyway —

PHOEBE: Why is that your favorite?

JANE: It's not *my* favorite, it's *a* favorite. Generally speaking. I don't know. I
thought you liked it.

PHOEBE: It's a love story. And then she dies.

JANE: Phoebe — gracious, what a thing to say. When did you get so cynical? I think it's a little more complicated than that, don't you?

PHOEBE: I'm not cynical!

JANE: . . . I'm sorry I wasn't here — I thought I'd be back before you.

PHOEBE: I'm sixteen, Mom.

JANE: I know.

PHOEBE: I'm old enough to look after myself.

JANE: —

*(Phoebe goes back to her box of pictures. Jane picks up her book, settles down
to read, but watches Phoebe instead. Phoebe has found a picture that inter-
ests her. She goes to the fourth wall mirror to look at herself, then looks down
at the picture she's holding, then looks back at herself.)*

JANE: What do you have there?

PHOEBE: A picture of you.

JANE: Can I see? My God.

PHOEBE: How old are you there?

JANE: Probably about your age.

PHOEBE: You look so happy.

JANE: I suppose so.

PHOEBE: You're laughing, you're laughing, look.

JANE: Yes I am.

PHOEBE: But Mom. What is going on with that hair!?

JANE: I know, we thought it was very attractive at the time.

PHOEBE: Do you think we look alike?

(They look at themselves in the mirror.)

JANE: You look more like your father, you always have.

PHOEBE: Not at all like you?

JANE: It's hard for me to say, I'm too close. *(They look again.)* A little bit around here. *(She points to their eyes.)* And this. *(She touches Phoebe's forehead.)* You get the same worried expression sometimes, I think.

(Phoebe backs away slightly from the touch, Jane puts her hands down.)

PHOEBE: But mostly like Dad.

JANE: I'd say. But ask someone else who can be more objective.

PHOEBE: Dad says you were the Homecoming Queen in high school.

JANE: When did he say that?

PHOEBE: Tonight.

JANE: But what possessed him — never mind.

PHOEBE: How come I didn't know that?

JANE: That I was Homecoming Queen?

PHOEBE: Yeah.

JANE: I don't know, I thought you did. It seems kind of silly now anyway.

PHOEBE: I can't really picture it.

JANE: No? Well . . . hm. *(Beat.)* You haven't told me, what books are they having you read for English this year?

PHOEBE: Oh. *The Great Gatsby, Beloved,* stuff like that. *Twelfth Night.*

JANE: That's quite a mix.

PHOEBE: Yeah. I'm going outside for awhile.

JANE: What? Phoebe, it's late.

PHOEBE: It's only ten o'clock.

JANE: Ish. Late-ish.

PHOEBE: I'll just be out here, I'm not going anywhere.

JANE: What about your homework?

PHOEBE: I did it already.

JANE: Phoebe —

PHOEBE: I don't want to be cynical, Mom.

JANE: . . . Oh Honey. *(Gets up.)*

PHOEBE: *(Abruptly turns to go.)* I'm going outside. I haven't seen the moon yet.

(Phoebe exits. Jane starts towards the door, hesitates. She considers her book, considers the box, perhaps starts to read, perhaps doesn't. End of scene.)

PHOEBE'S LIGHT

PHOEBE: Last night I had this nightmare that the moon crashed into the earth. It was very scary. It crashed and caused all of these tidal waves and earthquakes and typhoons and disaster and *everyone* was dying and I was trying to wake up Mom and I couldn't find my Dad. You know, in the dream. And then this thought popped into my head, while I was still asleep: "At least I'll die pretty." That was my thought. Everybody in the world was going to be dead soon, or dying and all I could think was, "at least I'll die pretty."

I used to dream of saving the Talking Horses of Narnia. I used to think I could be a great painter. I used to want to be Amelia Earhart or Louisa May Alcott or Harriet Tubman.

But in this dream I just wanted to be pretty.

(Lights shift.)

SCENE TWO

Phoebe approaches the steps, restless.

JESSE: *(Enters.)* Hi.

PHOEBE: Hi. *(He looks at her.)* What?

JESSE: I missed you at lunch.

PHOEBE: Sorry! I forgot.

JESSE: I was waiting for you.

PHOEBE: I just forgot. I was helping a, a friend of mine study for some math quiz. Sorry.

JESSE: *(Trying to shrug it off.)* It's OK, I was just standing there like a moron for half an hour.

PHOEBE: —

JESSE: It's too bad you're out of that English class.

PHOEBE: Yeah, I had to switch everything around.

JESSE: I haven't seen you anywhere.

PHOEBE: School's weird that way.

JESSE: Not even in the neighborhood.

PHOEBE: New York's weird that way.

JESSE: I was trying to figure out if you'd changed schools recently or something. Did you used to go to a different school?

PHOEBE: No. Why?

JESSE: I was remembering from class, how people seemed to know you but you didn't seem to know them in a way. Or vice-versa, I don't know.

PHOEBE: When were you doing that?

JESSE: Doing what?

PHOEBE: When were you watching me?

JESSE: I wasn't *watching* you, I was just noticing, it was my first or second day of school and I didn't have anyone to talk to, so I was just noticing people —

PHOEBE: Why didn't you just come up and ask me?

JESSE: I said — I hadn't even met you yet. I had noticed you . . . and then I met you.

PHOEBE: But why did you notice *me?*

JESSE: . . . I don't know . . .

PHOEBE: It's a big school, there are lots of kids.

JESSE: I know, but you stand out.

PHOEBE: In what way?

JESSE: I don't know, you're very, stand-out-ish. What's going on?

PHOEBE: I don't know what that means.

JESSE; It doesn't mean anything — you stand out because you're nice and smart and —

PHOEBE: And what?

JESSE: And pretty.

PHOEBE: Forget it.

JESSE: That a compliment.

PHOEBE: Forget it!

JESSE: I was just trying to —

PHOEBE: I don't care . . .

JESSE: I noticed you most because of English class that first day, because you asked Mrs. Dort if we could read *Titus Andronicus* instead of *Twelfth Night.* I liked that.

PHOEBE: Jesse —

JESSE: What is wrong all of a sudden?

PHOEBE: Nothing. My fault. I gotta get inside though.

JESSE: What did I do?

PHOEBE: Nothing.

JESSE: C'mon —

PHOEBE: I'm tired of people worrying about what I look like.

JESSE: I didn't mean —

PHOEBE: I'm so sick of it. You don't know what it's like —

JESSE: Phoebe —

PHOEBE: Jesse, would you just go away please? Leave me alone. Why do I have to spell it out — I, I like someone else, I'm sorry, but I like someone else, so just leave me alone.

JESSE: I do know what it's like.

PHOEBE: What?

JESSE: I do know what it's like.

PHOEBE: *(Upset.)* I'm really sorry I forgot about lunch. I'm really sorry about that. That was terrible . . . OK? I would never, I would never do something like that on purpose. OK?

JESSE: Are you all right?

PHOEBE: I'll see you around. At school! *(Jesse stares at her.)* I'll see you around! *(As he turns to go, Phoebe stands or takes a step towards him, upset. He hesitates, and they look at each other, not sure what to do. Crystal enters, breaking the moment. Jesse exits.)*

CRYSTAL: Hey gorgeous, ah, shoot, I was supposed to pick up the cat litter. I knew I forgot something. *(She starts to leave.)* I'm going back to the store, you want anything?

PHOEBE: —

CRYSTAL: Yoo-hoo.

PHOEBE: I was a jerk to that kid.

CRYSTAL: Who, the black kid?

PHOEBE: The *black* kid?

CRYSTAL: That black kid going down the street there —

PHOEBE: Why do you have to color him?

CRYSTAL: I was just identifying which kid you were talking about.

PHOEBE: He's the only kid in sight.

CRYSTAL: Is he black?

PHOEBE: I guess.

CRYSTAL: Then what's the problem, sugar.

PHOEBE: You don't have to identify him as the black kid. He's just a kid.

CRYSTAL: Look, if I were black, I'd probably call you the white kid, so don't be so touchy.

PHOEBE: Forget it.

CRYSTAL: What's wrong, Phoebe?

PHOEBE: —

CRYSTAL: What's wrong?

PHOEBE: . . . I don't know.

CRYSTAL: You've been having a hard time lately, haven't you, hon?

PHOEBE: —

CRYSTAL: Is it anything specific, anything you can put your finger on?

PHOEBE: . . . No . . .

CRYSTAL: How's school so far?

PHOEBE: Fine.

CRYSTAL: Have you been sleeping sweetie, you've got dark circles under your eyes.

PHOEBE: Don't look if it bothers you so much.

CRYSTAL: What did you say!?

PHOEBE: Sorry. I'm just getting old and mean, already.

CRYSTAL: Oh, come on.

PHOEBE: I feel like it.

CRYSTAL: Honey, you're way, *way* too young to worry about getting old. Good Lord.

PHOEBE: Mom's worried about it. So are you, you're getting a face-lift.

CRYSTAL: Eye-tuck. You're not allowed to use us as an example, sweetheart. You're a beautiful, beautiful girl, you always will be.

PHOEBE: Not always.

CRYSTAL: Always.

PHOEBE: Anyway, I'm not *worried* about getting old. I can't wait, it'll be a relief.

CRYSTAL: Honey —

PHOEBE: I can't wait.

CRYSTAL: Believe me, you can wait.

PHOEBE: I think Mom's beautiful.

CRYSTAL: You might want to tell her that.

PHOEBE: It shouldn't be important!

CRYSTAL: Maybe not, but she'd sure love to hear something from you. She misses you, you know. So do I.

PHOEBE: I'm right here!

CRYSTAL: No Ma'am, you've been very far away, lately.

PHOEBE: Daddy wants to marry Emma.

CRYSTAL: Oh Christ, what's the rush, the Fucker. Since when?

PHOEBE: Since today.

CRYSTAL: Does she know?

PHOEBE: Yes.

CRYSTAL: Is she all right?

PHOEBE: She's upstairs.

CRYSTAL: I'm going up. *(Starts up the stairs, pauses.)* Why don't you come with me?

PHOEBE: No thanks.

CRYSTAL: C'mon, honey.
PHOEBE: *NO!*
   (*Crystal goes inside; lights shift.*)

PHOEBE'S LIGHT

PHOEBE: I've been going to the museum every day now, to look at that paint-ing I told you about. The Barnett Newman, remember? With that bright orange line down the middle? I've had to make sure the orange wasn't disappearing, but I got in trouble today. I guess the guard kept telling me not to stand so close but I didn't hear him and he got mad. I think he thought I might steal it or deface it or something.

   I *was* standing very close but I had to — I had to see if it was really happening. If the orange line was really disappearing.

   It was. I saw it. You have to stand very close for as long as they'll let you and then you'll see what I mean.

   I used to love that museum.
   (*Lights shift.*)

SCENE THREE

Lights up on Crystal sitting on the steps, drinking a cup of coffee. It is eleven a.m. Jim enters, after a night shift at the firehouse. Neither notices Phoebe on the balcony and, if possible, the audience should not notice her immedi-ately either.

CRYSTAL: Hi.
JIM: Hi.
CRYSTAL: I called the station.
JIM: We were called out.
CRYSTAL: I hate it when no one answers the phone over there.
JIM: Yeah, well, we were called out.
CRYSTAL: I got so . . . upstairs I felt so . . . off . . . I felt so restless. So I came out here.
JIM: It's been a long night, I need to get some sleep.
CRYSTAL: You smell clean.
JIM: Turned out to be nothing much.
CRYSTAL: Guess what I did last night.

JIM: I have no idea.

CRYSTAL: I got Jezebel to wink at me. After all this time I had just about given up, and then she goes and finally winks back at me. Three times last night, and then this morning she did it again; I winked at her, she winked back.

JIM: I need to get some sleep.

CRYSTAL: *You* said it couldn't be done.

JIM: I just wasn't sure why you wanted to spend so much time teaching a cat to wink.

CRYSTAL: I didn't know it would take so much time when I started.

JIM: I don't know why you'd want to spend *any* time teaching a cat to wink.

CRYSTAL: Look at me Jimmy.

JIM: Could you explain it to me?

CRYSTAL: Look at me sweetie, please.

JIM: Just tell me why any sane person would want to waste so much time teaching a *God-damned cat to wink!*"

CRYSTAL: There is no *reason*. Because it *is* silly, it makes me feel giddy, because it made Jane laugh out loud last night and even made Phoebe smile.

JIM: I'm tired.

CRYSTAL: Jimmy look at me. Don't you dare not look at me. No matter how bad something gets we've always promised to look at each other. See each other. This isn't about a cat.

JIM: I can't look at you.

CRYSTAL: Of all the fights we've ever had, I don't understand why *this* bothers you so much.

JIM: Look in the mirror.

CRYSTAL: Why?

JIM: You're going to change that face and you don't understand why that might bother me?

CRYSTAL: Jimmy, my face is going to be the same, I told you!

JIM: I'm too tired for this.

CRYSTAL: My face will be the same.

JIM: Then why do it?

CRYSTAL: The same, just a little, fresher . . . younger, more awake. The way I looked ten years ago. I don't understand what's wrong with that.

JIM: Yes you do, you understand, you wouldn't have been so secretive if you didn't understand. It's an operation, Crystal! You're having it on Monday and you finally told me about it last night.

CRYSTAL: I told you two weeks ago!

JIM: I didn't realize you were serious, I thought you were just testing the idea, to see what it sounded like — it must have been obvious to you that I wasn't taking you seriously.

CRYSTAL: It was obvious.

JIM: And?

CRYSTAL: And . . . I'm sorry.

JIM: OK. Cancel the appointment.

CRYSTAL: No. It's too important to me.

JIM: It's Richard leaving Jane, isn't it?

CRYSTAL: No.

JIM: You think I don't love you enough or will stop loving you or —

CRYSTAL: It's the business, I told you.

JIM: You want to look like that woman at church? Mrs. Dunleavy?

CRYSTAL: You don't know anything about it. I'm only having my eyes done, she had . . . everything, I guess. Besides, I have a better doctor, I'm sure. I'm telling you, you will hardly even notice.

JIM: And in five years you'll want something else, and in ten years, more.

CRYSTAL: It's the business, honey, I keep telling you, it's this god-damned business. I'm not getting the work or even the auditions I used to. It's expected, almost, after a certain point.

JIM: Quit then, Crystal. Do something else.

CRYSTAL: How can you say that?

JIM: If you have to mutilate yourself for your job it's time to get another job.

CRYSTAL: What kind of simpleminded crap is that to say?

JIM: I'm going in.

CRYSTAL: I'm not going to *quit!* I haven't worked this hard for so long to quit now! I've finally . . . I finally feel that I'm good, I finally have some confidence, Jimmy; nobody knows more than you what that means to me — how could you say that! But I am losing opportunities — I lost that God-damned Levinson project last year to some *child.* That role was for a woman my age, a "Forty-ish Susan Sarandon type" or some casting director horseshit. I nailed that audition, they practically offered the role to me then and there. Remember how excited I was? And then they turn around and hire a *teenager,* practically. *(Beat.)*

Sometimes — rarely — but sometimes it doesn't seem so long ago that I was Phoebe's age, coming into full bloom. I hope she can enjoy it, use it, not be afraid of it . . . she's going to be so gorgeous . . . Jane was too. Is. Beautiful. Are you listening?

JIM: I took Phoebe to a game the other day.

CRYSTAL: What? I know.

JIM: I caught a couple of guys leering at her. At least three different guys. Leering.

CRYSTAL: What was she wearing?

JIM: One of them said, under his breath, "Nice catch."

CRYSTAL: Did she hear that?

JIM: I don't know, I don't think so, she was looking at something.

CRYSTAL: Did he think you were together?

JIM: Yeah, he thought we were together. She's just a kid.

CRYSTAL: She doesn't look like a kid.

JIM: She's just a kid!!

CRYSTAL: I know sweetie, I know. Don't worry about it, he was an idiot.

JIM: I've been feeling . . . kind of awkward around her lately.

CRYSTAL: We all have, she's at an awkward age.

JIM: I guess. But we've always had that thing, a bond.

CRYSTAL: Maybe — now don't get mad, but maybe, with her growing up . . .

JIM: What?

CRYSTAL: She's always had a special kind of, crush on you, maybe, maybe you find her attractive.

JIM: Crystal — Jesus, you're crazy.

CRYSTAL: I know.

JIM: What is going on in that head of yours?

CRYSTAL: I'm just saying that Phoebe is a pretty girl, it would be bizarre if you hadn't noticed, and that can be awkward sometimes —

JIM: That has got to be the worst thing I've ever heard you say.

CRYSTAL: I'm not insinuating anything, that's not what I'm saying — it's like, remember Jack, from the miniseries, remember? He was so attractive I found myself babbling around him for the first two days. I told you that. It doesn't mean I wanted to be with him —

JIM: Crystal — Jesus. Enough. The bottom line is you and me, this whole thing is about you and me and that's what the surgery is about too, you're obsessed —

CRYSTAL: It's not you and me, it's the business, how many times do I have to say that!?

JIM: So why stop with your face, why don't you get your boobs lifted, and while you're at it make them *big*, and ask them to suck the extra fat out of your ass, and I'll go too, I'll get my jowls clipped or trimmed or sucked out and maybe there's something they can do with my dick, let's make it *huge*, to match your new tits —

CRYSTAL: Jim!

JIM: You offend me, Crystal.

CRYSTAL: I wasn't trying to insinuate anything! I just want to work, Jim. I want to *work*, there is nothing I'd rather *do*, and I will do what it takes, you can bet your sweet ass that I will do what it takes. And if that seems 'obsessed' to you, too fucking bad.

JIM: That's right, Babe. You do what it takes. I'm going to bed. *(Turns to go up the stairs into the building, sees Phoebe on the balcony.)* Phoebe.

PHOEBE: Hi, I was just . . .

JIM: What are you doing?

PHOEBE: Nothing, I was just, sitting here . . .

CRYSTAL: Phoebe, God-dammit, this is a private conversation!

PHOEBE: I barely even noticed you —

JIM: If you had wanted it to be private, you should have stayed in the house.

CRYSTAL: I felt too restless in the house!

JIM: Why aren't you in school?

PHOEBE: It's Saturday!

CRYSTAL: What a pain in the ass.

JIM: Jesus.

PHOEBE: I was just sitting here! I was here first! I didn't know you were going to, do that in front of me!

JIM: You should have said something Phoebe — you should have something. It's not right. It's not right. I'm going to bed. *(Exits into the building.)*

PHOEBE: I'm sorry.

CRYSTAL: Don't worry about it. Excuse me, I need some fresh air. *(Exits down the street.)*

(Phoebe has climbed down from the balcony. She remains alone for a beat. End of scene.)

PHOEBE'S LIGHT

PHOEBE: *(Pause.)* I, I haven't really, been sleeping very well lately. *(Pause. Maybe she shrugs, as though there were nothing further to say. Lights shift.)*

SCENE FOUR

The Harris living room. The box is missing. Jane is in front of the mirror checking out her outfit. Phoebe is watching her mother.

JANE: This looks awful, *awful*. I thought you would be with your father. I never would have agreed to go tonight if I thought you would be here. What *ever* made me think I looked good in this? I'm going to cancel, this is absurd. What do you think of this skirt?

PHOEBE: It's nice.

JANE: I think it might look better with the gray jacket, don't you?

PHOEBE: I don't know.

JANE: I'll try that. *(Jane exits to her room. Phoebe approaches the mirror, looks at herself without expression. She goes to the couch, sits. Jane enters in gray jacket.)* It's quite a moon out there tonight, gorgeous, isn't it?

PHOEBE: I don't know.

JANE: Didn't you see it?

PHOEBE: No.

JANE: No? It must be the harvest moon, go look, you can see it from my window.

PHOEBE: I will.

JANE: I don't know if I have the right shoes for this anymore. I think I gave them away. Did I?

PHOEBE: —

JANE: I don't like this outfit. *(Starts back to her room.)* Your Dad was looking forward to seeing you tonight.

PHOEBE: I have a test tomorrow.

JANE: So you said. In what?

PHOEBE: English.

JANE: Are you ready for it? *(Phoebe stares straight ahead.)* Phoebe?

PHOEBE: —

JANE: *(Exits. She comes right back, jacket off.)* I could cancel this date. *(Phoebe is still staring at 'nothing.')* Phoebe?

PHOEBE: What?

JANE: I could cancel this date.

PHOEBE: Why?

JANE: Because you're here . . . and maybe we could —

PHOEBE: I have this test tomorrow.

JANE: Does it bother you? That I have this date? It seems kind of soon to me, I don't know.

PHOEBE: No, you should date.

JANE: We could talk.

PHOEBE: I told you —

JANE: Right. *(Beat.)* I don't know how to date. I don't know this person, who's *he?* I've never even met him, he's a friend of Crystal's — he works in the film industry — I hate this, I'm canceling — crap — it's too late to cancel. *(Starts back to her room. There is a quick tap at the door and then Crystal bursts in, drink and a camera in hand. Her face is very bruised.)*

CRYSTAL: You left your keys in the door, Jane. Second time this week. No more leaving the keys in the door. Do y'all have any oranges? *(Phoebe is staring at Crystal.)* What's wrong, sweetie?

JANE: *(Exiting to her room.)* Your face.

CRYSTAL: *(Simultaneously.)* Oh, my face, my face! I'm sorry, I forgot that I hadn't seen you yet. *(She goes to the mirror.)* It's a lot worse than it looks, I promise you. I mean it's not as worse as it — it's not as *bad* as it looks. We have a lot of blood in our heads, people do. What am I trying to say? You have a lot of blood in your face that's very close to the surface, which is why head wounds always bleed so much, and why I have all this bruising and general . . . You look so stricken! I'm fine sugar, really. Just a little sore. OK? So stop looking at me like that please.

PHOEBE: —

CRYSTAL: I'm sorry about the other day, honey.

PHOEBE: It's OK.

CRYSTAL: I'm sure Jim is too. I know he is.

PHOEBE: Uh-huh.

CRYSTAL: We were just, in the thick of it, you know? But we didn't mean to take it out on you. And the part about the, when you went to the ballgame, was just silly talk —

PHOEBE: It's no big deal.

CRYSTAL: You sure?

PHOEBE: I hardly even heard you, I was thinking about stuff.

CRYSTAL: OK . . . Jane I brought you some — where'd she go, I brought her some umbrellas from Chinatown. *Jane,* I brought you some umbrellas! *(Crystal goes off to the kitchen.)* Do y'all have any oranges? I have to have my slice of orange — here we go.

(Jane comes back to the mirror with her lipstick.)

CRYSTAL: *(Pokes her head around the corner from the kitchen.)* Where's that great little paring knife you have?

JANE: It's not in the knife block?

CRYSTAL: No.

JANE: Dish drainer.

CRYSTAL: No.

JANE: Maybe you left it at the bar the last time.

CRYSTAL: *(Peeks around again, brandishing a large knife and her orange.)* Never mind, I'll use the X-Caliber here.

(Jane has applied her lipstick and is studying her reflection. She starts back to her room.)

PHOEBE: You look nice, Mom.

JANE: What?

PHOEBE: I said you look nice.

JANE: I do?

PHOEBE: Yeah.

CRYSTAL: *(Comes back in, orange slice in drink.)* I think you're not supposed to drink alcohol for at least thirty hours after the operation, but hey, it's been about thirty-point-o-one so, Olé!

(Jane goes out.)

CRYSTAL: Are people noticing your new figure? It's a good thing sweetheart, don't look so horrified. My Mother used to say, with a good figure and a little bit of sense, a girl can do just about anything.

PHOEBE: What does that mean?

CRYSTAL: No, no. I'm lying. No, Mama used to say . . . what was it . . . with a good figure and a little bit of sense, a girl can *marry* just about anything. That's small town Texas for you. I thought that sounded just too old-fashioned, so I updated it.

PHOEBE: It still sounds stupid.

CRYSTAL: You know what honey? Stupid but true — with a good figure and a little bit of sense —

PHOEBE: Like you?

CRYSTAL: Sure, like me, more or less. I haven't had the lead in a feature yet, and I haven't been on the cover of *People*, but . . .

PHOEBE: —

CRYSTAL: What?

PHOEBE: What.

CRYSTAL: You're thinking something, what are you thinking?

(Jane has entered with her purse.)

PHOEBE: . . . you wouldn't really want to be on the cover of *People*.

CRYSTAL: I was being a little . . . what's the word —

JANE: Facetious.

CRYSTAL: — but yes I would. *People, Vanity Fair, Entertainment Weekly, Redbook* — something. Yes I do, I want to be on the cover of something. Jane, I want to be on the cover of something! *Guns and Ammo* . . .

PHOEBE: That doesn't have anything to do with anything.

(Jane exits.)

CRYSTAL: It has everything to do with it! Everything — everything — *Everything*, because it has to do with choice, visibility, and *God-damn fucking opportunity*. Sorry. Not that I have strong feelings on the subject — *Jane*, I want to be on the cover of *something!!* Where'd she go?

PHOEBE: People in those magazines always sound so stupid.

CRYSTAL: Yeah, but honey, you're different than the rest of us.

PHOEBE: I am not!

CRYSTAL: Not different, I didn't mean different! I meant . . . smarter. Smarter. OK, listen up. Are you listening? Phoebe. I'm serious now. You are a very special girl. If I could've had a girl like you I would have . . . I don't know what. People like you only come along once in a blue moon, I swear to God. I'm sorry, I don't mean to embarrass you. But you are. You can do anything you want to. Anything. Ignore the stupid stuff I say and just remember this: anything.

(Jane re-enters, ready for her date.)

CRYSTAL: There you are Jane, we're getting all maudlin here — come take pictures of me — Jane, you look fantastic!

JANE: Thanks.

PHOEBE: Mom?

JANE: Yes?

CRYSTAL: Look at her!

PHOEBE: Nothing.

CRYSTAL: What on earth — your date! Your date with Mitchell, it's tonight!? I'm sorry, I've been so pre-occupied with my own — you look gorgeous.

JANE: Thank you. I feel very odd. Oh well.

CRYSTAL: He's wonderful, everyone adores him. You'll see. *(to Phoebe.)* He's a Gaffer I know, did your mother tell you? Worked on a lot of commercials I've done, everyone *adores* him. Is he picking you up?

JANE: Pretty soon.

CRYSTAL: Take pictures of me real quick then, I can't let him see my face.

JANE: He's not coming up, I'll go down and meet him when he rings. Phoebe, did you want to ask me something?

PHOEBE: Huh? No.

JANE: I'll be back by eleven. *(To Crystal.)* Where'd you put my keys?

CRYSTAL: Not sure. Phoebe, take my picture.

PHOEBE: OK. *(She takes the camera.)*

JANE: Phoebe has a big English test tomorrow, do you want to come down and study with her?

PHOEBE: I'm fine, I'm fine. *(To Crystal.)* Ready?

CRYSTAL: *(Checking herself out in the mirror.)* God, what a sight. Jane, do these pants make my butt look fat?

JANE: Huge.

CRYSTAL: Well thank God. Your sense of humor's coming back. Good for you.

PHOEBE: There's no film in this camera.

CRYSTAL: Oh for God's sake.

PHOEBE: I think I have some in my room, somewhere. *(She exits.)*

CRYSTAL: Look at her — she's hanging out with the grown-ups a little bit.

JANE: I know.

CRYSTAL: Good for her. Good for us.

JANE: How are you feeling?

CRYSTAL: Oh . . . Jim's still mad at me.

JANE: What?

CRYSTAL: Jim hasn't spoken to me.
(The doorbell rings.)

JANE: Damn, he's early. Jim's not speaking to you?

CRYSTAL: Don't let him up!

JANE: Crystal —

CRYSTAL: It's all right, we'll talk later.

JANE: *(Presses intercom.)* I'll be right down. *(To Crystal.)* We'll continue this tomorrow. *(Calls down the hall.)* Phoebe, Phoebe — I'm leaving. *(The doorbell rings again.)* This damn thing, it never works. Does yours?

CRYSTAL: Just yell out the window.

JANE: I will *not* yell out the window. *(She presses the intercom again.)* I'LL BE RIGHT DOWN!! *(She starts down the hall.)* Phoebe! Her door's shut, it's always shut. Uhm . . .

CRYSTAL: Go on down and have a good time.

JANE: What's she doing?

CRYSTAL: She's finding the film for me, go on, I'll say good-bye for you. Have fun! Don't do anything I wouldn't do.

JANE: Oh please. *(The doorbell rings again, she turns to go.)* You know what though? I'm a little excited about this all of a sudden. It's absurd. *(Jane opens the door, just as Jim was about to knock.)* Goodness, you scared me, hi. Come on in, Crystal and Phoebe are here, I'm on my way out.

CRYSTAL: Hi Jimmy.

JIM: Hi.

(Jane exits.)

CRYSTAL: How was work?

JIM: Fine.

CRYSTAL: Good.

JIM: I wanted to check in on Phoebe.

CRYSTAL: She has a test tomorrow.

JIM: Oh. How's she doing?

CRYSTAL: Fine, I guess.

JIM: Good.

CRYSTAL: I was telling Jane . . .

JIM: What?

CRYSTAL: Something. I was asking her, I lost my train of thought.

JIM: —

CRYSTAL: Phoebe'll be right out.

JIM: OK.

CRYSTAL: She's getting film, she's going to take pictures of me. For posterity. Ha-ha. Do you think she has dark circles under her eyes, Phoebe, I mean?

JIM: I don't know. Something.

CRYSTAL: See if you think so when she comes in. Don't let her catch you looking though, she's extremely touchy about that.

JIM: Uh-huh.

CRYSTAL: And could you stop looking at me, please, I look awful.

JIM: It will heal. *(Jim touches her gently. Beat. Jane re-enters with Jesse in tow.)*

JANE: False alarm, it was a friend of Phoebe's. This is Jesse.

CRYSTAL: Hello Jesse, I'm Crystal! I'm eighty-nine years old but I just had plastic surgery, so I only look sixty.

JESSE: Hi.

JANE: Didn't I meet you? You're in Phoebe's English class, aren't you?

JESSE: I was before she switched all her classes.

JANE: What do you mean, she didn't switch her classes.

JESSE: Maybe it was just English she switched, but I, but, I never even see her — so anyway, so I just wanted to . . . say "hi," and give her this base-ball card I thought she might like.

CRYSTAL: That's very nice of you, Jesse.

JANE: I don't get it.

JIM: Who've you got there?

JESSE: Roberto Clemente, '55.

JIM: Clemente — you're kidding, I gotta see that.

JANE: I'd have to know if she switched her schedule around, wouldn't I?

JIM: This is his rookie card, you're *giving* her this, it must have cost a fortune. Where'd you get it?

JESSE: I traded an old Hank Aaron I had. I don't care about that stuff any-more, so.

JIM: Geez. How about that, she's always wanted that.

JANE: I'm calling Richard, something's wrong.

PHOEBE: *(Enters, calling from down the hall.)* Wait, did Mom leave, I wanted to say — *(To Jesse.)* Oh hi.

JANE: Jesse's the one from your English class.

PHOEBE: Yeah, hi.

JESSE: I was just saying —

PHOEBE: What are you doing here?

JESSE: I wanted you to have this, I brought you this Clemente —

JIM: It's his rookie card, Phebes.

JESSE: I was just saying —

JANE: It's nice you're in the same class, you'll be able to study for your test together.

PHOEBE: Sure, if he wants to, but, I usually study better alone.

JANE: Except that Jesse says you switched out of his class.

PHOEBE: Yeah I did.

JANE: What are you doing, Phoebe?

PHOEBE: Nothing. *(To Crystal.)* I found the film.

JANE: What's going on at school?

PHOEBE: Nothing. Jesse —

JANE: What is going on?

PHOEBE: Nothing. What's everyone doing, everyone can go now.

JANE: I'm calling your father. *(Phoebe starts for the door.)* Where are you going?

PHOEBE: —

JANE: Where are you going!? Come back here young lady, right now. *(Phoebe's at the door.)* Right. Now. *(Phoebe stops in her tracks.)* I'm calling your father — Crystal, when Mitchell comes could you tell him I'm very sorry, but —

CRYSTAL: Sure.

JANE: Tell him I'm very sorry, maybe another time —

PHOEBE: You don't need to cancel your date, I'm fine, I'm fine!!

JANE: Are you skipping school!?

PHOEBE: I'm fine!

JANE: OK, Crystal?

CRYSTAL: Of course, honey.

PHOEBE: I'm fine, I said I'm fine!

JANE: You're not fine, sweetheart, look at those circles under your eyes —

JIM: You look exhausted, Phebes.

JANE: What's going on?

CRYSTAL: We're just worried about you, sweetie.

JANE: Why aren't you going to school? What have you been doing?

PHOEBE: Nothing — I don't know — would you stop — I'm fine — just stop — can't you hear me — you've got to stop, looking at me! What do I have to do, Mommy, I can't stand this anymore, I can't stand it!!
(Lights shift, the other characters freeze. Phoebe walks away from them, downstage center.)

PHOEBE'S LIGHT

(Phoebe pulls out a kitchen paring knife. She brings it in a slow arc up to her face. Phoebe touches the knife to her cheek, right below the eye. Lights out. Except for intermission, this should probably be the first blackout of the play.)

SCENE FIVE

Lights up on Crystal sitting on the building steps, her face still bruised. Jim comes out of the house, sits next to her. He takes her hand. They continue to sit. Jane comes out of the house. She sits next to Crystal. They all continue to sit, looking out. Jesse walks into the light by the balcony, he also looks out. Finally, Phoebe walks into her light center stage. There is a slim strip of bandage on her face, running from her cheek to her jaw.

PHOEBE: I have this bandage on so you won't feel upset, too much. The cut is kind of upsetting right now, I have to admit. Thirty-nine stitches from my cheekbone to my chin. I'm not sorry I did it though, almost. Not that I'd recommend it.

Everybody's looking for an answer. I don't have one, really. I'm sorry about that. Especially for my Mom. And even my Dad. And Jim and Crystal. But especially for Mom. But I'm still figuring things out. The only thing I can say is, every since people got so interested in what I look like, I felt like they weren't, seeing me anymore . . . I don't know.

Guess what? I'm in an asylum! Or Psychiatric hospital. Or place to rest, as Jesse calls it. None of those words seem right, although I guess I am sleeping better. Don't worry though. I *will* get out of here.

That Jesse . . . he's been here everyday. Every day. Anyway, get this: Jesse went to the Museum of Modern Art, third floor. To see that Barnett Newman painting I've been telling you about. The one with that rust color everywhere and the orange part that was disappearing. You know what!? Jesse said the orange wasn't *dis*appearing at all. He said the orange was *appearing*. Like . . . like a person appearing out of all the rustiness and . . . affirming life and . . . beauty, and . . . life. That's how Jesse explained it anyway. He saw it completely differently. *(Phoebe finds this wonderfully and almost unbelievably moving.)* I can't wait to get out of here and see that painting again.
(Lights out.)

END OF PLAY

Landlocked

By Cusi Cram

For Peter, who makes me brave.

it is always ourselves
we find
in the sea and
the deep blue
dream of sky

     e.e. cummings

Things like to get lost and be
found again by others. Only
Human beings love to find themselves. . . .

    Yehuda Amichai

ORIGINAL PRODUCTION

Landlocked was first workshopped at South Coast Repertory as part of the Hispanic Playwrights Project.

DIRECTOR: Juliette Carrillo
DRAMATURG: José Rivera

CHARACTERS:
ANNA . . . . Svetlana Efremova
REPORTER/CAMILLA . . . . L. Scott Caldwell
CONSTANZA/LINDA . . . . Kadina Halliday
PIERRE-LUIGI . . . . Richard Coca
ALDO . . . . Michael Salazar
DR. BOB . . . . Jeff Allin

Landlocked was later produced by the Miranda Theater in New York City (Valentina Fratti, Artistic Director):

DIRECTOR: Jim Gaylord
SET: Warren Karp
LIGHTING: Chuck Cameron
COSTUMES: Polly Byers
SOUND: Crispin Freeman

ANNA . . . . Helen Wassel
REPORTER/CAMILLA . . . . Kate Mailer
CONSTANZA/LINDA . . . . Amy Wilson
PIERRE-LUIGI . . . . Matt Servitto
ALDO . . . . Michael Port
DR. BOB . . . . Peter Hirsch

ABOUT THE AUTHOR

Cusi Cram is of Bolivian and Scottish decent. Her plays include, *Landlocked* (South Coast Repertory Hispanic Playwrights Project/Pacific Playwrights Festival and The Miranda Theater), *The End of It All* (South Coast Repertory Hispanic Playwrights Project/Pacific Playwrights Festival), *Lucy and the Conquest* (Julliard and The O'Neill Playwrights Conference), *Fuente* (The Cherry Lane Alternative), and two solo shows, which she also performs, *Bolivia* and *Euripidames* (New Georgés).

Her plays have also been developed and performed at MCC, The Williamstown Theatre Festival, Naked Angels, Joe's Pub at the Public Theater, The Women's Project, Here, The Lark Theater, PS 122 and The Dag Hamerskjold Theater at the United Nations. She is a recipient of a fellowship and residency from the Lila Acheson American Playwrights Program at Julliard, a residency at Marymount College, and the LeComte du Nuoy Prize from the Lincoln Center Theater Foundation. She has been commissioned by South Coast Repertory, New Georgés and Theaterworks USA. She is a member of MCC's Playwrights Coalition and of New Georgés "kitchen cabinet." She writes for the children's television program "Arthur" and has been nominated for an Emmy and a Humanitas award for her work on the show. Ms. Cram is a graduate of Brown University. She lives in Greenwich Village with her husband, Peter Hirsch.

AUTHOR'S NOTE

Fact is *always* weirder than fiction. At lease it is in my universe. *Landlocked* is based on a true event that I heard over dinner while I was vacationing on an island in Greece. My friend, Kevin told me about a woman artist he knew from Switzerland who collected beach garbage from all over Europe and transformed the garbage into the most amazing and beautiful collages. He also told me that once this artist was having a show of her work in Paris, and a man came up to her and told her that the dentures in one of her collages were, indeed, his and that he had lost them on the beach where she had found this particular garbage. The coincidence, the weirdness, the dentures, the romantic settings, and the beauty of the collages (I later saw a catalogue) stuck with me. I knew there was a story here; I just wasn't sure what form it would take.

At the time, I was writing monologues. I began a monologue. I never finished it. Another friend suggested it would make a good movie. I started a screenplay but lost heart. Finally, my husband suggested that perhaps it was a play. I wrote *Landlocked* in a room of a monastery overlooking the Aegean. It was a fast and furious process. At the end, I almost had a play. I am deeply indebted to Juliette Carrillo, Director of the Hispanic Playwrights Project, and the supportive folks at South Coast Repertory for having faith in my first draft and helping me turn an "almost" play into a real, bona fide one.

CHARACTERS
ANNA: a Swiss German artist
REPORTER: a reporter of indefinable European descent *
CONSTANZA: an art dealer from anywhere, who could be any age *
PIERRE-LUIGI: a Bolivian restaurant manager
ALDO: an ex-garbage man from Rhode Island
CAMILLA: an English sculptor, ANNA's sister-in-law
DR. BOB: an American dentist
LINDA: an American underwater archaeologist

* The actors playing these roles can double with the roles of CAMILLA and LINDA.

LANDLOCKED

ACT ONE

SCENE ONE

Darkness. The sound of ocean waves. Lights fade up to reveal Anna, a Swiss-German woman in her late twenties. She has a light Swiss-German accent. The walls of the stage are covered with meticulously ordered garbage, the kind of garbage that could wash up on a beach.

ANNA: I collect things. I collect things that wash up on beaches. I collect dolls heads, sea glass, sea shells, rubber boots, wood shaped like arthritic fingers, rusted metal — I am particularly fond of the color and texture of rust — and plastic bottles so torn to pieces by waves that they can no longer contain. I recreate these beaches in places far from the sea, Paris, Basil, Vienna, and most recently Zurich. I collect lost things. Lost things feel different in the hand. (*Blackout.*)

SCENE TWO

Darkness. The sound of ocean waves. Lights up on a gallery opening in Zurich. People are milling about looking at the walls covered with the meticulously organized garbage. A reporter approaches Anna; she wears large thick black-framed glasses. She has an accent that could be from anywhere.

REPORTER: Anna, are you in contact with other people in the found art movement? You and Peter Specht have a very similar sensibility.

ANNA: I am in contact with very few people. Most of the time I spend at the beaches where I collect lost things. I like the sea, perhaps because I grew up by a lake. If there was a movement of people who grew up by a lake but dreamt always of the sea, I would be part of such a movement. I have never heard of Peter Specht.

REPORTER: Are you espousing an anti-lake platform?

ANNA: What?

REPORTER: Are you against lakes?

ANNA: Of course not.

REPORTER: Well, many of Europe's lakes are filled with rubbish. What exactly is your position on the lakes? *(Getting aggressive.)* What about the lakes, Anna?

ANNA: Perhaps I will leave the lakes to Peter Specht. Excuse me, I wish to try some of the hors d'oeuvres.

REPORTER: Are you aware there are plans to start a museum of found objects in Utrecht?

ANNA: I have never been to Utrecht. Right now I feel hungry. *(Anna crosses away from the Reporter. Anna is intercepted by Constanza, the gallery owner. She wears a turban. She is from everywhere.)*

CONSTANZA: Anna, Anna, carissima, Anna, everyone is saying that you are a vraiment genius. I put my thinking cap on, and I have an idea, a fabuloso idea. You're gonna flip.

ANNA: Really?

CONSTANZA: You need an agent.

ANNA: Why?

CONSTANZA: Because everyone needs an agent, amore. We have to think of a fucking way to sell these beaches. Scusa mei, I smell money and I get a dirty mouth.

ANNA: You can't buy a beach. It's one of the reasons I like them.

CONSTANZA: Anna — I want to be your agent, let me your agent, leibshein please.

ANNA: Constanza you don't know anything about being an agent.

CONSTANZA: What's to know, schmooze, schmooze, kiss, kiss, sign on the dotted line, time to go to the bank. I'm a natural.
(Pierre-Luigi, a Bolivian man in an Armani suit, stands transfixed in front of a pair of dentures glued to the wall. He looks at them from all sides. He opens and closes his mouth.)

ANNA: Excuse me.

CONSTANZA: Right, right, circulate, work the room, leibshein. I'm going to find someone very important to introduce you to.
(Anna crosses toward Pierre-Luigi. Constanza adjusts her turban. Anna tilts her head to one side observing Pierre-Luigi. He is transfixed by a pair of dentures in one of the collages.)

ANNA: Hello.

PIERRE-LUIGI: Oh, hello. Very beautiful painting, Not painting, beautiful garbage. I've never seen anything like this. It really speaks to me.

ANNA: And what does it say?

PIERRE-LUIGI: It says . . . that one of these lost things alone you would not even notice — but together they make something beautiful.

ANNA: Interesting.

PIERRE-LUIGI: Yes, it is. Do you like the sea?

ANNA: Very much *(Pierre-Luigi and Anna stare at each other transfixed.)*

PIERRE-LUIGI: Then why are you in Switzerland?

ANNA: I try to leave as much as possible. The mountains give me a headache.

PIERRE-LUIGI: Me too. And my country has higher mountains that Switzerland. I am always dizzy there.

ANNA: What country is that?

PIERRE-LUIGI: Bolivia, you know Bolivia?

ANNA: I know of it. I've never been there. But I've always been interested in countries that have no coast.

PIERRE-LUIGI: Excuse me, I must correct you, it is my duty to correct you. Bolivia once had a coast, not a big one, but once, once my country had a port, a beautiful port. My family is originally from that port, you know the name of that port?

ANNA: No.

PIERRE-LUIGI: I will tell you — the name is Antofagasta. My country lost this port in a war with Chile a long time ago in the War of the Pacific. Chile has so much coast, but she must also have my port. There are many songs in my country which speak of this. You know Zulma Yugar?

ANNA: No, I'm afraid I don't.

PIERRE-LUIGI: She is like Barbra Streisand, but Bolivian. Zulma sings one song that makes all Bolivians cry — the song is Busco el Mar, you never heard it?

ANNA: No.

PIERRE-LUIGI: You want me to sing it.

ANNA: Not right now.

PIERRE-LUIGI: Of course not. I am just so angry at my country. How can a country lose a coast? Only in Bolivia. Busco el Mar means I look for the sea, well you can spend all your life in Bolivia looking for the sea, and you never find it. I come from a family of fisherman.

ANNA: You don't look like a fisherman.

PIERRE-LUIGI: No, I manage a fish restaurant.

ANNA: Here in Zurich?

PIERRE-LUIGI: No, I live at sea level. I must live at sea level for my health. I came to this exhibition because I woke up queasy, you know? My house is on the beach of Rome, Ostia.

ANNA: You live in Rome?

PIERRE-LUIGI: Yes. La città eterna. Of course I would prefer to live on the spiagga eterna, the eternal beach, but a job is a job. I am here on business, a conference of seafood restaurants. Can I take you to dinner for fish, or what you prefer?

ANNA: Maybe.

PIERRE-LUIGI: You know what, I give you my card, when you come to Rome you will eat plenty of fish.

ANNA: I'm sorry, I never go to Rome.

PIERRE-LUIGI: But now you must come. You have a reason that likes you very much.

ANNA: I don't think so.

PIERRE-LUIGI: Please take my card. Maybe dinner tonight, I have a beautiful voice.

ANNA: Maybe. Excuse me, someone said the cheese is good.

PIERRE-LUIGI: Sure, sure, we chat later. My name is Pierre-Luigi. Funny name. French and Italian. But I am from Bolivia. I will tell you the story of my name, maybe later. What's your name?

ANNA: Maybe I will tell you that later too.

(Anna crosses away from Pierre-Luigi. Pierre-Luigi watches her and shakes his head, his attention shifts back to the dentures. Anna is intercepted by Constanza who is with Aldo, a tall muscular man from Rhode Island.)

CONSTANZA: There you are, amore mia. Look at this big American I found, not bad huh, he loves what you do with garbage. Go on, tell her, big guy. Come on, go, go.

ALDO: Yeah, I guess. I mean, I've never seen anything like it, that's for sure.

CONSTANZA: You two must charlar, parler, shoot the shit, so to speak. *(Whispering loudly to Anna.)* Americans always have a little extra dinero to spend on a souvenir of their trip, if you know what I mean, amore mia?

ANNA: But they're not for sale. And I don't need an agent, Constanza.

CONSTANZA: You do, you just don't know it yet.

(Constanza crosses up stage. Anna and Aldo smile politely at each other. A pause.)

ALDO: Wow, I mean, wow.

ANNA: In response to what?

ALDO: I mean . . . um these things on the wall. How'd you think them up?

ANNA: Well, I find things and then it's a lot of hard work with an occasional moment of inspiration.

ALDO: Wow. I, well . . . I didn't think I'd be saying this much. Actually, I thought I came to Switzerland to stop saying this, but I used to work in sanitation.

ANNA: Oh.

ALDO: I was um . . . a garbage carrier, you know, a garbage man.

ANNA: *(Intrigued.)* How interesting.

ALDO: Well, actually it was pretty interesting. So, all this . . . um . . . I never thought garbage could be so um . . . attractive, if that makes sense?

ANNA: Yes it does. I want people to see things that normally they would ignore, throw away even, to see them as something attractive, as you say. I have always been attracted to things we overlook.

ALDO: Wow. I could tell you some stories.

ANNA: Interesting. Are you in Zurich for some time?

ALDO: Oh yeah, I'm not going anywhere.

ANNA: Good. Are you working here also in sanitation?

ALDO: Oh no, that's all behind me. Mostly, I'm skiing. I love the mountains.

ANNA: Well, there are many of them here.

(Constanza pops her head out.)

CONSTANZA: Anna come quick. Pronto. There is a very important collector at the cheese table.

ANNA: OK, Constanza. Will you excuse me, I believe there is some good chèvre.

ALDO: Chever?

ANNA: Goat cheese, the soft white one.

ALDO: Oh it is good, superior. I don't know anything about cheese, but I know what I like. See you later . . . maybe?

ANNA: Maybe.

(Anna crosses away. Aldo drains his drink, shakes his head. Pierre-Luigi is gingerly trying to remove the dentures from the wall. He pulls, pushes, trying not to be noticed. Aldo stands next to Pierre-Luigi, taking in the beauty of the garbage. He notices Pierre-Luigi.)

ALDO: Hey, mister, I don't think this is interactive art work. I think you're just supposed to look at it.

PIERRE-LUIGI: Please mind you own business.

ALDO: Excuse me, I um . . . happen to know the artist and I don't think she would appreciate you making off with her work.

PIERRE-LUIGI: You could never understand.

ALDO: If you don't stop it, I'm going to have to make you stop.

PIERRE-LUIGI: Look, Mr. America, something here belongs to me. I hear there is good cheese, perhaps now might be the moment to try it.

ALDO: I'm not trying any cheese.

(Pierre-Luigi gives a last tug to the dentures, they fall off. He puts them in his pocket.)

PIERRE-LUIGI: Excuse me, there is a young lady her who was very beautiful and I need to find her to make dinner arrangements.

ALDO: You are not going anywhere. Give me the dentures.

PIERRE-LUIGI: No.

ALDO: Give me the dentures, man.

PIERRE-LUIGI: No.

ALDO: I am going to make you give me the god damn dentures. *(Aldo shoves Pierre-Luigi. Pierre-Luigi shoves Aldo.)* Give me the teeth before I knock the ones in your mouth out.

PIERRE-LUIGI: Impossible!

(Aldo takes a swing at Pierre-Luigi. Pierre-Luigi groans and begins to yell loudly.)

PIERRE-LUIGI: I must speak to the artist. Help, I can explain. I must speak to the artist before this man kills me. I am honorable. I am an honorable man.

(Constanza and Anna move toward Aldo and Pierre-Luigi.)

CONSTANZA: Please stop the man screaming please, screaming's not good for selling.

ALDO: This man is trying to steal the art work.

CONSTANZA: OK, Mr. Honorable, you have drunk enough of the free wine. I think it's time to say arrivederci.

PIERRE-LUIGI: I must speak to the artist. I am not stealing.

CONSTANZA: If you don't leave now, you will tell your story to the police, capice?

PIERRE-LUIGI: *I must speak to the artist!*

ANNA: I am the artist.

PIERRE-LUIGI: No, not you? Dios mio. May I speak to you in private?

ALDO: Give her back the friggin teeth first. He's got the dentures in his pocket.

PIERRE-LUIGI: Here. *(He hands her the teeth.)* This is very private matter, you understand.

ANNA: I'm not sure I do.

ALDO: Be careful. He's a nut job. I know a nut job when I see one.

PIERRE-LUIGI: Am I talking to you? No, I am talking to the beautiful artist. This is a matter between the two of us, OK Mister Man?

ANNA: *(To Aldo.)* Thank you for your help.

CONSTANZA: OK tout le monde, everything is peachy. Back to drinking. Look at the pretty pictures. Anna, I have it all under control. No problem.

Bene. Bene. Bene. Fun. Fun. Fun *(Constanza and Aldo cross away from Pierre-Luigi and Anna.)*

PIERRE-LUIGI: This is difficult for me. Sometimes I feel I have no luck. Sometimes I feel I have all the luck.

ANNA: And what do you feel now?

PIERRE-LUIGI: No luck. I think the life of Pierre-Luigi is the hardest in the world and that you cannot escape the curse of a family. My family is known as the unluckiest family in Cochabamba. Tonight, I met woman who is so beautiful and talented and then I must tell her immediately the most painful thing in my life. This is no luck.

ANNA: And what is the most painful thing?

PIERRE-LUIGI: Those teeth you are holding are mind.

ANNA: But you have teeth. I noticed them right away.

PIERRE-LUIGI: They are not mine, the ones in my mouth now. I mean they belong to me, but they are false, very good no?

ANNA: You do have a strange smile.

PIERRE-LUIGI: I know.

ANNA: How do you know these ones are yours?

PIERRE-LUIGI: I know, believe me I know. I wish I didn't know. I wish I could take you to a fish dinner, sing for you and never speak of my teeth. Every time I come close to something beautiful, I lose it.

ANNA: How did you lose your teeth?

PIERRE-LUIGI: I lost them in the sea on that Greek beach that you also visited. Life is always easy for me at the sea, or so I thought. I have false teeth. I cannot tell you why, not now. It's too much. That day, I ate calamari. It was not fresh, it was like rubber, my teeth felt a little loose. I took a swim in the sea, it was a day with wind, the water was rough, and a wave hit me in the face and kaput, I lose my teeth. I also lost the woman I loved. She was on the beach. She said she could not love a man without teeth. There is more. Not now. Perhaps in Rome.

ANNA: I'm afraid it won't be in Rome. That is a lost city for me. As lost as your teeth.

PIERRE-LUIGI: Perhaps I can help you find it again.

ANNA: I don't think so. But, we could still have dinner tonight. You could sing.

PIERRE-LUIGI: You are very kind but I've lost my appetite. I couldn't sing tonight. *(Pause.)* May I take the teeth?

ANNA: No. I'm afraid that is not possible.

PIERRE-LUIGI: But they have a value of great sentiment for me.

ANNA: Yes of course, but they are very important to the ambiance of that particular beach. In my mind they are the centerpiece. You can have them back after the show closes.

PIERRE-LUIGI: All right, I don't want to mess up your beautiful garbage. You make very magical things. I would be grateful for the teeth, I don't actually need them, but they are in my family for some time.

ANNA: Are they from Bolivia?

PIERRE-LUIGI: Yes.

ANNA: Wow, Bolivian dentures on a Greek beach. I always hate it when people say the world is small because there is so much of it I will never get to see, but the distances have become shorter. Don't you think? *(Pause.)* I've enjoyed talking to you.

PIERRE-LUIGI: You know where I am. If you would like to talk more.

ANNA: I like what you said about my work.

PIERRE-LUIGI: I meant it. You've got something good going on here. You must keep doing it — no matter what.

ANNA: Really?

PIERRE-LUIGI: Yes, really. OK, I go now.

ANNA: Good-bye, Pierre-Luigi, I promise to send them.

PIERRE-LUIGI: Good-bye. *(Pierre-Luigi exits quickly. Anna holds the teeth and looks at them. She shakes her head. Aldo approaches her.)*

ALDO: Strange guy, huh?

ANNA: Not really.

ALDO: I'm sorry. I didn't mean to cause a scene or anything.

ANNA: I don't mind. I like scenes. So much of life is avoiding scenes. It is quite a relief when one actually happens.

ALDO: I don't know, scenes seem to follow me like flies.

ANNA: I never did get to the cheese.

ALDO: Hungry?

ANNA: Yes.

(Blackout.)

SCENE THREE

Anna's studio/apartment later that night. Anna and Aldo in bed. Aldo sleeps like a baby. Anna sits on the edge of the bed; she is awake, but in a dream state.

ANNA: Tell me anything. Tell me my teeth are bad, they are. I've smoked since I was twelve. Tell me that you have loved better than this, that all this, the years, the waiting, the tears, the hushed phone calls, the letters, the secrets, the meetings during siesta, the afternoons on your desk, tell me it means nothing. Tell me you don't think about it. Discourage me. Tell me once again that you will never leave her. I am just a diversion. I have diverted you in front of statues, fountains and Renaissance palaces. I go home to stone, and clay and work till my hands ache and I think, I think if I can make something beautiful, you'll stay, you'll stay through the night. Tell me anything. I can't live waiting. Don't promise. Don't speak about the future. Don't call me in the middle of the night. Don't wake me with your voice that sounds so intimate. It is not intimate. Tell me anything, as long as it's bad.

ALDO: Hey Anna, um . . . you're laughing or crying or something. Are you awake or asleep, or what?

ANNA: I'm not sure.

ALDO: Bad dream.

ANNA: Sort of.

ALDO: Don't you just hate that? Life's hard enough, right?

ANNA: Yes.

ALDO: Well, I feel wide-awake.

ANNA: I'm sorry. Would you like coffee?

ALDO: Why would I want a cup of coffee?

ANNA: Because it's hot, because it is dark, because usually when I'm awake I want a cup of coffee.

ALDO: I don't drink coffee.

ANNA: What a shame. *(She moves to get up).*

ALDO: It'll keep you up.

ANNA: Exactly. I'll get more rest if I'm awake. *(Anna exits offstage to make coffee.)*

ALDO: Hey, um, I'm skiing Mount Uetliberg tomorrow, you wouldn't want to come?

ANNA: *(Offstage.)* No, I wouldn't.

ALDO: I don't get it. Here you are in this country with the best skiing in the world, and you just met a devil of a skier who would be tickled to get you on skis, and you want to spend all day arranging garbage. *(Aldo gets out of bed and begins to do sit-ups.)* Don't get me wrong, I told you that you have an uncanny knack for making garbage look attractive. I might even start investing in art, I like it so much.

ANNA: It's not for sale.

ALDO: How do you get by Anna, if you won't sell?

ANNA: I don't need much. *(Anna enters.)* What are you doing, Aldo?

ALDO: Oh . . . a set of sit-ups. I feel awake. You drink coffee, I usually do sit-ups or watch cable TV. No matter how many I do, my stomach never gets hard. I want abs of steel, but mine are more like play dough.

ANNA: What is play dough?

ALDO: Something soft. *(Aldo finishes sit-ups, comes over to Anna. He strokes her arm.)* I think I like you.

ANNA: I think I like you too.

ALDO: Give me a reason.

ANNA: Because you have abs of play dough. Stomachs are not meant to be hard.

ALDO: Hit me again.

ANNA: You have good teeth.

ALDO: I need another one, Anna.

ANNA: Because you were once a garbage man.

ALDO: Those are the strangest reasons I've ever heard. However, I like them. The question is do you think you can like me now that I am no longer a garbage man? Kick me, if I'm not living the life of Riley.

ANNA: Why are you living Riley's life and not your own?

ALDO: Because of a startling combination of good and bad luck.

ANNA: What do you mean?

ALDO: Well, Anna I have a knack.

ANNA: A knack?

ALDO: An ability, I have an ability to find things, like you I guess. Only sometimes, what I find gets me into trouble.

ANNA: Are you a criminal? A garbage man with a past? *(Anna begins to see Aldo as a possible canvas for her work. She begins to pick up objects to place on him.)*

ALDO: No, no, of course not. I don't think I am. Not technically speaking. OK. Basically, Rhode Island, where I come from, is heavily controlled by the Mafia, the government of Rhode Island is not unlike the government of Italy, except smaller and more corrupt.

ANNA: Is the food as good?

ALDO: My guess is no. So, over the years, doing my rounds I've picked up various, let's call them items, items of trash that belong to the Mafia. Which I really should not have seen, but by chance, fate, or what you will, I did.

ANNA: What kind of items?

ALDO: I think it's better not to be too specific. Let's just call them items.

ANNA: *OK.*

ALDO: *(Aldo removes stuff from his head and neck.)* Is this stuff clean? It smells funny. So, one day I found a very incriminating item and I felt like I should go to the police, even though I knew that could mean some big trouble for me.

ANNA: What did you find Aldo?

ALDO: Let's just say, it wasn't good, Anna. Let's just say that. So I go home to wash up before going to the police and right inside my door is a brown paper bag with more money that I've seen my whole life and a brief, but to the point note that said get out of the country fast.

ANNA: Wow.

ALDO: So I did. I figured it was my safest bet.

ANNA: Why Switzerland?

ALDO: Because I could go anywhere. Because Switzerland is clean and un-corrupt, or at least all the corruption takes place in the safety of a nice big bank, which now that I have something to bank, is all right by me. I also love to ski.

ANNA: *(Anna sculpts Aldo's face.)* Aldo — please tell me what the incriminating item was.

ALDO: *(Aldo a little uncomfortable.)* A very hairy left arm with a wedding band on the ring finger.

(Blackout.)

SCENE FOUR

A dentist office in Rome. Lights up on Pierre-Luigi in a dentist's chair. Dr. Bob, an American dentist, is looking in Pierre-Luigi's mouth.

DR. BOB: They look good Pierre-Luigi. You say that bully was an American?

(Pierre-Luigi tries to answer, but cannot. He clenches his fist.)

DR. BOB: They are sticking very nicely. That extra-emollient gum seems to do the trick. All in all, I'd say your mouth is a pleasure to behold. And if I don't say so myself, displays some of my finest work to date.

(Pierre-Luigi still with various dental equipment protruding from his mouth, nods and gurgles in agreement.)

DR. BOB: You are welcome, my friend. You were a fascinating case. The most complicated and intricate bridgework I have ever done. If I were back home, you might make the cover of Dental America, but here in Italy these things are not important. The tooth in all its complexity, is not as cherished as in the States. American dentists, Pierre-Luigi, are artists in their own right, and don't you forget it.

(Pierre-Luigi spits and sits up.)

PIERRE-LUIGI: I am very thankful to you, Dr. Bob. These new dentures you make for me remind me of my old teeth. They fit with my face, it's not like I am wearing someone else's smile.

DR. BOB: Exactly! I'd like you to buy a rotary brush, Pierre-Luigi, with elmo florescence.

PIERRE-LUIGI: Yes, of course, Dr. Bob. May I ask you a question, Dr. Bob? Something in confidence.

DR. BOB: Pierre-Luigi, of course. . . if it has to do with teeth, I may very well be able to answer it. If it's something else, I'm probably less qualified, and most likely won't give you good advice. Shoot!

PIERRE-LUIGI: Dr. Bob, have you many younger patients who wear dentures?

DR. BOB: Not many, but a few. There's the odd accident that knocks a mouth full of teeth out, certain trauma-related incidents. In Italy most commonly auto and vespa accidents. However, in this line of work you see everything. Why do you ask, Pierre-Luigi?

PIERRE-LUIGI: I came to you Dr. Bob, so I could forget my past, all the things that happened to me in Bolivia, that brought me to Rome. I spend so much money, but you must pay a lot to forget a past.

DR. BOB: Pierre-Luigi, my rates are reasonable, perhaps a little higher than the Italian rates, but it all pays for the shipping and handling of American dental products. Now what was it you wanted to ask, I have a complicated root canal at three and I like to focus before I go in.

PIERRE-LUIGI: Have you ever had a colpo di cuore, Dr. Bob, you love someone the second you see them?

DR. BOB: Yes.

PIERRE-LUIGI: You have?

DR. BOB: Yes.

PIERRE-LUIGI: Your wife Giuseppina?

DR. BOB: Nope.

PIERRE-LUIGI: So you know when you have it, something in you heart goes ba-ba-boum.

DR. BOB: Ba-ba-boum, yes.

PIERRE-LUIGI: Tell me of this love, Dottore?

DR. BOB: No, not now. Not before a root canal.

PIERRE-LUIGI: Maybe one day, I buy you dinner at the restaurant. And you will tell me over fish and wine about your colpo di cuore?

DR. BOB: I don't know about that.

PIERRE-LUIGI: Well, I had ba-ba-boum last week.

DR. BOB: Really?

PIERRE-LUIGI: Yes. I met a woman at an exhibition. She was something else. And the art was something else. It spoke to my soul, Dr. Bob. Each wall is covered with garbage from a different beach. And then I notice there is garbage from a beach I spent my vacation on last summer. And then, Dr. Bob, I see my teeth!

DR. BOB: The teeth you lost before you came to me?

PIERRE-LUIGI: Claro que si! I am thinking! I must find the artist to talk to her or maybe I just take the dentures because they are mine. So, I tried to take them and the American man hits me on the mouth and I scream for the artist. And the artist, Dr. Bob, is the ba-ba-boum!

DR. BOB: Ba-ba-boum found your teeth?

PIERRE-LUIGI: Yes, ba-ba-boum. She was very beautiful to me. Perhaps no matter how much money you pay, your past is in your smile. Yes, Dottore?

DR. BOB: I don't know if I'd put it quite like that, not good for business.

PIERRE-LUIGI: We were supposed to have dinner, but I was afraid that man did something to my mouth when he punched me. When I first met her I was like OK here we go, but then I felt so afraid of her, Dr. Bob, I wanted to run away. But I'm not going to be a wuss anymore. So the question I ask you, Dr. Bob, is can this woman love me, knowing that all but five teeth in my mouth are from plastic?

DR. BOB: Not plastic, Pierre-Luigi, a hybrid of cyberplastocine treated at a high temperature . . .

PIERRE-LUIGI: Yes, yes, I told her about my hot plastic teeth. So, can a beautiful woman with a vision, because she has a vision Dottore, can she love a manager of a fish restaurant with no teeth? Can she?

DR. BOB: Easy, easy, hot sauce. Did she seem to like you?

PIERRE-LUIGI: Yes.

DR. BOB: Did she have a husband?

PIERRE-LUIGI: I didn't see one.

DR. BOB: Well, it was a ba-ba-boum, right? Not just a ba or a boum?

PIERRE-LUIGI: *(Over excited.)* Ba-ba-boum! Dottore, Ba-ba-boum!

DR. BOB: Well, I don't see why not. I'm all for people chasing the ba-ba-boums! Holding onto them, because they don't happen every day, Pierre-Luigi.

PIERRE-LUIGI: I have your blessing, you know of teeth, and surprisingly, you know the heart, so you say yes!

DR. BOB: Yes! Yes! Yes! I'll do my best to keep what you got in there! All right, pal?

PIERRE-LUIGI: Ba-ba-boum!

(Blackout.)

SCENE FIVE

Anna's studio/living space. Camilla, an Englishwoman in her thirties, puts the finishing touches on a clay beetle she is sculpting. She is Anna's sister-in-law.

CAMILLA: Anna, I've just finished the most hideous dung beetle! You must have a look! *(Camilla finesses the beetle. Anna enters. She is holding a mauled yellow rubber boot and a rusted tin can. She approaches the clay beetle and looks at it from several angles. Camilla nervously awaits her approval.)*

ANNA: It is very ugly. I congratulate you.

CAMILLA: *(A little disappointed.)* Well, I always say, not all of us can make beautiful things. So why not make something truly hideous and scary? Mind you, I get a good price for them at the shop. Tourists somehow think they're very Swiss.

(Anna places the boot and can on a large canvas and looks at them.)

ANNA: You have a knack, Camilla. You married a rich man, and your hobby makes you richer.

CAMILLA: *(A little hurt.)* It's not really a hobby is it? I mean if you're getting paid?

ANNA: Of course not. I'm sorry. I didn't mean anything.

CAMILLA: Of course you did. You're right and it irritates me. *(Pause.)* We all pay in different ways. Your brother is no picnic in Provence. Ernst is difficult to the core. Rich and difficult. Most rich men are.

ANNA: I never understood my brother.

CAMILLA: The dung beetle's tentacles are very hard to sculpt. They're terribly thin! Ernst was the tidiest man I'd ever seen. I know that doesn't seem like a very romantic thing, but I thought 'That man could make me — the unruliest, wildest of wrenches — ordered, calm and correct.' Oh damn, this tentacle is too thick!

(Anna is meticulously moving the boot and can around the canvas, placing them in different areas around the canvas and removing them as she tries to find the perfect spot.)

ANNA: What do you think, like this? *(As Anna moves the boot.)* Or like this?

CAMILLA: The first, definitely, the first. *(Camilla works for a second and stops suddenly.)* Here I am going on about dung beetles and your tidy brother and you haven't said a word about *it*.

ANNA: About what?

CAMILLA: The show, your Zurich debut. How was it, darling tell me everything. Ernst insisted we go on a ski weekend which nobody enjoyed. Sorry, the show, you, every last word. I'm silent with anticipation.

ANNA: I think it went well.

CAMILLA: And? And . . . I need a little more Anna. A morsel!

ANNA: People seemed to like it. I was surprised.

CAMILLA: Surprised my foot, of course they liked it, you are oozing talent. My question for you is: Are they going to pay you? When is the green going to grow, darling? I hate you living on cous-cous and meusli and tiny government grants.

ANNA: I don't need much. I just want people to see the sea as I see it.

CAMILLA: As a big rubbish bin?

ANNA: No, as a place where everything converges — a place where things are redefined, or as someone at the show said, a place where lost things you would never have noticed come together and are somehow newly beautiful.

CAMILLA: And who said this?

ANNA: Someone.

CAMILLA: Is that the American someone who phoned earlier.

ANNA: No.

CAMILLA: Sometimes, I look at you Anna and I wonder what it must be like to be you. I have no mystery; I'm not an enigma, that's my charm.

ANNA: Yes. Your face is wide open. You don't say anything and I know your thoughts.

CAMILLA: And what am I thinking now?

ANNA: The American — I met him at the show. He used to be a garbage man, he's from Rhode Island. He came to Switzerland to ski and to get away from the mafia.

CAMILLA: How thrilling. Is he lovely and brutish?

ANNA: He has very good teeth. Americans have such big teeth.

CAMILLA: Yes they do, they certainly win out over the English. Most of my family can't even close their mouths, because everything is so criss-crossed and fang-like. Thank god I had an American Grandmum who insisted on teeth braces.

ANNA: I met someone else at the show, but he has no teeth.

CAMILLA: An old man Maybe a toothless sugar-daddy?

ANNA: He's quite young. He really understood my work. Camilla, it was as if he was explaining it to me. I felt very comfortable with him and terrified at the same time.

CAMILLA: Sounds exciting.

ANNA: Yes and no. Anyway, he lives in Rome. But, I'm not sure I could love a man with no teeth. Is that shallow of me?

CAMILLA: Of course not, darling. But who knows, a toothless Italian could be Mr. Right?

ANNA: He's not Italian. He's from Bolivia. He sent a smoked salmon to the gallery yesterday with a note that said, "I am in Rome now, but my heart is swimming upstream to you."

CAMILLA: Ah, a toothless poet, I knew one of those once. You lived in Rome, didn't you?

ANNA: Yes I did.

(Silence.)

CAMILLA: All right, I'll be very English and keep my distance. I can't bear to look at this beetle another second. I have to get back home. The nanny has a bad foot, and she's taking some sort of water therapy at the clinic. I'm off. Dinner Sunday, little Ernie is so fond of you. You bring him such treasures. I often find him with his ear pressed to a seashell you've given him, laughing. *(Camilla kisses Anna and exits. Anna looks at the beetle and picks up a piece of clay. She holds it in her hands for a few seconds, puts it to her cheek and then quickly puts in down. Blackout.)*

SCENE SIX

Half-lights come up on Aldo and Anna; Aldo is sleeping like a baby. Anna sits at the foot of the bed. Anna is in a dream state.

ANNA: I'm leaving. You can't stop me. All day I've been walking, walking on marble steps, the Campidoglio, the Spanish steps up and down, smooth ancient steps. I'm packing. Don't look at me sideways. Don't say you're sorry, because you're not sorry. Along the Pincio, in to Villa Borghese, down the Via Veneto, to Piazza del Tritone. The fountain, all the fountains. I'm taking everything. Everything I taught you to see. Your eyes will be dead and lonely like when I met you. I had never seen such a handsome dead man before. I thought, 'maybe there is something moving in the gray of his eyes.' You had forgotten what it was like to laugh with your whole body. You will forget again, because I am leaving this city; this city which persists in living. This city which I love more than you, this city which I'm learning to hate. *(Anna snaps out of her trance-sleep. Aldo also stirs.)*
ANNA: I'm sorry. I don't know what's happened to me. All I do is wake you up.
ALDO: I can't think of anybody I'd rather have keep me up. Coffee?
ANNA: Sit-ups?
(Blackout.)

SCENE SEVEN

A table in the restaurant Pierre-Luigi manages in Rome. Dr. Bob is sitting with him.

PIERRE-LUIGI: You ate good fish, Dr. Bob?
DR. BOB: Yes indeed, I haven't had such a variety of fish in years.
PIERRE-LUIGI: You must remember to floss, Dr. Bob.
DR. BOB: Right you are, Pierre-Luigi. Usually I carry floss, but this afternoon I felt impetuous. Giuseppina and the kids are visiting their aunt in Frascati. I had a difficult appointment today, the end of a very complicated capping job, a young American woman, an underwater archeologist, lost her two front teeth and four on the upper left; an on-the-job accident, something involving a large amphora.
PIERRE-LUIGI: Ouch. Poor woman, but these things happen all the time.

(*Dr. Bob nods in agreement.*) So, this is where I live, Ostia, the beach of Rome. Not so beautiful, but for me it's okay. I wake up, I smell the sea. Sometimes it smells more like a bathroom. This okay until I am saving up enough to have my own very good fish restaurant.

DR. BOB: And where will you have that, Pierre-Luigi? In Bolivia?

PIERRE-LUIGI: No, no, Dr. Bob. There is no sea in Bolivia. Bolivia lost her coast 128 years ago. I will never return to Bolivia until she has her own port. For now, I find the most beautiful beach in Europe and there I make my restaurant.

DR. BOB: You certainly are fond of the sea. Well that's good, Pierre-Luigi. Every self-respecting man has to have a passion outside of his profession, something that takes his mind off the day-to-day chores; the strain of brining home the bacon.

PIERRE-LUIGI: And Dr. Bob, what is your passion? Maybe a little ba-ba-boum?

DR. BOB: I'm a married man, Pierre-Luigi. I cherish those vows. My family comes first, before dentistry even.

PIERRE-LUIGI: Of course, Dottore, only the other day in your office you said you knew about ba-ba-boums. I asked it if was Giuseppina, your beautiful wife and receptionist because I could understand Dr. Bob if it was. Giuseppina, entre nous, Dr. Bob, is a very sexy lady.

DR. BOB: Yes she is. She has kept her figure and her teeth intact. She has good genes, and even better gums.

PIERRE-LUIGI: So tell me Dottore, tell me of your ba-ba-boum. It is Saturday. The restaurant is no busy. We ate fish. We floss later.

DR. BOB: Do you like sculpture, Pierre-Luigi?

PIERRE-LUIGI: Yes, Dottore. Michelangelo, the Davide, beautiful naked people, what's not to like?

DR. BOB: Well, Pierre-Luigi, what brought me to Rome in the first place, was a love of sculpture. Now you may find this hard to believe, but as a young man of twenty-two, just having finished college, I wanted to be a sculptor. Now my family, they are just about the sweetest people you ever met, but they are professionals, lawyers, doctors, accountants, one of my uncles is a judge. In Indiana, people just don't lose their head for Italian Baroque sculpture. They are reasonable in Indiana, Pierre-Luigi, reasonable to *the point of unreasonableness*. Well, I came over here with my graduation money and looked at sculpture. Mostly I just stared. I was mad for Bernini. He could make marble seem like it was moving. Do you know how hard that is? I would look at his work and weep.

PIERRE-LUIGI: Like me and the sea. I cry like a baby.

DR. BOB: Yes, infantile, Pierre-Luigi, I had an infantile response to the sculpture of the Baroque period. And then I met Giuseppina.

PIERRE-LUIGI: This is the part I am waiting for.

DR. BOB: She was lovely, just lovely. In bloom. I met her in Piazza Navona. Both of us were staring at the Fountain of the Four Rivers. Well actually, I was staring at the fountain, and Giuseppina was staring at me.

PIERRE-LUIGI: Claro que si! I bet she was.

DR. BOB: Well, she was lively and full of sex appeal — and I left Rome to come back, marry Giuseppina — and become a sculptor.

PIERRE-LUIGI: You devil. This is muy romantico!

DR. BOB: Well, that's when the romance ended. My family was appalled at both ideas. My mother threatened to throw herself under a train; my father said he would never speak to me again; my grandparents, they just looked confused. And Pierre-Luigi, I am not a brave man. My parents' approval, the love of my family, I couldn't turn away from that.

PIERRE-LUIGI: This is hard — I know this — it is hard for a man.

DR. BOB: So I agreed to go to dental school. It seemed the closest profession to sculpture I could find. It seemed there was some artistry involved. I wasn't dedicated enough to medicine to become a surgeon. I considered architecture, but that was even too out there for my parents. It all seems silly now, but I was desperate then.

PIERRE-LUIGI: Ay, probrecito, I think you are an artist Dr. Bob. I say this all the time.

DR. BOB: And I appreciate that Pierre-Luigi, more than you could ever know. *(Dr. Bob begins to cry. Blackout.)*

SCENE EIGHT

Aldo is doing sit-ups. Anna reads a large book entitled Bolivia.

ALDO: Fifty-eight, fifty-nine, sixty. *(Aldo stops.)*

ANNA: I don't see it doing anything. Perhaps you eat too much cheese.

ALDO: Well — I'm a big guy — I'm not like you. I need to put a lot in to keep the motor running. Where's Bolivia?

ANNA: In South America, between Peru and Chile. It has no sea — I want to go there.

ALDO: Is it clean?

ANNA: Not like Switzerland. I like the landscape. *(Anna holds up a picture.)*

ALDO: Bleak.

ANNA: Yes.

ALDO: I don't get you. I like you. But I don't get you. Why do you want to go there . . . what's there? I'm here, why would you want to go anywhere else?

ANNA: Sometimes I just need a trip.

ALDO: Oh.

ANNA: I met someone from there at the opening. He reminded me that I wanted to go to Bolivia.

ALDO: You liked him that much, huh.

ANNA: He had a friendly face. You don't find so many friendly faces in Switzerland.

ALDO: Do you have anything nice to say about your country? I think it's pretty amazing.

ANNA: The mountains are very beautiful, but I don't want to have anything to do with them.

ALDO: But you'd go half way around the world to see some other mountains, which are most likely pretty similar, if not inferior to the ones outside your back door.

ANNA: But I know the ones here already.

ALDO: So?

ANNA: I get excited by the puzzle of places.

ALDO: I don't get it.

ANNA: What don't you get? I want to go to Bolivia — because it's a country with no sea and high mountains, like Switzerland — but halfway around the world. I want to know what's different there. I want to talk to people who have never seen the sea and ask them what they think it's like. I want to visit the highest place in the country and the lowest, and compare their garbage.

ALDO: Sounds pretty good, except for the garbage part. Can't we do that here?

ANNA: You can't do that in your own country. Even if you don't have a map — you have one in your head.

ALDO: I see. Anna, I mean I like the garbage, I like it just fine, but what does it all mean?

ANNA: I can't tell you that, Aldo.

ALDO: What do you mean?

ANNA: I shouldn't have to explain it to you.

ALDO: No need to get all hoity toity with me.

ANNA: I don't know what that means.

ALDO: It means, tell me what this *(Referring to garbage round him.)* is all about.

ANNA: Fine. I think that we are more what we have lost than what we have — what we throw away, leave behind, lose — tells us more about who we are than what we hold on to.

ALDO: So what did you lose, Anna?

ANNA: Everyone has lost something they really regret. Maybe you haven't yet.

ALDO: Look, I understand you. I've lost more than I care to remember. I'm not an idiot just because I used to haul trash. I could tell you some stories.

ANNA: When?

ALDO: When you tell me why you wake up screaming every night.

(Blackout.)

SCENE NINE

Dr. Bob and Pierre-Luigi an hour later in the fish restaurant. Much brandy has been drunk.

DR. BOB: I was the best dental student Indiana had seen in years. My bridge-work, my dentures, extraordinary!

PIERRE-LUIGI: You are the Michelangelo of dentistry, senza dubbio.

DR. BOB: I insisted on marrying Giuseppina. I married her to annoy my parents. I'll be candid with you, Pierre-Luigi, that is not a good reason to marry someone.

PIERRE-LUIGI: For other things yes, but not marriage, because *you* live with the wife, not your parents.

DR. BOB: Giuseppina was miserable in Indiana. She couldn't eat anything. She refused to learn English properly. We had to move back to Rome. Giuseppina was pregnant with Bobby and I was certain she would lose the baby because the only thing she could eat was Frosted Flakes.

PIERRE-LUIGI: They are very good.

DR. BOB: Well yes, I've always enjoyed them myself. However, I was not happy back in Rome, it was a place — so filled with everything that I had not become — the difference between a sculptor and a dentist is large, Pierre-Luigi.

PIERRE-LUIGI: Hey, you got a job, many people have no jobs. I don't want to rush you, but you came here, I think you came to tell me the story of your ba-ba-boum. Soon the Saturday night rush, you know, it doesn't look like I am working, but I am working.

DR. BOB: Of course, of course, excuse me. I get long-winded with brandy. Well, Pierre-Luigi, I met someone.

PIERRE-LUIGI: Here we go.

dr. bob: She was a patient of mine. She came to me with a cracked tooth. Her mouth was a mess. She was a smoker. She needed a root canal, ten cavities, as I recall, and advanced gingivitis.

PIERRE-LUIGI: Ah, the dreaded gingivitis.

DR. BOB: She was an art student.

PIERRE-LUIGI: And very beautiful with yellow teeth?

DR. BOB: Well, not beautiful, or exactly full of sex appeal in the way Giuseppina is, she was the kind of pretty that every time you looked at her you would notice something new. Her beauty was shy; it didn't reveal itself all at once.

PIERRE-LUIGI: A shy beauty — the best.

DR. BOB: Besides being lovely to behold, she also was a sculptress. She had talent. Boy, oh boy, did she.

PIERRE-LUIGI: And?

DR. BOB: And I fell head over heels, knock your socks off, take your breath away in love with her. I loved her pretty much the first time I looked into her mouth. I think it took her some more time. I was never exactly sure what she felt until the end.

PIERRE-LUIGI: She loved you. You shared sculpture, a love of stones is very strong, like my ba-ba-boum and me, we love the sea. These loves bring people together. Can I tell you what my ba-ba-boum made for me? She wrote me a letter on seashells, thanking me for the fish I sent her. Each shell has a word in it. How did she think that up. I'm sorry, go on.

DR. BOB: Well, she somehow managed to make all the dead stones of Rome come alive for me again. For the first time in years, I was happy to be where I was. She was enough, Pierre-Luigi, she was enough.

PIERRE-LUIGI: Why are you not with her?

DR. BOB: Because I'm from Indiana, Pierre-Luigi, and you don't leave a wife and two small children for a twenty-two-year-old sculptress when you're from Indiana. I am many things, Pierre-Luigi, but I am not brave.

PIERRE-LUIGI: Nonsense. You are a big brave American dentist. Dottore, great love requires great courage. I will make you brave. You must see this lady again. I insist. One ba-ba-boum on the house.

(*Blackout.*)

SCENE TEN

Anna's studio. Anna holds a pair of dentures. She looks at them. She cleans them. Anna looks at the dentures again. She puts them down. She exits. Camilla enters with a bottle of wine. She suddenly sees the dentures and screams.

CAMILLA: Anna! What on earth are you doing with someone's teeth? Are you trying to kill me with terror? I've had a beastly fight with your brother. He's having an affair. That's why he's so bloody awful to me — because he feels so bloody awful. He better not be in love. I married Ernst because he was rich and tidy. Some young, long-legged thing would be messy. *(Anna enters holding seashells to her ears. She has heard nothing Camilla has said.)*

ANNA: I didn't know you were here.

CAMILLA: Open this. I can't. What are those *(Pointing to the teeth.)*

ANNA: The Bolivian's teeth.

CAMILLA: Now that is a rather primitive expression of love!

ANNA: I'm sending them back.

CAMILLA: Of course darling, I'm sorry. I've had a hell of a day. Little Ernie has impetigo. And Big Ernie is a motherfucker. He's fucking some skinny banker from Torino. I don't want to talk about it and if you're kind and sympathetic, I'll kill you.

ANNA: All right, what's the best thing to pack these teeth in? I also want to send this shell, and a message in a bottle.

CAMILLA: Packing things are in the cupboard. Let's go out to dinner and charge it on his card. Better yet, I feel a shopping spree coming on. I need something cashmere, something big and cashmere. You wrap up your teeth in peace. I'll just sit here and polish off this Mouton de Rothschild. I took it from Ernst's goddamn wine cellar. That filthy, tightfisted, fucking bastard! I'm sorry Anna, I know he's your brother.

ANNA: I much prefer you to him.

CAMILLA: Now that's loyalty. So the teeth are going to Rome. But you of course, are not.

ANNA: No, but I want to go somewhere soon. Listen to this shell, it always soothes me when I feel upset.

CAMILLA: Do you think you love the toothless man in Rome? I so used to love being in love.

ANNA: I liked him very much the minutes we spoke. He sent me fish. We write notes. But he's not here.

CAMILLA: And the skiing garbage man is. Be careful of convenience my dear, it can wind up being very inconvenient. What does your message say, read it to me? Distract me, darling.

ANNA: *(Reading.)* "Here are your teeth. I will miss them. They were one of my best finds. Perhaps you are another one. Anna"

CAMILLA: I think that's very romantic, but I'm not sure because it's all about false teeth. What about the garbage man? Is it sex? They say the sex doesn't last, but I wish I had found out for myself, because it might not last, but it must make everything much easier while it does.

ANNA: He is very physically able. He surprises me. I'm going to the post. Would you like something?

CAMILLA: No. I'll just lie here. *(She lies on the floor and listens to a seashell.)*

ANNA: Are you sure, you're all right? *(No reply. Anna exists. Camilla snoozes on the floor with a seashell to her ear. Aldo enters carrying a huge broken mirror.)*

ALDO: Anna! Anna! I've got the mirror. It gave me a gash you wouldn't believe. I was bleeding down the Keltenstrasse. I don't think people bleed very often down the streets of Zurich. The looks I was gettin! Hey Anna! *(Camilla gets up.)*

ALDO: Oh!

CAMILLA: Oh is right! Anna has exquisite if impractical taste. I am Camilla.

ALDO: Oh yeah, the sister-in-law. Nice to meet you. I'm Aldo.

CAMILLA: Well, I'd offer you a drink, but Anna doesn't even have Pernod.

ALDO: Well, I don't know what that is anyway. What I'd really like is some first aid.

CAMILLA: Of course, of course. I'm an expert at this sort of thing. I'll just get some gauze. *(Camilla exits. Aldo looks at the empty wine bottle and tries to pronounce it.)*

ALDO: Motown dee rothschild?

(Camilla returns with a huge roll of gauze, tape, scissors, disinfectant.)

CAMILLA: You just sit right down here.

ALDO: I think some of that pink stuff and a Band-Aid would do the trick.

CAMILLA: Nonsense, it's very deep. It requires a dressing. *(Camilla wraps a huge amount of gauze around Aldo's thumb.)*

ALDO: Anna saw that mirror lying against some fence in the suburbs. She kept on talking about how beautiful broken mirrors were. I thought it might make her happy. Strange things make her smile, you know?

CAMILLA: Yes.

ALDO: It's funny, I moved to Switzerland to get away from garbage, but now I'm picking it up for free.

CAMILLA: I moved to Switzerland to clean up my act. And look at me . . .

ALDO: Can I ask you something? I mean you know Anna pretty well, right?

CAMILLA: Yes, of course.

ALDO: Do you know if something bad happened to Anna, some trauma? I mean, an accident, a sudden death, something in her family?

CAMILLA: Well, her brother is a truly horrible human being, and I can say that because I am his wife. However, they barely speak. How thankful I am for her. It's been lovely having a place to escape to . . . to do a little work. I'm a sculptor, you know. I used to be quite good, but one gets distracted from the things that one is really good at. I'm not a very good mother. I'm terribly impatient. I'm not a good wife. Oh dear, it's all so sad.

ALDO: So, you don't know if anything happened to her?

CAMILLA: Well, she doesn't reveal much. Wait, I know she hates Rome. Something happened there.

ALDO: Rome, huh?

CAMILLA: Yes. It must have been an affair, a liaison of some sort.

ALDO: You think so?

CAMILLA: Don't worry. Darling, whatever it is, it's long over, and now you're here to carry her garbage, what a blessing!

(A knock at the door.)

CAMILLA: Who could that be? It's open.

(Constanza enters breathless, holding a letter.)

CONSTANZA: OK, allora. Big News. Where's Anna? I'm so excited I don't know what to do with myself. Where's Anna? I need to talk to her, pronto.

CAMILLA: I'm sorry, do I know you?

CONSTANZA: I'm Anna's agent, sort of. She doesn't have an agent, but if she did it would be me, if I were an agent. I want to be an agent.

ALDO: What she talking about?

CONSTANZA: OK, entre nous, bottom line, we have a helluva offer on the table. I'm talking big money.

CAMILLA: How big is big?

CONSTANZA: So big, I'm all jumpy and crazy inside *(to Aldo.)* You look familiar.

ALDO: We met at Anna's show.

CONSTANZA: Right, looks like you've become an art lover. That Anna, she gets all the breaks. OK time is money, bene, bene, where is Anna?

(Anna enters.)

ANNA: I'm here, Constanza. What do you want?

CONSTANZA: Leibshein, we have to talk. Time for a tête à tête. I've been working for you, all I do is work for you. Currently, you are my only client.

ANNA: That's too bad because I'm not your client.

CONSTANZA: That's what you think. I'm here to talk money, mi amor, soldi, dinero, a lot of it. The Museum of Found Art in Utrecht, they are crazy about you, loco, cocoo, they can't get enough of you. The man there, Ono somebody, I forget his name, he's like Anna, blah blah blah genius, Anna blah blah blah virtuoso, it's un peu trop, like cool your jets Ono . . . But the bottom line is . . . they want three pieces. Am I a pro or what? Time to Pat Constanza on the back. So maybe now you're my client?

ALDO: Wow.

CAMILLA: It's about time.

ANNA: A museum wants to buy my work? Are you sure?

CONSTANZA: Yes I'm sure. It's too good. I know you have principles, I love principles — I don't understand them, but this is a museum, leibshien, say it after me a museeeumm.

ALDO & CAMILLA: Museeeumm.

ANNA: I feel uncomfortable selling, everything belonged to someone else before. I see myself as the host of a big beach party. You can't charge for a party.

CAMILLA: Oh, yes you can. Right Aldo?

ALDO: Best parties I've ever been to had a cover charge.

CONSTANZA: I won't go to a party unless I have to pay for it.

ANNA: But it would be nice to know that people could always look at my beaches if they wanted to.

ALDO: This is the big time, baby.

CONSTANZA: Big is not the word.

CAMILLA: And it means you could travel to any beach, anytime you wanted.

ALDO: You've been talking about needing a trip.

CAMILLA: You barely survive on those tiny grants.

ANNA: I don't feel ready. *(Pause.)* I'll think about it.

CONSTANZA: OK, OK, no capisco. Can't get my head around this. Elaborate, amor. I want to be on the same page with you.

ANNA: I'll let you know, Constanza.

CONSTANZA: You'll let me know? Fuck, this is a hard job. Does this mean I'm your agent?

ANNA: I don't know.

CONSTANZA: *OK.* I go. Je vais. I tried. I'm going home and putting two bottles of Don Perignon on ice, because I hope to be celebrating very soon. Anna, you say no, enough people stop asking. *(Constanza exits.)*

ALDO: She's a piece of work.

CAMILLA: She certainly is. I would like to propose a toast. *(Toasting.)* To museums and taking the motherfucker to the cleaners. Now, I'll put my head under the tap and then I'm taking everyone to an exorbitant dinner. I insist. *(Camilla exits.)*

ALDO: Hey baby, you happy?

ANNA: I feel strange. A part of me doesn't want to let these beaches go.

ALDO: But think about it, you could go wherever you want. You could leave Switzerland.

ANNA: It seems so easy.

ALDO: I got a mirror for you. I was wounded in action. I think I just needed a Band-Aid, but Camilla seemed to think it was a war wound.

ANNA: Thank you. It's beautiful.

ALDO: No, you're the one who's beautiful.

ANNA: I am not beautiful. You are beautiful. Beautiful people are always trying to tell the normal people that they are beautiful — it's sort of a consolation prize.

ALDO: I think you're beautiful. I like everything about you. It's pretty simple. I like the way you drink coffee in the middle of the night, I like the way you try to hide your smile, I like the way you didn't give that crazy woman what she wanted. I like you, Anna.

ANNA: You're being silly.

ALDO: I even like the way you refuse to take a compliment. So, you want someone to spend that money with, if you decide to take it?

ANNA: What do you mean?

ALDO: I mean I like you to the point of following you to every beach in Europe. And I don't even swim, but I'll learn. I like you enough to pick up any piece of garbage you find. Anna, I would like to carry your garbage for a long, long time.

ANNA: How long is long a long time?

(Blackout. End of Act One.)

ACT TWO

SCENE ONE

Dr. Bob's office, Linda, a young enthusiastic American is in the chair. Dr. Bob is finishing up.

DR. BOB: So I think you should really invest in a rotary brush with elmo-fluorescence. I always say there's no investment like an investment in your teeth.

LINDA: Well, I'll take a look. I already use a rotary brush and I know how expensive they can run. As much as I'd like to — I appreciate your consideration and kindness Dr. Bob — but underwater archeologists don't make a lot of money.

DR. BOB: All right, Linda —I understand your predicament. So, how long are you in Rome?

LINDA: Well, I'm working off the coast of Ostia for at least another month. Unless of course there are any more accidents.

DR. BOB: I'm sure that won't be the case.

LINDA: If only you knew, Dr. Bob — if only you knew. I'm not sure if there's a tooth in my mouth that's mine. All my life I've been getting accidentally 'hit in the mouth.' I have yet to have someone actually punch me, but in some way that would be a relief.

DR. BOB: Well, Linda, I've had experience in that arena and let me tell you it's not fun at all. If I can be candid with you, because I feel I can, three of my own teeth are not my own. I lost them in the line of fire, so to speak.

LINDA: Well, I know the feeling. I've been popped in the mouth by a tennis ball, a Frisbee, a large rock, a squash racket, a skateboard, and most recently a third century Roman amphora. Someone up there just doesn't want me to have teeth.

DR. BOB: But you still have one of the nicest smiles I've come across.

LINDA: Thanks, Dr. Bob. I've been fortunate enough to work with some of the finest Doctors of Dentistry — like yourself.
(Pierre-Luigi enters.)

PIERRE-LUIGI: Scusa-mi, Dr. Bob, Giuseppina said I could come in; she said you are running late.

DR. BOB: Yes, of course Pierre-Luigi, you know me — I get distracted. Everyone has such interesting stories. Ah, Pierre-Luigi, this is a fellow countryman of mine — Linda; Linda, this is a friend and patient, Pierre-Luigi. If you are looking for a good fish dinner, Pierre-Luigi manages a terrific restaurant specializing in seafood.

LINDA: *(Quite taken with Pierre-Luigi.)* Great, I love seafood. I'm there.

PIERRE-LUIGI: And I love beautiful women who leave seafood. You and Dr. Bob, and of course the sexy Giuseppina will be my guests tonight.

LINDA: Excellent.

DR. BOB: Oh dear, I can't. I have a previous engagement. Perhaps I could join you for a drink after . . .

PIERRE-LUIGI: Of course. I am at the restaurant all night.

LINDA: Well, I better go. I need to get back to Ostia and do some work.

PIERRE-LUIGI: But I live and work in Ostia. Why do you stay there?

LINDA: I am an underwater archeologist. I'm diving for a third-century bathhouse off the coast.

PIERRE-LUIGI: Wonderful. You love the sea?

LINDA: Yes . . . I'm usually in it.

PIERRE-LUIGI: Here is the card of the restaurant. After ten, there are fewer people.

LINDA: Cool. See you next week, Dr. Bob.

DR. BOB: Yes, of course. Be sure to make an appointment with Giuseppina. *(Linda exits.)*

DR. BOB: You have a flair, Pierre-Luigi — a flair for the ladies — I didn't realize.

PIERRE-LUIGI: Nice smile.

DR. BOB: Not a tooth in her mouth is her own.

PIERRE-LUIGI: Interesting.

DR. BOB: What about your ba-ba-boum?

PIERRE-LUIGI: What about her? She never comes to Rome. I can't leave because the restaurant is so busy. It seems like if it is meant to be, it should be easier. In short, the ba-ba is not very booming. So, I've been trying to find your old ba-ba-boum. There is no Clara Springer listed in Lucerne, Zurich, Basil or Lugano.

DR. BOB: Well Pierre-Luigi, thank you for your help . . . perhaps we should just let it rest.

PIERRE-LUIGI: No, Dr. Bob — I want you to be happy in this life. I want you to see this woman again.

DR. BOB: But Giuseppina — I have Giuseppina.

PIERRE-LUIGI: Yes you do — but this is not enough. I have a friend in

Zurich. I'll make him do investigations. Don't you worry I will find your ba-ba-boum, Dr. Bob. What's the girl with no teeth's name again?

DR. BOB: Linda.

PIERRE-LUIGI: Linda, nice name. Dr. Bob. I must find Clara.

DR. BOB: You certainly are headstrong, Pierre-Luigi.

PIERRE-LUIGI: You think so? You're right. I can be unstoppable if I want to. I must remember this.

(Dr. Bob goes into Pierre-Luigi's mouth. The sound of a dentist's drill. Blackout.)

SCENE TWO

Half-light up on Anna and Camilla in bed in Anna's studio. Camilla snores. Anna sits bolt upright in bed.

ANNA: I can't. I can't.

CAMILLA: What darling?

ANNA: I can't marry Aldo. Not that he really asked me. I think he did last night, but I can't anyway.

CAMILLA: All right, darling, I will. Now go back to sleep.

ANNA: Camilla, he said he would carry my garbage for a long, long time. What does that mean, exactly? *(Anna gets up and exits.)*

CAMILLA: God, I've got a helluva hangover. Maybe you should just shoot me, or if guns make you squeamish, hang me —I feel unafraid of death. What are you doing?

ANNA: *(Offstage.)* Coffee . . .

CAMILLA: Make me one too. I suggest marrying someone you love. I didn't, and it's not much fun. I don't know if love conquers all, but it makes the bloody mess that life is more palatable . . . lots of milk, no sugar. Maybe love is a panacea, maybe it isn't; it's terribly pleasant as I recall with really horrid bits. I was in love with a painter from Sweet Home, Oregon. I met him at art school. He was lovely, full of talent. He mostly painted breasts, very large breasts, mostly my breasts. However, he smoked marijuana all the time. He wanted me to go back to Sweet Home with him, and you know I really wanted to. I was such an idiot, I just couldn't imagine having a family with him. I had this notion that you weren't a woman, a real proper bona fide woman without houses, babies, husbands. *(Anna enters.)* Now I know, it's all just something that one can do. I wish I'd known that when I said I couldn't go to Sweet Home. *(Anna enters with two coffees.)* Do you love him?

Anna: I'm not sure.

CAMILLA: One usually knows.

ANNA: I think I've only known once.

CAMILLA: Who was it?

ANNA: An American dentist in Rome.

CAMILLA: Oh, how unlikely.

ANNA: Yes, he was just that.

CAMILLA: And . . .

ANNA: And . . . I know I loved him.

CAMILLA: How did you know?

ANNA: He felt . . . he felt like home to me. After I met him, everything made sense, at least for a while. I didn't want to be anywhere else. It was enough. I loved him, but . . .

CAMILLA: Oh god, don't say it.

ANNA: He was married . . .

CAMILLA: So . . . your home had other tenants. How did you meet this two-timing Yankee dentist?

ANNA: I was studying sculpture in Rome and went to him for some cavities. He had wanted to be a sculptor. I think he actually had talent. He was a very good dentist. His bridge and denture work were exquisite. He was a good person, except for the wife. He seemed like someone you should love, except for the wife.

CAMILLA: And it didn't end well.

ANNA: No, not at all — I punched him — knocked out his three bottom teeth. I just got so angry that I had found this . . . home and it wasn't really mine. I left Rome after that. He didn't even know my real name.

CAMILLA: Really? Why not?

ANNA: In Rome I used a different name. I thought I would be a better artist if I disassociated myself with my past, as I never felt very connected to it. After I left, I stopped doing sculpture, I took back my old name . . . And I cut off that part of my life. Rome, I've never loved a place like that. In the last few weeks, I have these dreams about him and the city. Last night I dreamt I was a stone and on the outside, I was one shape, but inside I was a completely different shape. I need to find out more about that shape.

CAMILLA: Only one thing to do. Go to Rome. Go, Anna. And while you're there, look up the toothless man you talk about all the time.

ANNA: I'm not sure if I can. Rome, was so many things to me.

CAMILLA: Go to Rome. See the city you love again. See them both . . . Find out if you love either of them. Get it all straightened out — run away with one or the other of them or stay there and do sculpture again, or come back and marry that lovely garbage man, or not. There are so many things that you can do. Anna, go to Rome. Please go. Go for me.

ANNA: Should I tell Aldo?

CAMILLA: Leave that to me. I might stay here for a few days — get Ernie — until I'm sorted out.

ANNA: Of course.

CAMILLA: Time to pack. You've got to look smashing. I'm giving you Ernst's platinum card to tide you over.

ANNA: Thank you, Camilla. Thank you. I'm scared.

CAMILLA: Nonsense, la città eterna awaits you.

(Blackout.)

SCENE THREE

The fish restaurant. Pierre-Luigi and Linda are sitting over wine.

PIERRE-LUIGI: So — how did you happen to choose a profession where you are always losing your teeth?

LINDA: Oh — probably because I have four older brothers.

PIERRE-LUIGI: What do you mean?

LINDA: Well — they were always forcing me to do scary things. You know — dive from high places, walk along steep precipices, jump between wide gaps. It seemed like those were the only tings that ever got any respect from them. So when I was thinking about what I wanted to be — I chose something that I knew would impress them. I've also always liked finding things, I feel like a detective — an underwater detective.

PIERRE-LUIGI: Oh — I like this — sounds mysterious.

LINDA: Can I ask you a question? Not to be forward, but I find it easier to be up front about these things. In most of the countries I've worked in, very charming interesting men take me out to dinner and I'm charmed and interested until a wife or fiancée or a live-in girlfriend surfaces a week or sometimes a month or two later . . . That is not so charming or interesting to me.

PIERRE-LUIGI: No, no — this is not charming. I will be frank

LINDA: Please.

PIERRE-LUIGI: I do not have a ragazza or a wife or a fiancée.

LINDA: Great.

PIERRE-LUIGI: Yes, great . . . but . . .

LINDA: Here we go . . .

PIERRE-LUIGI: I have a situation, yes a situation. I have a correspondence with a woman who lives in another city.

LINDA: You write letters?

PIERRE-LUIGI: Yes. However, she never comes to Rome. It's difficult.

LINDA: Well, *(Linda thinks for a minute.)* I guess I'm OK with that. Great.

PIERRE-LUIGI: Good. *(They lean in to kiss; Dr. Bob enters.)*

DR. BOB: Oh, Gosh. Three's a crowd, excuse me. I better go. It's late. Giuseppina will get in a temper.

PIERRE-LUIGI: No, no Dottore, please. I bring out the grappa. Linda and I are just becoming friends.

LINDA: You bet.

(Pierre-Luigi exits.)

DR. BOB: Good fish?

LINDA: Oh, yes. Fried, boiled, in a risotto, why there was even some sort of a fish mousse.

DR. BOB: Well . . . Pierre-Luigi is fond of fish.

LINDA: Yes, he seems very fond of fish indeed. *(Silence.)*

DR. BOB: I think the world of Pierre-Luigi.

LINDA: So, I have your blessing, Dr. Bob?

DR. BOB: Well it's none of my business. However, you're a fellow countryman, and foreign men often don't always have the best motives.

LINDA: I can take care of myself, Dr. Bob.

(Pierre-Luigi enters with grappa.)

DR. BOB: Now doesn't that look yummy!

LINDA: Certainly does. Will you excuse me for a second? *(Linda exits.)*

PIERRE-LUIGI: Fantastico, Dr. Bob — To Dr. Bob.

DR. BOB: Linda is a swell girl. She's the real thing. I hope your intentions are um . . . honorable. I know there was that garbage collector artist woman . . . just reminding you.

PIERRE-LUIGI: And I thank you, Dr. Bob. However, I've been thinking maybe we are not supposed to be with the ba-ba-boums in our life, maybe the best we can hope for is to find a ba or boum and settle down. I feel comfortable with Linda. She lost her teeth so many times. I want to thank you, Dr. Bob. *(Pierre-Luigi kisses Dr. Bob on both cheeks.)*

DR. BOB: Now, now.

    (Linda enters. Pierre-Luigi stands.)

LINDA: I'm back.

DR. BOB: So you are.

PIERRE-LUIGI: And the grappa is waiting. I would like to make a toast. To new and old friends.

    (Linda lunges at Pierre-Luigi and kisses him. Anna enters.)

DR. BOB: Clara! Oh, my God.

PIERRE-LUIGI: Anna?

    (Anna looks from person to person. Pierre-Luigi untangles himself from Linda. Anna runs offstage. Dr. Bob and Pierre-Luigi follow. Linda stands alone. She drains her glass of grappa as well as the other two glasses. Blackout.)

SCENE FOUR

    Anna runs onstage. She stops to catch her breath. Dr. Bob enters running.

ANNA: I didn't come to see you.

DR. BOB: I didn't think you did.

ANNA: I came to see Pierre-Luigi. I'm thinking about a trip to Bolivia.

DR. BOB: I wish I could explain how good it is to see you.

ANNA: I'm not sure why I came. I think I came to see Rome again. That's really why I came.

DR. BOB: You look exactly as I remember you.

ANNA: I don't ever change. It's a problem. People should change. You got new teeth?

DR. BOB: Um, why yes I did.

ANNA: They look good, almost real.

DR. BOB: Thanks.

ANNA: I spent the whole day walking. When I lived here, I was inspired by every stone. I wanted so much to make something as beautiful as this place.

DR. BOB: And have you?

ANNA: I'm not sure. I got a lot of ideas today. I shouldn't have stayed away so long.

DR. BOB: Rome's a good place for ideas. A lot of people seem to have them here.

ANNA: It was the first place I learned about inspiration. The city inspired me to be greater than myself — to reach up. Well, it wasn't just the city

. . . I never understood why you had so much confidence in me. I had so little.

DR. BOB: You had plenty, you just didn't know it. Scared people can see confidence from a mile away.

ANNA: I went to Piazza Mattei today, to the Fountain of the Turtles.

DR. BOB: You always liked that one. The turtles are very nicely executed.

ANNA: Remember the story about the fountain, it's probably not true. You know the one about the beautiful Mattei princess that had many suitors, but one of them, who was not really a contender, decided to build the Fountain of the Turtles outside her window in the middle of the night. So, the Princess woke up the next morning to the sound of running water. She looked out her window and the suitor was standing in the piazza with the fountain he had made her. And he looked up at her and said he had tried to make something as beautiful as her. And she married him.

DR. BOB: In some accounts she didn't. But I like it better your way.

ANNA: I'd have married him, for something that beautiful. I kept on thinking today who I wanted to be more in that story — the princess or the suitor, I couldn't decide.

DR. BOB: You know, I always wanted to make something for you. I thought about it a lot. I even did some sketches. But, I was shy. I mean you were the real McCoy. I remember watching you in your studio and you had this assurance, this naturalness, which . . . well it knocked my socks off. I'm not sure I've ever loved anything so much as watching you work. It inspired me, it was as if all of a sudden someone turned the lights on. I miss that feeling.

ANNA: I do too.

DR. BOB: Really?

ANNA: I don't feel like anything I've made has been as good as when I lived here. It's strange, because recently I've been getting a lot of attention for my work, but I don't feel I deserve it. I know I've done better. I lost something when I lost you. Sometimes, I think you were my muse.

DR. BOB: I never knew. *(Pause.)* Look, would you like to get a hot chocolate and . . . do you still like hot chocolate?

ANNA: I told you I never change.

DR. BOB: (*Dr. Bob looks for his wallet.*) Damn, I left my wallet, my jacket, at the restaurant. We could walk back over there then go somewhere . . . catch up.

ANNA: I don't want to go back to the restaurant.

DR. BOB: Please, let me buy you a hot chocolate. I'll just go get my jacket. *(Dr. Bob begins to leave.)* You'll be here?

ANNA: Be quick.

DR. BOB: I'll run all the way.

ANNA: Good, I haven't had a cioccolato caldo in seven years.

(Dr. Bob runs offstage. Ana waits a minute. She begins to walk offstage and then runs.)

SCENE FIVE

The restaurant. Linda sits drinking grappa. Dr. Bob enters.

DR. BOB: Hello, Linda. I forgot my jacket.

LINDA: Yup.

DR. BOB: Quite an evening. Full of surprises. Well, I better be going!

LINDA: Uh-huh.

DR. BOB: Is Pierre-Luigi here?

LINDA: Nope.

DR. BOB: Oh, I'm sorry.

LINDA: Yup.

DR. BOB: Well . . . I best be going.

LINDA: Home to your wife?

DR. BOB: Right. *(Dr. Bob exits. Linda exits through a door to get some more grappa. Aldo enters.)*

ALDO: *(Reading from a piece of paper.)* Da Silvano's, this is it. *(Calling.)* Anna, Anna are you here? *(He moves toward the kitchen; he pushes the door open. Linda is on the other side. He somehow manages to hit Linda in the mouth.)*

LINDA: Aw, God!

ALDO: I am so sorry.

LINDA: *(Linda is not lisping.)* It's all right, it happens to me all the time.

ALDO: Did I get you in the nose?

LINDA: No, no the mouth, where else? That'll teach me to walk through swinging doors drinking a bottle of grappa. Am I bleeding? Any cracked or missing teeth?

ALDO: Not that I can see.

LINDA: Phew. *(Linda smiles in disbelief.)* Woow!

ALDO: You have a great smile.

LINDA: Well, it's fake. Not one of my teeth is real. Impressive huh? I'm not violent or anything. I'm just unlucky. I'm not sure where everybody went. I was being kissed, skillfully, I might add, and my dentist yelled Clara and my date yelled Anna.

ALDO: Anna was here?

LINDA: I guess so. I only saw one person, but whoever she was ran out, and my dentist and my date followed them or her.

ALDO: Do you always travel with a dentist?

LINDA: No but I should, it might end up being cheaper. I think one of my caps is loose.

ALDO: So you're sure Anna was here?

LINDA: I'm not sure of anything. Who is she, anyway?

ALDO: The first woman I every volunteered to carry garbage for anytime, anywhere in the world, for as long as she wanted.

LINDA: Okay, that's enough for me, I'm leaving. Buenasera.

ALDO: I think she said no.

LINDA: How do you know?

ALDO: She skipped town in the middle of the night.

LINDA: That is a bad sign, take it from me, I know all the bad signs.

ALDO: I shouldn't have asked her. I knew that I shouldn't have while I was doing it. I just really like her. I shouldn't be here even — Italy was the last place I wanted to come to, let me tell you. However, her sister-in-law told me she might be here, so here I am, like an idiot. It's like, I thought she was my fresh start, my sign that I was finally in the right place, at the right time, doing the right thing.

LINDA: What do you mean?

ALDO: Got an hour or three.

LINDA: Yup.

ALDO: You don't want to hear this. I should try and find Anna. God knows what she's up to, I probably don't want to know. You've got better things to do, with your time.

LINDA: I wish that was the case.

ALDO: Geeze, I duno. All my life I've been trying to keep my nose clean. But I'm always in the wrong place at the wrong time, finding things I don't want to find. And that's the least of it.

LINDA: Elaborate.

ALDO: I am always the guy who gets punched by mistake in a bar, some idiot mistakes me for someone else, or I'm coming out of the bathroom at the wrong time, or someone just doesn't like my face.

LINDA: I hear you, Pal. Go on.

ALDO: I've eye witnessed three murders, found a thumb, an index finger, and eventually a hairy left arm with a wedding band on the ring finger — that one was my ticket out. I figured if someone was going to pay me to leave town, maybe I would stop seeing things I wasn't supposed to. I did the wrong thing, because I thought maybe it was right. And then I meet Anna. I felt like I was in the right place for the first time in my life. Wow, did that feel good. She was opening up a whole new world for me. Now it's lost. Maybe it was never there. Or it wasn't mine to have.

LINDA: Look, I don't know your name, and I've drunk a bottle of Chianti and several glasses of this dreadful grappa which tastes like a combination of turpentine and mouth wash, but I want to tell you something stranger. Anna/Clara, whatever her name is, didn't open up any world for you — she just brought out something that was already there. *You* chose to see what she showed you, you wanted to see something new. It's all still yours. And you can still make a fresh start. I'm making one right now. Would you like to join me? *(Linda winces.)*

ALDO: Are you OK?

LINDA: I'm fine. My mouth hurts, I have the beginning of a migraine and my hopes are dashed yet again. But when you've been hit in the mouth as many times as I have, you learn to smile through excruciating pain. Otherwise, people would just feel so sorry for you all the time.

ALDO: Maybe you should just stop trying to smile so much.

LINDA: But I've paid so much for this smile. So, what about you? Are you going to chase this woman from city to city, hoping for a glimpse, waiting for the final rejection that will set you free?

ALDO: I have no idea what I'm going to do.

LINDA: Would you like to see the beach of Rome?

ALDO: Why?

LINDA: Because that's where I live. I'm not proposing anything, but my couch. I've had my weekly dose of rejection and humiliation. Do you like the water?

ALDO: I am more of a mountain person.

LINDA: Oh.

ALDO: But I always seem to be on a beach these days. I came to Europe to ski and stop finding limbs . . .

LINDA: I came to Europe to stop being hit in the mouth, but . . .

ALDO: Hey, you said it, fresh start. Right here, right now.

LINDA: Right. To new beginnings and being in the wrong place at the wrong time, but somehow it's right.

ALDO: I should get some ice for your mouth. Your upper lip is swelling.

LINDA: Don't worry. I can't feel a thing. I'm sort of self-anesthetized.

ALDO: I should get some ice, anyway. *(Aldo gets up.)*

LINDA: Get a glass for yourself and we can toast and toast the night away.

ALDO: I'd like that. I'd really like that.

(Blackout.)

SCENE SIX

Dr. Bob holds his jacket.

DR. BOB: Clara? Clara?

(Pierre-Luigi enters.)

PIERRE-LUIGI: What did you do with my ba-ba-boum?

DR. BOB: Listen you, she also happens to be my ba-ba-boum. And you've scared her off. Do you have to have every interesting woman in Western Europe? You've already left one tonight, drinking herself into a stupor.

PIERRE-LUIGI: You trying to make me feel guilty, Mr. Married man? Well, what is the sexy Giuseppina doing this evening? Huh? And your two boys?

DR. BOB: You're the one who told me I needed my own ba-ba-boum. You opened the whole can of worms.

PIERRE-LUIGI: I did not tell you that you could take mine.

DR. BOB: You toothless gigolo.

(Pierre-Luigi moves to punch Dr. Bob. Dr. Bob ducks; Dr. Bob moves to punch Pierre-Luigi; he suddenly stops. Dr. Bob tests out Pierre-Luigi's jaw.)

DR. BOB: Close. Open. I can't punch you. It's like taking a hammer to the David. My greatest work to date, Pierre-Luigi, is your mouth. I don't want to hit you. Aw, gosh, I don't know what I want. *(A pause.)*

PIERRE-LUIGI: I know what I want.

DR. BOB: What?

PIERRE-LUIGI: I want Anna. I told you great love requires great courage, Dr. Bob, but I was scared like a baby. But I am ready now, to dive off this cliff, take the plunge, come what may. I don't care if she hits me in the face and knocks out every tooth in my head. Anna. She is the only thing I want.

DR. BOB: We've lost her. She doesn't want either of us, pal.

PIERRE-LUIGI: I don't care. I want her, Dr. Bob. *(Pierre-Luigi runs offstage. Dr. Bob follows. Blackout.)*

SCENE SEVEN

Anna's studio a day later. Camilla sits and sculpts a devil. There is a knock at the door.

CAMILLA: Oh, God it's impossible to ever get anything done. Impossible. It's open.

DR. BOB: Does Clara or umm . . . I mean Anna live here?

CAMILLA: Who wants to know?

DR. BOB: Her friend, her former dentist.

CAMILLA: Oh yes, you. What are you doing in Zurich?

DR. BOB: Well, there was a conference of . . . No actually I am lying, there was no conference. I came to see Anna. I've been to every gallery in Zurich asking about an artist named Anna who works with garbage. The last one I went to gave me this address.

CAMILLA: She's not here. I am not expecting her back any time soon. I suggest you phone next time, maybe when your wife goes out for milk?

DR. BOB: You know about Giuseppina?

CAMILLA: I know, oh yes I know. You are talking to the wrong person if you want sympathy, or anything resembling compassion. I've just left my husband because he's been having an affair with his Italian co-banker. This is a bust of him. I don't know when Anna will be back. She wouldn't tell me because I can't keep a secret. If you'll excuse me, I've got some work to do. I used to be a very good sculptor and then it became a hobby. I am trying to remedy that. Sorry if I am rambling on. I haven't seen a grownup in days, just my son. He's at the daycare. I sacked the nanny. She was too pretty.

DR. BOB: Could I ask a favor? It may sound a little strange.

CAMILLA: What? I'm not into anything strange, particularly with somebody who has a wife.

DR. BOB: Can I just watch you work, maybe hold a piece of clay? I think I'd like to. I used to work with clay. I haven't allowed myself the pleasure in over twenty years.

CAMILLA: Are you all right?

DR. BOB: I'm fine, just fine. Everything is upside down, but I am doing fine. Here I am in Zurich and seems I came here just to see you make something out of nothing. I thought I would come here and have something to say to Anna. I thought I might tell her that I miss and that I know I will always miss her. I didn't come to Zurich to win her back or promise her anything, it's too late for promises, just to tell her that I miss her. She has scarred me, but I am grateful for the scars, if that makes sense?

CAMILLA: It makes a lot of sense. It's what we do with those scars that's so difficult. I'll tell her.

DR. BOB: Thank you. Could I just watch you work for a little while, pretend I'm not here.

CAMILLA: I'm not much good at that sort of thing.

DR. BOB: All right. I'm sorry. I'll leave.

CAMILLA: No, no please stay. But if you stay, I'll have to chat. I just can't pretend you're not here. *(Camilla hands Dr. Bob some clay. Camilla continues to work with the clay.)*

CAMILLA: I like Americans. I should have married an American. A painter. I wanted something safe. Now I know nothing is safe. He was from Sweet Home, Oregon. It seemed so far away. Now nothing seems far away. New Zealand seems close.

(Blackout.)

SCENE EIGHT

Greece. The stage is cleared. Blue Light is reflected on the back walls covered in garbage. The sound of the sea and Greek Bouzouki music. Anna sits with a sketchpad, sketching a large seashell. Pierre-Luigi enters; he is out of breath.

PIERRE-LUIGI: Anna! I knew you would be here. I knew you would be in Greece. I just knew it. I went to the hotel and asked for you, I said have you seen the pretty Swiss lady artist and the man said . . .
(Anna holds up her hand for Pierre-Luigi to be quiet and continues sketching.)

ANNA: Not bad. I've been finding things I like and drawing them. I think next I'll sculpt them and then maybe put them all together, in a sort of three-dimensional collage.
(Pierre-Luigi looks over Anna's shoulder at the sketch.)

PIERRE-LUIGI: I like the seashell. It looks powerful.

ANNA: It is powerful. *(Anna sketches some more.)*

PIERRE-LUIGI: I found you.

ANNA: You seem to find a lot of things.

PIERRE-LUIGI: What do you mean?

ANNA: You found me, you found that pretty girl in Rome, and maybe you found another one on the ferry coming here, who knows. You're such a finder.

PIERRE-LUIGI: It was nothing, Anna, believe me.

ANNA: You said your heart was swimming upstream to me.

PIERRE-LUIGI: It was, it is. It's just a long way up, you know? That girl was just a distraction.

ANNA: Well, I had a distraction of my own in Zurich.

PIERRE-LUIGI: I see.

ANNA: He offered to carry my garbage for as long as I wanted.

PIERRE-LUIGI: Oh, did he? That's a good line.

ANNA: But I realized I didn't want anyone else to carry it. And that maybe I should stop thinking about lost things and think about what I have.

PIERRE-LUIGI: You have me, Anna. You have me. *(He leans in to kiss her, but then pulls away.)* I can't. I want to, I really want to, but I can't. I have some problems.

ANNA: Is it me?

PIERRE-LUIGI: No, no. It's me. When I love a woman, something always happens to my teeth. Once, I was almost married but the bad luck got in the way.

ANNA: What happened?

PIERRE-LUIGI: I almost married the most beautiful girl in Cohabamba. Maria Belen, flowers bloomed when she walked into a room. We had a wedding with five thousand white carnations and incense . . . lots of incense.

ANNA: So, you were married?

PIERRE-LUIGI: I said I had a wedding. The priest, Padre Gustavo, was a holy man, but old with cataracts. He got carried away with swinging the incense holder and he hit me in the mouth before the vows. That's how I lost my teeth.

ANNA: How horrible. What did you do?

PIERRE-LUIGI: The only thing I could do, I ran away. Maria Belen looked ant me and roared with laughter. I had never seen her look like that before. My grandmother followed me out of the church. She said I could only break the bad luck if I left Cohabamba. Then she gave me some cash and her dentures.

ANNA: And those were the ones I found?

PIERRE-LUIGI: Yes. It's too weird right? I think I will leave now.

ANNA: Pierre-Luigi, don't go. We lose things, so we can find new things.

PIERRE-LUIGI: I'm not sure it's so easy, Anna. Some things cannot be replaced.

ANNA: What things, Pierre-Luigi?

PIERRE-LUIGI: Big things, Things you can't put in your hand . . . all my life I dreamt of the sea, Anna. Mostly I dreamt of fish. Sometimes I was the fish. Even before I almost got married, I knew I would leave Bolivia, because at night I dreamt only of the sea. And then . . . I finally got there. Anything was possible, I could be anyone. I became Pierre-Luigi. Pedro Luis and all his bad luck was gone . . . But you take your country with you, I am now Pierre-Luigi, but at night alone in my bed, I am still Pedro Luis. I speak many languages, but now I dream only of Bolivia, in Spanish.

ANNA: You should go back. It's your home.

PIERRE-LUIGI: I don't know if home is a place anymore. I'm a little bit of everything now, like a tapas.

ANNA: Do you think another person can be your home?

PIERRE-LUIGI: I hope so . . . Is that what Dr. Bob is for you? He is a wonderful dentist and a wonderful man too. Do you still love him, Anna?

ANNA: That's a difficult question.

PIERRE-LUIGI: Believe me, it was hard to ask.

ANNA: Growing up, I never felt at home, I always felt like I was just passing through, that the mountains outside my window were too large to understand. I also dreamt of the sea. Sometimes I was a seashell in my dreams. Bob pulled me out of that seashell and made me see myself. He made me feel I could do or be anything. But, Bob is not my home anymore. I'm homeless.

PIERRE-LUIGI: Let me be your home. Anna, I think you found my teeth, so you could find me. I have something for you. *(Pierre-Luigi hands Anna a package.)* Take them Anna, cut them up, throw them away, whatever, I want you to have them.

(Anna opens the package. It is Pierre-Luigi's dentures. The same dentures that were in Anna's exhibition.)

ANNA: Thank you, Pierre-Luigi, thank you. *(Anna kisses Pierre-Luigi.)*

PIERRE-LUIGI: Everything OK with the teeth?

ANNA: They're perfect. But I can't accept these, they brought you to Europe.

PIERRE-LUIGI: Please, they were mi abuela's, maybe she brought us together from heaven. Anna, do you think you could possibly be Mrs. Pierre-Luigi? I don't have a ring. Take the teeth instead.

ANNA: Can I take the teeth and promise to consider your offer. I need some time. You see, I'm changing what I'm doing in my work, I want to experiment with stone again and my head is full of ideas.

PIERRE-LUIGI: Time? OK. Stone, garbage, whatever you do is beautiful. *(He kisses her.)* Where will you go next? *(Pierre-Luigi and Anna keep kissing each other through these lines.)*

ANNA: Here.

PIERRE-LUIGI: Me too. Everyday I will ask you.

ANNA: What about your job?

PIERRE-LUIGI: I have no job. I left. I have a little money, maybe now is the time to open a fish restaurant. *(Pierre-Luigi stops kissing Anna. Very serious.)* Anna.

ANNA: What?

PIERRE-LUIGI: Do you like fish?

ANNA: I love fish. *(They kiss again.)* And I am inviting you to a big fish lunch. I'll meet you at the taverna in a minute.

PIERRE-LUIGI: So, you haven't said no?

ANNA: Yes, I haven't said no.

PIERRE-LUIGI: I am known for my stamina.

ANNA: Good.

PIERRE-LUIGI: Please do not disappear again.

ANNA: I'll try not to.

PIERRE-LUIGI: I won't move until I have your word.

ANNA: You have my word. I won't go anywhere until after lunch.

PIERRE-LUIGI: Well, that's something.

ANNA: Encouraging, Pedro Luis?

PIERRE-LUIGI: Demasiado. Almost, I am almost happy. *(Pierre-Luigi exits singing, Busco El Mar. Silence. Anna looks at the sea.)*

ANNA: To saying yes to museums and to muses old and new, to eternal cities and cities I have yet to see, to finding what I've lost and knowing what I've found. And to a long, long lunch.

(She pulls back her arm to throw the teeth into the "sea." Blackout. The sound of the teeth hitting the water.)

END OF PLAY

Two-Headed
A play of History

By Julie Jensen

To the 19th century women of Mormon Utah,
brave, bold, and hard-working,
my great-great grandmother among them, Phidelia Dame Farrer.
And to Juanita Brooks, historian and writer,
who always told the truth.

ORIGINAL PRODUCTION
February 2 – March 12, 2000, Salt Lake Acting Company
Salt Lake City, UT

EXECUTIVE PRODUCERS: Allen Nevins and Nancy Borgenicht
DIRECTOR: Keven Myhre
SET DESIGN: Keven Myhre
COSTUME DESIGN: K.L. Alberts
LIGHT DESIGN: Jim Craig
COMPOSER/SOUND DESIGN: Kevin Mathie
STAGE MANAGER: Barbara Sturgis

CAST:
LAVINIA . . . . Anita Booher
HETTIE . . . . Valerie Kittel

SUBSEQUENT PRODUCTIONS
May 3 – 28, 2000, Women's Project and Productions, New York, NY

ARTISTIC DIRECTOR: Julia Miles
DIRECTOR: Joan Vail Thorne
COSTUME DESIGN: Carrie Robbins
LIGHTING DESIGN: Michael Lincoln
MANAGING DIRECTOR: Patricia Taylor
SET DESIGN: David P. Gordon
STAGE MANAGER: Paul A. Kochman

CAST:
LAVINIA . . . . Dierdre O'Connell
HETTIE . . . . Lizbeth Mackay

January 11 – February 25, 2001, TimeScape Arts Group
In collaboration with LA County Arts Commission
and ASK Theatre Projects, Los Angeles, CA

DIRECTOR: Veronica Brady
PRODUCERS: John J. Flynn, Sandy Kenyon and Patty Briles
SET DESIGN: Patty Briles
LIGHTING DESIGN: Robert Fromer

SOUND DESIGN: Shark
PROPS: Chuck Olsen
COSTUME DESIGN: Sandy Kenyon
STAGE MANAGER: Amy London
DRAMATURG: John J. Flynn

CAST:
LAVINIA . . . . Mary Mara
HETTIE . . . . Colette Kilroy

DEVELOPMENT HISTORY
This play was commissioned by ASK Theatre Projects in Los Angeles and received an in-house reading there. It was workshopped at Shenandoah Playwrights Retreat and at ASK's Spring Retreat. It was given staged readings at Salt Lake Acting Company in Salt Lake City, Bottom's Dream in Los Angeles, New Dramatists in New York City and the Women's Project in New York City. It was given a workshop production as part of ASK's Common Ground Festival and another as winner of the playwriting competition at Mill Mountain Theatre in Roanoke, VA.

Early in 2000, it was produced by Salt Lake Acting Company and later by the Women's Project in New York City, where it received enthusiastic reviews. Early in 2001, it was produced In Los Angeles by TimeScape at the Anson Ford Theatre, was nominated for three Ovation Awards, won three *LA Weekly* Awards, and was named one of the best plays of the year by *LA Times*.

ACKNOWLEDGEMENTS
The playwright owes special thanks to Ann Loux, Elizabeth Murphy, Frank Dwyer, Elissa Adams, Mead Hunter, Davey Marlin-Jones, Lee Mikeska Gardner, Jane Ridley, Wendy Liscow, Veronica Brady, Christine Dunford, Colette Kilroy, Joan Vail Thorne, Jere Hodgin, and Julia Miles.

ABOUT THE AUTHOR
Julie Jensen's play *Two-Headed* was commissioned by ASK Theatre Projects in Los Angeles and was developed the Common Ground Festival and the Shenandoah Playwrights Retreat. It won the Mill Mountain Theatre Playwriting Competition and has had successful productions at Salt Lake Acting

Company, Salt Lake City, UT; the Women's Project in New York City, where it received enthusiastic reviews, and TimeScape Arts Group in Los Angeles, CA, where it won the *LA Weekly* Award for best writing.

Jensen's earlier plays include *Last Lists of My Mad Mother*, produced widely and published by Dramatic Publishing; *The Lost Vegas Series*, winner of the Joseph Jefferson Award for Best New Work; and *White Money*, winner of an award from the Fund for New American Plays. Currently the recipient of an Artist Residency Grant from NEA/TCG and a major grant from the Pew Charitable Trust, she is Resident Playwright at Salt Lake Acting Company in Salt Lake City.

CHARACTERS

LAVINIA: a woman between ages of 10 and 50, from rural southern Utah; feisty, opinionated.

HETTIE: a woman between the ages of 10 and 50, from rural southern Utah; a believer, salt-of-the-earth.

SETTING

The play is set outdoors in the back lot of a large rock house in rural southern Utah in the 19th century. The central focus is a root cellar and a tree. The action covers 40 years, and in simple ways, the passage of time might be suggested in the set.

HISTORICAL NOTE

In the fall of 1857, ten years after the first Mormons arrived in the Salt Lake Valley, a wagon train of 127 immigrants from Missouri and Arkansas were slaughtered in southern Utah by Mormon zealots. The event is known as the Mountain Meadows Massacre. Only one man, John D. Lee, was ever tried for the crime. The jury could not reach unanimity in his first trial, but in a second, he was convicted and executed.

TWO-HEADED

SCENE ONE — LAVINIA'S TREASURE

DATE: 1857
AGES: 10

> *This scene takes place out-of-doors, near a root cellar. It is evening in late*
> *summer. Lavinia, age 10, is climbing a tree, a branch of which hangs over*
> *the cellar. Her friend, Hettie, the same age, is sitting on the cellar door.*

LAVINIA: If Jane was a animal, what would she be?

HETTIE: *(Having played this game too many times already.)* Ah . . . Ah . . . Horse.

LAVINIA: No! Guess again.

HETTIE: Ah . . . sheep.

LAVINIA: Hettie, you have no imagination. Horse, sheep. Them are both awful. Ugly, huge and clumsy.

HETTIE: She reminds me of something I can't remember.

LAVINIA: What is it?

HETTIE: I don't know, do I? I can't remember, can I?

LAVINIA: I'll tell you what it is.

HETTIE: What?

LAVINIA: Mourning dove.

HETTIE: Oh.

LAVINIA: Remember that mourning dove I raised in a box?

HETTIE: Yeah.

LAVINIA: You never seen a smoother, softer thing than the neck of a baby mourning dove . . .

HETTIE: So when are we gonna see the two-headed calf?

LAVINIA: . . . That's like Jane. Very smooth and soft. What do you think?

HETTIE: I guess.

LAVINIA: She acts like that, too. She acts smooth and soft. Mourning dove behavior. Don't you think?

HETTIE: I don't think I know what you're talking about.

LAVINIA: Jane! I am speaking of Jane!

HETTIE: Oh. Well, when are we gonna see the two-headed calf?

LAVINIA: I don't want to show it to you before I show it to Jane.
 (Hettie, butt in air, tries to see through the cracks in the cellar door.)
 (Lavinia grabs the tree branch and dangles a few feet off the ground.)
LAVINIA: When I look at Jane doing something ordinary, I think, "Oh, that ain't one bit ordinary, that is beautiful." That's how I think when I see Jane. What do you think when you see Jane!
HETTIE: Huh?
LAVINIA: What do you . . . Oh, never mind. *(She drops from the tree branch.)*
HETTIE: I can't stay out here too long, you know.
LAVINIA: How come?
HETTIE: That wagon train of emigrants.
LAVINIA: What about them?
HETTIE: No one knows where they are.
 (A pause as Lavinia ponders a decision.)
LAVINIA: I know where they are.
HETTIE: They ain't at Mountain Meadow. They was supposed to be camped at Mountain Meadow. But they ain't at Mountain Meadow.
LAVINIA: And . . .
HETTIE: And well, they could be anywheres. They could be hiding.
LAVINIA: So . . .
HETTIE: Well, things could get stoled.
LAVINIA: What could get stoled?
HETTIE: Children, small animals, pret-near anything. *We* could get stoled.
LAVINIA: Who would want to steal you? *(Lavinia ducks behind the tree.)*
HETTIE: Them emigrants are from Missouri. They would steal anything. They stoled Nolan's dog. And they ate it. If they ate a dog, they could eat a child.
 (Lavinia jumps out from behind the tree.)
LAVINIA: *(Softly.)* Boo.
 (Hettie leaps and screams.)
LAVINIA: In the afterlife, the beast will eat of the man.
HETTIE: Meaning?
LAVINIA: Two words: Be. Ware.
HETTIE: Anyways, I ain't supposed to stay out past dark.
LAVINIA: Well then, you'll have to wait till tomorrow to see the two-headed calf.
HETTIE: I ain't waiting till tomorrow! I *can't* wait till tomorrow.
LAVINIA: Sorry. But you will have to.

HETTIE: I tell you, I am a crazy peson when it comes to two-headed things. I just can't stand it till I see them.

LAVINIA: Then it's too bad you won't be able to see the two-headed calf till tomorrow.

HETTIE: So far, I have seen three two-headed things. Course, Ezra, he's seen four. I have seen a two-headed sheep, a two-headed pup and a two-headed snake.

LAVINIA: But you ain't seen a two-headed calf.

HETTIE: No.

LAVINIA: There's lots of other things, too. Besides the two-headed calf.

HETTIE: What other things?

(Lavinia invents an answer.)

LAVINIA: Scissors and dolls.

HETTIE: You mean, under this here cellar door, there is scissors, dolls *and* a two-headed calf?

LAVINIA: Pickled.

HETTIE: Pickled two-headed calf.

LAVINIA: In a vinegar jar.

HETTIE: In a vinegar jar.

LAVINIA: That's right.

HETTIE: I can't hardly imagine it. Where you think it come from?

LAVINIA: I think it could be a miracle.

HETTIE: Oh no.

LAVINIA: Miracle. Like pillar of salt.

HETTIE: Miracle. Like the Three Nephites. Like the Golden Plates. Like the seagulls eating the grasshoppers.

LAVINIA: Miracle. Like the answer to a prayer.

HETTIE: No! You *prayed* for a two-headed calf?

LAVINIA: God's will be done. *(Lavinia jumps off the cellar.)*

HETTIE: I'm gonna start praying. I tell you, I just love two-headed things.

LAVINIA: You think Jane will like it?

HETTIE: I don't think there's nothing that's two-headed I don't like.

LAVINIA: You think Jane will find it inter-esting?

HETTIE: Yeah. Probably.

LAVINIA: I think she will find it "irresistible."

HETTIE: If I was gonna pray for a two-headed thing, I would pray for a . . . a two-headed horse.

(Hettie kneels, ready to pray.)

LAVINIA: Wanna hear this idea?

HETTIE: Or maybe I would pray for a two-headed bob cat.

LAVINIA: *(More insistent.)* Wanna hear this idea?

HETTIE: Oh no. I would pray for a two-headed Ezra. Then me and Jane could divide him up.

LAVINIA: I said. Do you want to hear this idea?

HETTIE: I guess.

(Lavinia stands up high on the cellar roof, proclaiming a great truth.)

LAVINIA: There are toads of life. And there are doves of life.

HETTIE: Oh.

LAVINIA: You wanna know what it means?

HETTIE: I know what it means.

LAVINIA: What?

HETTIE: Everyone's a dove, if they want to be.

LAVINIA: No. *(She jumps off the cellar.)* Everyone's toads, the whole world is toads! Except for Jane.

HETTIE: Oh. *(Pause.)* So how long we got to wait for her?

LAVINIA: As long as it takes, Hettie.

HETTIE: How long *is* that?

LAVINIA: As long as it takes to get four cows from the bottom of the pasture, put them in the shed, milk them and come back.

HETTIE: Let me just sneak one look at the two-headed calf, and then I'll leave. You can show everything to Jane. By yourself.

LAVINIA: No. *(Lavinia jumps up and grabs the tree branch. She dangles there.)*

HETTIE: Please . . .

LAVINIA: Hush up.

HETTIE: Oh please, Lavinia.

LAVINIA: No whining.

HETTIE: I'll just look at it. I won't even touch it.

LAVINIA: No!

HETTIE: I'll give you that clear glass marble with the hole in it.

LAVINIA: No.

HETTIE: I'll give you one of them robin eggs my sister found.

LAVINIA: No.

HETTIE: I'll give you them three rabbit ears on a string we got from the Indians.

LAVINIA: No. Change the subject.

HETTIE: I'll give you . . .

LAVINIA: Hettie.

HETTIE: What.

LAVINIA: *Change the subject.*
    (Hettie collapses in misery on the cellar door.)
    (Lavinia lets herself drop from the branch, landing in front of Hettie.)
LAVINIA: I wonder what I'd be saying right now if I was looking at Jane instead of you.
HETTIE: I don't know. What?
    (Lavinia looks at Hettie for a long time.)
LAVINIA: The mind belagos!
HETTIE: What's a belago?
LAVINIA: I'll explain it to you when you're older.
HETTIE: Oh.
LAVINIA: In the meantime, you've gotta study your vocabulary words. Otherwise, life is gonna pass you by.
    (Hettie moves her attention to the lock on the cellar door. She fumbles with it.)
HETTIE: What's this lock doing here?
LAVINIA: Guarding other treasures.
HETTIE: What else you got down there?
LAVINIA: Many a marvelous work and wonder.
HETTIE: Like what?
LAVINIA: Many objects of great and exceptional beauty.
HETTIE: Name one.
LAVINIA: I am sworn to secrecy.
HETTIE: I don't believe you.
LAVINIA: I have swore a blood red oath.
HETTIE: To who?
LAVINI: I am not allowed to speak of it to you or any human youth.
HETTIE: Just name one other thing you got down there.
    (Lavinia ponders whether to tell.)
LAVINIA: A locket in the shape of a heart . . .
HETTIE: Oh.
LAVINIA: . . . That you can put two pictures in. And when you close it, they kiss.
HETTIE: *(Laughing.)* Oh no. If I had that, I would put Ezra in it. Kiss. *(She laughs again.)* What else you got down there?
LAVINIA: Swear you will never tell.
HETTIE: Swear.
LAVINIA: Even unto death and after.
HETTIE: Even unto death and after.
    (The both do a ritual gesture of promising. Long pause.)

LAVINIA: Silk underwear.

HETTIE: Nooooo.

LAVINIA: Blue, pink and salmon.

HETTIE: I don't believe you.

LAVINIA: I got one in my pocket.

HETTIE: You have not.

LAVINIA: You want to see it?

HETTIE: I don't know. You ain't supposed to look at other people's underwear.

LAVINIA: This here's fancy. It ain't like temple garments, nothing like that. Close your eyes. *(She pulls a salmon-colored camisole from the crotch of the tree. She stands in front of Hettie, hands behind her back.)* Open! *(She makes a rainbow arch with the garment.)* You ever see anything like that?

HETTIE: No.

LAVINIA: You wanna see how it works? *(Lavinia puts the camisole over her clothes.)* And in here goes the bosoms. *(She pokes her hands in the garment.)* It is worn by women of the night.

HETTIE: Oh no!

LAVINIA: They have love in every port.

HETTIE: Is that pure real silk?

LAVINIA: Yes, it is pure real silk. It costs one dollar per thread.

HETTIE: No.

LAVINIA: *(Vamping.)* Hey, lady, you want to make a beast with two backs?

HETTIE: *(A small giggle.)* What does that mean?

LAVINIA: What does it sound like it means?

HETTIE: I don't know.

LAVINIA: Well then, you'll have to think about it, won't you? *(Lavinia continues to strut around in the camisole.)*

HETTIE: It looks like there's light inside of it.

LAVINIA: It is magic. You put this on, and you will have your greatest love come true.

HETTIE: Oh no! They wear them things when they are sexing.

LAVINIA: And they do not wear anything else.

(Hettie laughs hysterically. Then she stops abruptly.)

HETTIE: We're not supposed to be thinking about this.

LAVINIA: Why not?

HETTIE: It gives me the fan-toads.

LAVINIA: What gives you the fan-toads?

HETTIE: Just thinking . . . just thinking about it gives me the fan-toads. *(Hettie shivers.)*

LAVINIA: It gives you the fan-toads when he kisses your neck? Kiss, kiss, kiss. *(Lavinia comes after Hettie. Hettie, screaming and laughing, runs away.)*

HETTIE: No. No.

(Lavinia pursues her.)

LAVINIA: It gives you the fan-toads when he rubs his face on your bosoms? *(Hettie runs behind the tree.)*

HETTIE: No. Stop.

(Lavinia pursues her again.)

LAVINIA: It gives you the fan-toads when he wiggles around on your stomach?

(Hettie slides to the ground in front of the cellar.)

HETTIE: Please . . . Please . . . No.

(Lavinia jumps in front of her.)

LAVINIA: It gives you the fan-toads when he lays his thing upon your leg.

(Hettie screams and beats her feet on the cellar door.)

(Lavinia watches as Hettie's "fit" subsides, then stops abruptly.)

LAVINIA: You've got to work harder on your maturity, Hettie. *(Lavinia takes off the camisole.)* Do you think Jane will like this?

HETTIE: Are you going to give her that?

LAVINIA: Yes I am. Because I am "devoted" to Jane.

HETTIE: You can't give her that. It's for a grown-up.

LAVINIA: Do you know the reason why I am *not* devoted to you? Because you are still a child.

HETTIE: I am three months and four days older than you.

LAVINIA: But . . . you still have the mind of a child. You are scared and jumpy. And you scream around.

(Hettie stands up to her.)

HETTIE: That's not even part-way true. Who touched those snakes? Who faced down Wylie's dog?

LAVINIA: I might be able to tell you something, then. But if you cry or run, neither me or Jane will speak to you again. So long as we both shall live.

HETTIE: Tell me what?

LAVINIA: First you have to take a solemn oath.

(They cross their hearts, lick their hands and clasp hands.)

HETTIE: Swear.

LAVINIA: If I speak.

HETTIE: If I speak.

LAVINIA: If I speak of this to anyone.

HETTIE: If I speak of this to anyone.

LAVINIA: I will sleep.

HETTIE: I will sleep.

LAVINIA: I will sleep with a snake.

HETTIE: I will sleep with a snake.

LAVINIA: And I will drink.

HETTIE: And I will drink.

LAVINIA: And I will drink raw vinegar.

HETTIE: And I will drink raw vinegar.

LAVINIA: If you ever break this oath. If you ever speak of this to a living soul, I will set your hair on fire. Do you swear?

HETTIE: Swear.

(Lavinia takes Hettie to the cellar door, where they kneel and look out.)

LAVINIA: *(Quietly.)* This silk underwear was once wore by a woman from Missouri.

HETTIE: A emigrant?

LAVINIA: Yes, a emigrant. It was owned by a emigrant woman from Missouri on her way to California.

HETTIE: How'd you get it?

LAVINIA: It was rendered up.

HETTIE: Rendered up?

LAVINIA: Rendered up by the sons of perdition.

HETTIE: Oh.

LAVINIA: Because the emigrants from Missouri are dead.

HETTIE: No. They're just hiding.

LAVINIA: They're dead. They all got killed.

HETTIE: Who killed them?

LAVINIA: Who do you think killed em?

HETTIE: God.

LAVINIA: No.

HETTIE: Your pop.

LAVINIA: No. *(Inventing the answer.)* Indians.

HETTIE: Indians killed em?

LAVINIA: This morning at sunrise.

HETTIE: At Mountain Meadow.

LAVINIA: Killed em all. All except for seven small children. Too young to speak the truth of what they saw.

HETTIE: I don't believe you.

LAVINIA: They all died in agony on the meadow.

HETTIE: How do you know all this?

LAVINIA: My pop is the commander.

HETTIE: So what?

LAVINIA: He is called upon to use his bravery.

HETTIE: He is crazy with a gun, that's what my pop says.

LAVINIA: He's supposed to be crazy with a gun. He's the commander. He had to bury the bodies. The dead and mangled bodies of the dead and mangled emigrants.

HETTIE: Did your pop tell you this?

LAVINIA: He had to bury them. Or else the wuffs would eat their flesh.

HETTIE: Wuffs? *(Hettie sits transfixed.)* Lavinia, I think I got the fan-toads again.

LAVINIA: Jist remember one thing. They deserved to die.

HETTIE: Because they was from Missouri?

LAVINIA: The people from Missouri shot the Prophet Joseph Smith and his beloved brother Hyrum.

HETTIE: I seen that emigrant train when it come through town. Them people from Missouri, they had dogs.

LAVINIA: Yes.

HETTIE: Cuz they eat dogs.

LAVINIA: They named their oxen Joseph Smith and Brigham Young. They deserve to die.

HETTIE: They snapped the head off a chicken and called it the Mormon Church. I seen them do that with a bull whip. Snap.

LAVINIA: And they cast aspersions on the godhead.

HETTIE: Yeah, aspersions on the godhead.

LAVINIA: They deserve to die.

HETTIE: The Lord's will be done.

LAVINIA: On earth as it is in heaven.

HETTIE: *(Searching for more.)* And they poisoned that spring.

LAVINIA: When they were a guest in the territory, they poisoned that spring. Which killed the Indians. And so the Indians hated them.

HETTIE: Yes, the Indians hated them. And so the Indians killed them.

LAVINIA: Yes.

HETTIE: What if the Indians hated us?

LAVINIA: They do not hate us. We never poisoned a spring.

HETTIE: And the emigrant children, they never poisoned a spring. That's why they never got killed.

LAVINIA: A hundred and twenty-seven souls. They all died on the meadow this day, their blood mixed with the water of the slew. *(Lavinia pulls the camisole through her hand, like it is a magic trick.)* Now then, look all over this salmon slip.

HETTIE: What for?

LAVINIA: See if you can find her blood.

HETTIE: Blood of the Missouri woman?

LAVINIA: Blood of the damned.

HETTIE: Lavinia . . .

LAVINIA: What.

HETTIE: I got the fan-toads again.

LAVINIA: Shhh. Examine the salmon slip. *(Lavinia drops the camisole on her. Hettie recoils.)*

HETTIE: Oh! *(Hettie sits transfixed. Quietly.)* Lavinia.

LAVINIA: What?

HETTIE: What about the two-headed calf?

LAVINIA: What about it?

HETTIE: Is there blood on the two-headed calf?

LAVINIA: Might be. Might not be. We don't know, do we?

HETTIE: Please, can I see if there's blood on the two-headed calf?

LAVINIA: No.

HETTIE: Please, Lavinia.

LAVINIA: You cannot see the two-headed calf. But . . .

HETTIE: But what?

LAVINIA: But later. After I show the calf to Jane. And after I give the pink slip to Jane. After that. After all that, I might give this salmon slip to you.

HETTIE: You might give it to me?

LAVINIA: I might.

HETTIE: What for?

LAVINIA: Because I love you.

HETTIE: You do?

LAVINIA: Of course I do.

HETTIE: Are you sure it's pure real silk?

LAVINIA: It's pure real silk and there's blood on it. *(Lavinia waits for a moment for the information to sink in. Hettie rubs the silk.)* Treasure it.

HETTIE: I will. I will.

LAVINIA: And now I'm gonna leave you here.

HETTIE: No, Lavinia, don't leave me here! Don't leave me alone.

LAVINIA: I must go help Jane with the cows.

HETTIE: I can't stay here by myself. There's too much going on. There's emigrants. There's Indians. There's blood on this slip.

LAVINIA: Shhhh. I must go help Jane so she will not be killed.

HETTIE: No, Lavinia, please don't leave me.

LAVINIA: Hush up. No whining. By the time you find the blood on that slip, we will both return. Me and Jane. The "incomparable" Jane.

HETTIE: And then we'll take a look at that two-headed calf?

LAVINIA: Only if you've found the blood. Blood of the Missouri woman.

HETTIE: Blood of the emigrant.

LAVINIA: Blood of the damned. *(Lavinia rushes off.)*

(Hettie is left alone and breathless. She studies the camisole, looks out and whimpers.)

(Sound of wolves bleed into the music.)

(Lights dim.)

SCENE TWO — ICE MAIDEN

DATE: 1867
AGES: 20

This scene takes place in the same back yard ten years later. It is a hot day in late summer.

Lavinia and Hettie, both now 20, are busy at work on a small quilt, just the size to bury with the woman whose crude casket is on the cellar door under the tree. The casket is covered with a large piece of canvas, over which is ice. Over that is another larger piece of canvas.

There are several moments of silence. Tension is thick in the air. Sound of crows.

LAVINIA: There are crows in that box elder tree.

HETTIE: I know, I saw them.

LAVINIA: You know why, don't you?

HETTIE: Yes, Lavinia, I know why.

LAVINIA: Why?

HETTIE: *(Trying to distract her.)* Remember you used to call them magpies, and Jane called them red-winged black birds?

LAVINIA: I am asking you a simple question.

HETTIE: . . . That's because half the town says magpies. The other half says red-winged black birds.

LAVINIA: Why!

HETTIE: Why what?

LAVINIA: Why are those crows waiting in that box elder tree?

HETTIE: Let's think about the good things, the lucky things. She was . . . funny and she was brave. It's lucky we knew her.

LAVINIA . . . Carrion. The crows smell carrion.

HETTIE: She was married before she died. That's a lucky thing.

LAVINIA: It's been three days. The crows are ready to feed.

HETTIE: We've had enough time to make her a quilt. That's a lucky thing.

LAVINIA: The crows are patient, but they cannot wait forever.

HETTIE: And Ezra will be back by nightfall!

(Pause. Sound of crows.)

LAVINIA: "That's a lucky thing." Because the crows are eager to feast.

HETTIE: Put your mind on something else, would you? *(Pause.)* Think about Ezra.

LAVINIA: No.

HETTIE: My heart goes out to him.

LAVINIA: Not mine.

HETTIE: You have to feel sorry for him. All he's lost.

LAVINIA: I do not feel sorry for him.

HETTIE: You feel sorry for yourself.

LAVINIA: I feel sorry for Jane. And I feel sorry for that crow.

(Hettie looks up from her work. She's losing patience.)

HETTIE: Lavinia, please . . .

LAVINIA: It's only got one leg. Ha! *(Pause of several seconds as the two return to their work.)*

HETTIE: What to tell Ezra, that's what worries me.

LAVINIA: Tell him the truth.

HETTIE: Obviously. But . . . how to put it.

LAVINIA: *(With a grin.)* Jane was smothered.

HETTIE: Jane was attacked and bit.

LAVINIA: By a diseased wolf.

HETTIE: It wasn't a wolf.

LAVINIA: What was it?

HETTIE: There are no wolves here. No one has seen a wolf. In five years, no one has ever seen a wolf.

LAVINIA: It was a wolf.

HETTIE: Wolves are further north. There are no wolves in the desert.

LAVINIA: Must have been a crow then.

HETTIE: What?

LAVINIA: Must have been a crow that got Jane.

HETTIE: Don't start.

LAVINIA: Was it crows dug up those bodies at Mountain Meadow?

HETTIE: Lavinia, we're not talking about that.

LAVINIA: Was it *crows* that dragged the limbs to the edge of town then repeatedly buried them and dug them up, buried them and dug them up?

HETTIE: You have a way of saying the awfullest things.

LAVINIA: It was crows that scattered the bones at Mountain Meadow! Yes, it was crows. And it was a crow that got Jane, a crow that will scatter her bones. You are so right, Hettie. Crows! Ha-ha.

(Long pause. The women continue working.)

HETTIE: Jane was not bit by a wolf.

LAVINIA: I know. *(Lavinia looks up from her work and then back down. With mock seriousness.)* Jane was bit by a diseased rabbit.

HETTIE: This is no time for joking.

LAVINIA: A diseased squirrel, a chipmunk, a field mouse.

HETTIE: You're irreverent.

LAVINIA: No, Hettie. I'm furious!

(Long, tense pause. The women continue to work.)

HETTIE: More than likely it was a coyote.

LAVINIA: *It does not matter, Hettie!*

HETTIE: We cannot spread the word that it was a wolf. People will think we live in the wild. We do not live in the wild. We are a civilized people. This is a civilized place.

LAVINIA: Civilized.

HETTIE: Yes. All the wolves have been killed.

(Lavinia moves to the box. She lifts up a piece of wet canvas. She rearranges something in the box, perhaps the woman's hair.)

LAVINIA: Jane is turning black.

HETTIE: We cannot put her in the ground before her husband comes. It would not be right. Not proper. Ezra needs to see her dead. Otherwise, he will live a haunted life.

LAVINIA: There's no more ice.

HETTIE: It takes three days from Salt Lake City. He'll be here tonight.

LAVINIA: Unless something has happened to him.

HETTIE: Lavinia. You are not to talk that way.

LAVINIA: *(False sentiment.)* But I worry about him. Something could happen. He could fall from his buckskin mare into Wildcat Gulch. He could break both legs, both arms, his back. He could lie in agony till nightfall when *diseased wolves* take after him. Bite by bite.

HETTIE: You're just upset.

LAVINIA: Up set. You have no words, Hettie. Up set?

HETTIE: It fixes nothing when you talk like that. Ezra is a fine, fine man.

LAVINIA: He should have been here.

HETTIE: He was on Church business.

LAVINIA: The goddamn Church.

HETTIE: And I don't want to hear nothing against the Church, neither.

LAVINIA: *(Blankly, quietly.)* Howl, Lavinia, howl.

HETTIE: And no more public spectacles like Jane's wedding day.

LAVINIA: Howl, howl.

HETTIE: Sitting in a tree pelting the wedding guests with bits of food.

LAVINIA: Howl.

HETTIE: You are not the only one affected by this. Of course, you're going to miss her, but . . .

LAVINIA: I don't miss her. I am with her. I only seem to be here.
(Hettie leans in toward her friend.)

HETTIE: Lavinia. Look at me.
(Lavinia does.)

HETTIE: It may be fine for you to talk like that to me. But you don't say those things to others. You understand?

LAVINIA: I understand. I understand everything. My beloved Jane is turning black.

HETTIE: Shhhh.

LAVINIA: *(Tears well up in Lavinia's eyes.)* She looks like a corpse. She used to look like someone sleeping. Not herself. Not Jane. But someone. Now she looks like a corpse. Dead calf in the desert. The smell, the flies. *(Lavinia replaces the canvas.)*

HETTIE: Shhh. She was always happy, never one to worry. Let's think about that.

LAVINIA: *(Turning on a dime.)* Jane would have been a great woman. What do you think?

HETTIE: Yes. She would have had a wonderful family.
(Lavinia looks at her.)

LAVINIA: She would have taught school.

HETTIE: She might have taught school.

LAVINIA: We would have taught school together.

HETTIE: She wasn't as fixed on teaching school as you are.

LAVINIA: Jane wanted to teach school.

HETTIE: She wanted to marry Ezra and have a big batch of children. That's really what she wanted.

LAVINIA: We would have taught school together. We would have talked about our students.

HETTIE: Maybe so.

LAVINIA: We would have discussed great books, great ideas, the greater meanings of things.

HETTIE: I'm sure you would have.

LAVINIA: Yes. And on Sunday afternoons we would have opened the windows and read books in the quiet breeze of our house.

HETTIE: That's a lovely thought.

LAVINIA: And on winter nights we would have built a fire and cooked a soup. We would have wrapped ourselves in blankets and discussed the meaning of the universe.

HETTIE: Do you know what I thought . . . what I thought every time I saw Jane?

LAVINIA: What?

HETTIE: That she was like . . . She was like . . . like a singer with a song.

LAVINIA: Like a singer with a song?

HETTIE: Don't make fun.

LAVINIA: Like a singer with a song. That's beautiful, Hettie.
    (Hettie grins.)

LAVINIA: The most beautiful thing you ever said. She was like a singer with a song. I love you for saying that.

HETTIE: I don't know where it came from . . .

LAVINIA: Shhhh. She was like a singer with a song. *(Turning on a dime.)* How could you do it, Hettie?

HETTIE: We all agreed on it. You were there. We all agreed.

LAVINIA: I did not agree.

HETTIE: It was her wish. She begged to be shot.

LAVINIA: But you did not shoot her. You smothered her.

HETTIE: She could not be saved. And no one could shoot her.

LAVINIA: I could have shot her. Like shooting a horse with a broken leg. Like shooting a cow with Bang's Disease. Like shooting . . . a mourning dove.

HETTIE: Let's think about something else.

LAVINIA: I can shoot anything. I have shot many things.

HETTIE: Let's think about Ezra. Poor man will be home soon.

LAVINIA: And his wife is dead.

HETTIE: Yes.

LAVINIA: She said to me. Before she was raving. After the bite but before the raving, she said, "If I get it, if I get the hydrophobia, I want you to shoot me. I want you, Lavinia. I want you to shoot me."

HETTIE: She said nothing of the sort.

LAVINIA: I am not the one that lies!

HETTIE: She refused to speak of the possibilities of the disease. That was part of her lovely spirit in the last few days. She maintained a lovely, positive spirit.

LAVINIA: Hog swill.

HETTIE: The Church was a comfort to her at the end. It was a comfort to all of us at the end.

LAVINIA: Mormons can make apple sauce from horse piss. "Go take her cows," you said. "Go take them to the milking shed. We'll wait with her."

HETTIE: I wanted to spare you.

LAVINIA: You smothered her.

HETTIE: It was the kindest thing.

(Lavinia grabs Hettie's face.)

LAVINIA: It was the most unkindest thing. *(Pause.)* For the rest of my life, Hettie Edison, every time I see you, every time, I will wonder what it would be like if Jane were in your place instead of you.

HETTIE: You're talking crazy now.

LAVINIA: It runs in my family.

HETTIE: Hush. Your family is not crazy.

LAVINIA: My father's as crazy as a rip saw.

HETTIE: Shhh. Everyone must pray for him.

LAVINIA: Pray for my mother if you want to pray for someone.

HETTIE: You've had too much grief. And now the trial. I am forgetting what you're going through.

LAVINIA: This trial does not concern my father.

HETTIE: If you say so.

LAVINIA: My father was not there that day.

HETTIE: No, of course not.

LAVINIA: And in all other ways my father did what he was told to do.

HETTIE: I'm sure he did.

LAVINIA: What he was told by Brigham Young to do.

HETTIE: Brigham Young had nothing to do with that thing.

LAVINIA: Massacre. The word is . . .

HETTIE: Shhh.

LAVINIA: Massacre.

HETTIE: There's no need to speak of it. I'm sure your father's suffered quite enough.

LAVINIA: Because they stripped him of his rank? That does not concern him. He wears his uniform just the same. And drills his regiment just the same.

HETTIE: He's a proud and proper man.

LAVINIA: He is a pompous ass.

HETTIE: He is your father.

LAVINIA: And a pompous ass.

HETTIE: He deserves your respect. Now he deserves your prayers.

LAVINIA: My prayers? My father threw me in a wagon. There was blood and mud in there.

HETTIE: Pray for him, Lavinia.

LAVINIA: It smelled like a pig slaughter. "Speak of this to no one."

HETTIE: We must pray for them all.

LAVINIA: He put something in my hand. Something metal. A necklace or a pin. Could have been a locket. Could have been a bone. "Speak of this to no one. Speak of this to no one."

HETTIE: Pray nothing is uncovered at the trial . . . nothing implicating him.

LAVINIA: He has a declaration. Signed by twenty men. He was not there that day.

HETTIE: But he must suffer at the thought that someone else is suffering.

LAVINIA: He does not suffer at the thought.

HETTIE: He is a caring man. He cares for John D. Lee.

LAVINIA: I doubt it.

HETTIE: They ran cattle together.

LAVINIA: So what?

HETTIE: They tell stories on one another.

LAVINIA: My father was not there. John D. Lee was there. John D. Lee must suffer for them all. Waiting for the axe to fall. Waiting for the wolves to bite. John D. Lee is being punished. And I am being punished. Jane is turning black. *(Lavinia returns to the casket. Long pause.)* That locket you're wearing. I want it back.

HETTIE: What?

LAVINIA: I want it . . . back.

HETTIE: What for?

LAVINIA: I gave it to you. Now I want it back.

HETTIE: Please, Lavinia . . .

LAVINIA: I gave you that locket. But before I gave it to you, I gave it to Jane. She had to give it back. Her mother said it came from the Mountain Meadow Massacre. That's when I gave it to you. But now I want it back.

HETTIE: It's got the pictures of my parents in it.

LAVINIA: Take them out.

HETTIE: Whatever you say. *(Pause.)*

LAVINIA: *Now!* I want it now.

HETTIE: I don't have it now.

LAVINIA: You wear it all the time. You're wearing it now. It's under your collar. I want it.

(Pause. Lavinia is fixed on Hettie, and she means business.)

(Hettie fumbles with her collar and takes off the locket. She hands it to Lavinia.)

LAVINIA: *(Grabs the locket and Hettie's hand.)* And stay away from my father.

HETTIE: What are you talking about?

LAVINIA: He's watching you.

HETTIE: He barely knows my name.

LAVINIA: I watch him watching you.

HETTIE: It is completely innocent, I assure you.

LAVINIA: You stay away from him. You resist his *courtly charm.*

(Hettie says nothing.)

LAVINIA: And now that silk camisole.

HETTIE: Silk camisole . . .

LAVINIA: The silk camisole I gave you. I want that too.

HETTIE: What on earth . . .

LAVINIA: I want it back.

HETTIE: We do not need to discuss this now.

LAVINIA: You never wear it. You can't wear it. You'd be afraid to wear it. I want it back.

HETTIE: I don't have it. That was ten years ago.

LAVINIA: You have it. I want it.

HETTIE: What for?

LAVINIA: I want to cut it up. All three of us had them. I had one. It was blue. Jane had one. It was pink. You had one. It was salmon. I want yours back.

HETTIE: You get worked up like this, it only makes things worse.

LAVINIA: I didn't like yours. I didn't like that color. That's why I gave it to you. Now I want it back. I'm going to cut it up.

HETTIE: Whatever you say. You can have it back. Now could we have an end to this?

LAVINIA: Do I give you the fan-toads? I'm going to cut the bosoms out of it. I'm going to sprinkle the petals on her grave. I'm going to dance in a circle, tromping the dirt on her grave . . . *(Lavinia rises and twirls. Hettie grabs her.)*

HETTIE: Lavinia, I understand you. I know your intensity. But I'm warning you, right now, you are not to talk like this any more. And especially in front of Ezra. You're not to talk like this to him.

LAVINIA: And why not?

HETTIE: He's gone through too much himself. He will not understand.

LAVINIA: Under. Stand.

HETTIE: We must be mindful of his pain. We must help him to bear up beneath the strain.

LAVINIA: You think you're going to marry Ezra, don't you?

HETTIE: The man's wife just died.

LAVINIA: You're not going to marry him, Hettie. I am.

HETTIE: My god, Lavinia . . .

LAVINIA: And do you know why, Hettie?

HETTIE: Oh, Lavinia.

(Lavinia laughs in exhaustion.)

LAVINIA: Why shouldn't I marry him? Jane is turning black.

HETTIE: Please be quiet now. We're almost finished.

(The women work. First Hettie finishes. Then Lavinia. They both sit back and study the quilt. Tears well up in Lavinia's eyes.)

LAVINIA: Oh, Jane . . .

(Hettie embraces her.)

(Lights fade.)

SCENE THREE — INSANE

DATE: 1877
AGES: 30

This scene takes place in the same back lot, another ten years later. Vegetation around the cellar is less planned. Things show signs of wear and tear. It

*is late autumn. A chill is in the air. Lavinia is about 30. She's washing clothes,
using a barrel, a washboard and a bar of lye soap.*

LAVINIA: *(Yelling back into the house.)* Janie, you keep those twins away from
that stove, ya hear? *(Brief pause as she waits.)* Then wash out the milk cans
and set em out for Grandma. Janie, you hear me?

HETTIE: *(Hettie appears from inside the house. She wears a long coat and is
clearly pregnant.) I* hear you.
*(Lavinia studies her in disbelief, then throws a wet garment at the tree. She
stands against the tree, refusing to look at her. Pause.)*

HETTIE: Did you get my letter?

LAVINIA: You didn't come through the house, did you?

HETTIE: The child let me in.

LAVINIA: Did you run into my mother?

HETTIE: No.

LAVINIA: That's a blessing.

HETTIE: If you say so.
(Lavinia studies her stomach.)

LAVINIA: What do you want?

HETTIE: Did you get my letter?

LAVINIA: Yes, I got your letter. We do not live in the wild, you know. This
is a civilized place. We are a civilized people. The post comes twice a week.
(Total silence. A long one.)

HETTIE: Your father sends his love.

LAVINIA: Hush. Up.

HETTIE: He's very sorry this has . . .

LAVINIA: I said, hush up!

HETTIE: He and I both think it's time we . . .

LAVINIA: I want you out of here as soon as possible.

HETTIE: Your father sent me.

LAVINIA: Of course he did. Got himself in prison or something.

HETTIE: Asylum.

LAVINIA: Yes, asylum. For doing what exactly?

HETTIE: Well, he went there to preach the gospel to his family.

LAVINIA: His family is here.

HETTIE: His family in Connecticut.

LAVINIA: Superlative job, too. An overwhelming success, I'd say.

HETTIE: Please, Lavinia, please don't talk to me in words.
(Lavinia throws something in the wash. A pause of several seconds.)

LAVINIA: I can't do a damn thing, Hettie. He's crazy. You shouldn't have married him. My mother shouldn't have married him.

HETTIE: He thinks you can get him out.

LAVINIA: I think he belongs there.

HETTIE: You do not. He is your father.

LAVINIA: And he's crazy as lightning.

HETTIE: He believes in you. He believes you can intervene.

LAVINIA: What did he do to get himself in there?

HETTIE: He was just trying to share the blessings of the gospel . . .

LAVINIA: Yes but what did he *do*?

HETTIE: He bore his testimony as to the truthfulness of the restored gospel . . .

LAVINIA: Quit dancing behind your chair. What did he do?

HETTIE: Took over the pulpit at a Catholic Church.

LAVINIA: I see. And what did he tell them?

HETTIE: He testified about the institution of plural marriage.

LAVINIA: *(Laughing.)* He told them he was a plig?

HETTIE: He testified as to the wisdom of the divinely inspired institution of plural marriage.

(Lavinia nods knowingly.)

HETTIE: That upset the Catholic people that were there that day. They sent up a call for the constabularies. And he was taken from the pulpit.

LAVINIA: To the prison?

HETTIE: No. To the asylum.

LAVINIA: To the asylum, right. Thank god for that. They think he's just crazy not criminal.

HETTIE: No call to speak so harshly.

LAVINIA: And what do they call it? What's the exact name of his "disease"?

HETTIE: Religious intolerance.

(There is a long pause. Hettie is uncomfortable.)

LAVINIA: You've just lied to me, haven't you?

HETTIE: What?

LAVINIA: They did not throw him in the asylum because he *talked* about polygamy.

HETTIE: No. *(Carefully.)* Someone. A friend of his sister . . . has family in Missouri.

LAVINIA: I see.

HETTIE: Word . . . got around.

LAVINIA: That he'd been up to more than multiple wives.

HETTIE: Word got around.

LAVINIA: That he's crazy but also a killer.

HETTIE: He's very frightened, Lavinia. He's afraid he'll have to spend the rest of his life in there. You can't imagine what it's like. The noises. Screaming. Banging. The smell.

LAVINIA: I can't get him out of there.

HETTIE: I don't know what to do with him.

LAVINIA: Neither do the rest of us.

HETTIE: I think he should come back here.

LAVINIA: Why? Because here everyone's as crazy as he?

HETTIE: Because here people understand his intensity.

LAVINIA: Intens-ity. *(Lavinia throws something in the wash.)*

HETTIE: I want to come home. He wants to come home.

LAVINIA: My father cannot come back here.

HETTIE: Why not?

LAVINIA: Second trial is about to begin.

HETTIE: Mountain Meadow?

LAVINIA: Mountain Meadow.

HETTIE: John D. Lee again?

LAVINIA: John D. Lee again.

HETTIE: Oh, that poor man.

LAVINIA: One more trip to the table of justice.

HETTIE: They acquitted him before. Pray God they do it again.

LAVINIA: That was ten years ago. This time they'll convict. He was solely responsible for the massacre. That's what we're to understand, what we're to believe. Typical Mormon justice. Kill as few Mormons as you can. Kill as many others as possible.

HETTIE: I feel so sorry for his family.

LAVINIA: Suffice it to say, my father should not be around.

HETTIE: Your father had nothing to do with it.

LAVINIA: He planned it. Commander in the Mormon Militia. That was his job! He got his cut of the loot.

HETTIE: Every drop of blood shed that day was but another rung on the ladder of salvation.

LAVINIA: Now you're quoting him.

HETTIE: Shedding the blood of the enemies of Christ is no sin in the sight of the Lord.

LAVINIA: The principle of blood atonement. I will not listen to this.

HETTIE: I believe it to be the truth.

LAVINIA: A hundred and twenty-seven people, Hettie.

HETTIE: And what had they done to deserve it?

LAVINIA: Nothing! A few taunts, a few jibes.

HETTIE: They bragged about killing Joseph Smith. I heard that myself.

LAVINIA: You do not kill people with words.

HETTIE: What about their *deeds* in Missouri a dozen years before? Those people from Missouri killed my grandmother. Made her walk across the frozen river. Middle of winter.

LAVINIA: It wasn't those people.

HETTIE: Of course it was.

LAVINIA? No, it wasn't, Hettie.

HETTIE: What difference does it make. They all hate us!

LAVINIA: I've got to say one thing. You are dumb, Hettie Edison. Stupid as a stump. Dumber than a chicken. Slow as a sheep. And you always were! There, I've said it.

HETTIE: Are you're finished?

LAVINIA: Yes.

HETTIE: Good. *(Right back at her.)* Because some of us don't find it worth our time being smart. We don't want to end up being tedious like you. There. *I've* said it. *(Deep pause.)*

LAVINIA: You've got to understand, Hettie, that you and my father have wreaked a big of havoc in this family.

HETTIE: What have we done? We're not even here.

LAVINIA: *(Inhaling, then controlling an explosion.)* Since my father took himself another wife, my *mother* has been "upset." Since my father picked *you* to be his second wife, *I* have been "upset." Since my father and second wife have taken themselves to Connect-icut, we have *all* been "upset."

HETTIE: That wasn't my idea. Your father wanted to see his family. He wanted me to meet his family. He wanted to preach the gospel to his family.

LAVINIA: *We* are his family.

HETTIE: His family back in Connecticut.

LAVINIA: And it sounds like he's been a great success with his family back in Connect-icut. They got him where?

HETTIE: State House for the Feeble Minded and the Insane.

LAVINIA: The feeble minded and the insane. You should not have married him, Hettie.

HETTIE: Your father has many fine qualities.

LAVINIA: So does that dog asleep on the porch out there. You gonna marry him?

HETTIE: Your father had stature in this town. People thought highly of him. They respected him. They respected me when I was with him.

LAVINIA: Whatever crumbs of respect there were should have belonged to my mother. She put up with him for twenty-four years. Exactly what had you done? *(Pause.)*

HETTIE: *(An admission.)* My parents had eight daughters. Eight.

LAVINIA: You could have said no.

HETTIE: I thought I'd be well cared for.

LAVINIA: And you were right, so right. Probably living in a palace back east.

HETTIE: I thought, when I married your father, I'd finally be the equal of you.

LAVINIA: So you are. What exactly do you want from me? *(An awkward moment.)*

HETTIE: *(Changing the subject.)* I brought Tess with me.

LAVINIA: All the way on the train? Must have cost a fortune.

HETTIE: I thought maybe she could get to know her cousins. Janie, the twins.

LAVINIA: They're not cousins. Your daughter is my sister.

HETTIE: Well yes, technically.

(Pause. Lavinia washes on a scrub board.)

HETTIE: And how's Ezra?

LAVIIA: Had typhoid last winter, but it didn't kill him.

HETTIE: Does he still look the same?

LAVINIA: Shoulders more stooped. His knees are bad.

HETTIE: I'll bet he enjoys the children.

LAVINIA: Can't tell the twins apart.

HETTIE: Rising in the Church.

LAVINIA: Yes. Oh, yes.

HETTIE: I look forward to seeing him.

LAVINIA: I should have let you have him.

HETTIE: Lavinia, please.

LAVINIA: Well, it's the truth.

HETTIE: I'm perfectly satisfied with the lot I have.

LAVINIA: Your life's been a comfort, has it?

HETTIE: Some of it, yes. Tess has. Tess has been a comfort to both of us.

LAVINIA: Then what in hell do you want from me?

HETTIE: *(Hettie cannot say it yet.)* Your mother, how is . . . your mother?
(Lavinia tosses the garment she's been working on into the rinse tub. Then she fishes another one from the scalding wash. She rubs a bar of soap on it and scrubs it on the board.)

LAVINIA: Mother looks at the sky all day. She's trying to find God. So far, he has eluded her.

HETTIE: Neither one of us understand what it's like to leave the world behind and come west.

LAVINIA: No, I'm sure we don't.

HETTIE: To sacrifice everything for the Church. Load all your belongings into a wagon.

LAVINIA: Please save us your handcart story, Hettie.

HETTIE: They walked more than a thousand miles. Your father and mother both.

LAVINIA: And ain't it a blessing that "in these, the latter days," we have the railroad.

HETTIE: Please give my good wishes to your mother.

LAVINIA: Oh, I will, I will.

HETTIE: And your father sends . . .

LAVINIA: Yes.

HETTIE: Your father sends his best to her. His warmest regards.

(Lavinia looks at her blankly.)

LAVINIA: No more la-dee-dah, Hettie. What do you want?

HETTIE: *(A difficult admission.)* I have . . . I have no means of support.

LAVINIA: If you can work, we can feed you.

HETTIE: I need ready money.

LAVINIA: No one's got ready money.

HETTIE: They want a hundred dollars.

LAVINIA: Ah.

HETTIE: For the indigent tax. If I pay the tax and promise not to let him come back to the state of Connecticut, they'll let him out.

LAVINIA: A hundred dollars. Out of the question.

HETTIE: Can't you sell something?

LAVINIA: Why don't *you* sell something? Start with that coat.

HETTIE: *(An admission.)* It's borrowed.

LAVINIA: And you're also pregnant again.

HETTIE: Well, yes . . .

LAVINIA: It's barbaric how many children we have. Even the Indians have fewer children than we do.

HETTIE: The Commander wanted more children.

LAVINIA: The Commander? The old man is running around the east calling himself the Commander.

HETTIE: I didn't feel I could deny him.

LAVINIA: Oh no, of course not.

HETTIE: The last one. After Tess. It . . . was not whole.

LAVINIA: Was it two-headed?

HETTIE: *(Tears up.)* Your father was . . . very hurt. His pride.

LAVINIA: His pride is the size of Great Salt Lake.

HETTIE: Well yes, I suppose it is. But he cares for you. He does.

LAVINIA: He is a crazy son of a bitch. And the Church did nothing but make him crazier.

HETTIE: He is haunted by Mountain Meadow. Sometimes he hears wolves. They speak to him in nightmares. They tell him to bury it deeper. But he has no shovel, no tools, just his hands.

LAVINIA: In my own nightmare, I am the one that gets shot. Never one that shoots. A bearded man with kindly eyes shoots me in the neck, and I die slowly, my blood leaking drop by drop into the water of the slew.

HETTIE: The Lord has tested us. Tested us all.

LAVINIA: You say he suffers then?

HETTIE: More than you can know. His life is a torment.

LAVINIA: *(Lavinia considers this. Nods. Then decides.)* It'll take a week or more to get the money together.

(Hettie rushes to her, but Lavinia turns away.)

HETTIE: Thank you! Your father thanks . . .

LAVINIA: In the meantime, you better stay with your mother.

HETTIE: I planned to. Please understand how grateful . . .

LAVINIA: And you are not to see *my* mother.

HETTIE: No.

LAVINIA: You should go now.

HETTIE: Yes. *(Makes a move to leave, then stops.)* The child inside, the girl, she's yours and Ezra's.

LAVINIA: Yes. Janie. She and the twins. The sum total of what Ezra and I have in common.

HETTIE: And is she very much like our Jane?

LAVINIA: No.

HETTIE: She looks like Ezra.

LAVINIA: She's quiet like Ezra.

HETTIE: And she's six?

(Lavinia nods.)

HETTIE: Same age as Tess. Tess reminds me of you. She has two little friends, like we were. Like you and me and Jane. She orders them around.

LAVINIA: *(Smiles then fights back tears.)* I think you better go now.

HETTIE: (*Touches her face, comforting.*) I know how hard it is for you. (*Hettie moves to leave. Then returns, having remembered one more thing.*) Lavinia . . . there's something else.

LAVINIA: What?

HETTIE: That necklace.

LAVINIA: Yes.

HETTIE: Your father would like it back.

LAVINIA: This locket?

HETTIE: Yes. He wants it back.

LAVINIA: What for?

HETTIE: He says it's worth good money.

LAVINIA: Good. Money.

HETTIE: He says it's his to bestow.

LAVINIA: You see that. He has no regret for what he did.

HETTIE: He wants to give it to Tess.

(*Lavinia reaches up and removes the locket. She dangles it above Hettie's hand.*)

LAVINIA: Make sure she knows where it came from.

(*Hettie takes the locket and leaves.*)

LAVINIA: (*Calling after her.*) See to it Tess knows! (*Exhausted, Lavinia sits on the cellar door and stares at the ground.*)

(*Then lights fade.*)

SCENE FOUR — ANIMAL TRAP

DATE: 1887
AGES: 40

In the darkness, we hear a loud crash. It is the sound of a large wooden chest full of hand tools falling from the second story.

The sound of barking dogs erupts in the distance. Then we hear tools being tossed and moved.

Lights up on the same scene. It is an autumn night, ten years later. The leaves are yellow. Tools are scattered around the broken wooden chest.

Lavinia is pawing through the rubble. She is holding an animal trap in her hand.

HETTIE: (*Off.*) Is someone hurt?

LAVINIA: Not yet.

HETTIE: Do you need some help?

LAVINIA: I don't think so. *(Pause. More pawing.)*

    (Finally, Hettie enters on the run, carrying a lantern.)

HETTIE: What on earth is going on over here?

LAVINIA: I pushed Ezra's tool box off the porch upstairs.

HETTIE: And set every dog in this valley to barking.

LAVINIA: I was looking for something.

HETTIE: That animal trap?

LAVINIA: I think so.

HETTIE: *(Picks up some of the scattered tools and tosses them in the box.)* I knew
    you were gonna be upset.

LAVINIA: I ain't upset.

HETTIE: No, of course not.

LAVINIA: *(Slams shut the lid on the chest.)* I'm as calm as a cow.

HETTIE: Calm as a volcano between eruptions.

LAVINIA: Hettie, I want you to promise me something.

HETTIE: What's that?

LAVINIA: See to it I'm not buried next to him.

HETTIE: Where do you want to be buried?

LAVINIA: Anywhere but next to Ezra.

HETTIE: But you're still married to him. Polygamy doesn't change that.

LAVINIA: Anywhere but next to him.

HETTIE: You can't be buried next to Jane. She's buried in Gunnison.

LAVINIA: Bury me alone then. Bury me next to the Indian woman we found
    dead last winter.

HETTIE: I'll do nothing of the sort.

LAVINIA: It is my desire. No, it is my command.

HETTIE: And exactly who do you think listens to your commands?

LAVINIA: You do.

HETTIE: Our job is to search for the blessings, that's what we need to do at
    a time like this.

LAVINIA: It's immoral.

HETTIE: It's a burden, I know.

LAVINIA: No, it's criminal.

HETTIE: The Church is a blessing, Lavinia. I really do believe that.

LAVINIA: And the divinely inspired institution of plural marriage?

HETTIE: Is a challenge. *(A slight pause.)*

LAVINIA: Is an old man's nocturnal emission!

HETTIE: Lavinia, if you were a child of mine, I'd wash your mouth out with soap. *(Hettie slowly, deliberately picks up some more of the scattered tools.)*

LAVINIA: Exactly when did he have time to carry out this little interest, this little preoccupation with the flesh of teenage children?

HETTIE: Tess never let on, never told me a thing. A couple of month ago, I had an inkling of something between them. But then I figured they'd get over it.

LAVINIA: That's the nice thing about polygamy. Old men don't have to "get over it." Do you think it's a passion? The great passion of his life?

HETTIE: I don't think so.

LAVINIA: Pity! But I never promised to put up with this. And I won't. From now on, he is married to Tess, not me. Quicker than a Goshute Indian. He no longer has a place at my fire.

HETTIE: You are not taking this at all well.

LAVINIA: *(Slams shut the lid on the chest.)* He is marrying someone three and a half months younger than his own daughter!

HETTIE: Must you tell me things I already know. At full volume? *(Kicks the chest.)* I dug up the garden today. Quarter of an acre.

LAVINIA: And why? Do tell us why, Hettie.

HETTIE: Tess should marry someone young.

LAVINIA: Everyone should marry someone young.

HETTIE: I know what it's like to marry someone old.

LAVINIA: What is it like?

HETTIE: Never mind.

LAVINIA: Oh please, pretty please, do tell us, do.

HETTIE: I wouldn't touch it with a pitchfork.

LAVINIA: Everyone should marry someone young. Except for Janie. Who should marry no one at all. *(She makes a big swipe with the trap in her hand.)*

HETTIE: Oh, Lavinia, don't talk like that.

LAVINIA: Don't listen, then. Janie is going to be a schoolteacher. Live in a house by herself. Read books in the quiet of her house on Sunday afternoons.

HETTIE: We cannot control the arc of an arrow. And we cannot control the lives of our children. Your father used to say that. About you.

LAVINIA: She's going to find him dull.

HETTIE: I told her as much. But I think she loves him.

LAVINIA: Someone should love him before he dies.

HETTIE: He's hard-working, kind.

LAVINIA: Smells like a suckling calf.

HETTIE: What's that got to do with it?

LAVINIA: Nothing. Nothing at all.

HETTIE: He's good with children.

LAVINIA: Children make him nervous.

HETTIE: She'll be well cared for.

LAVINIA: Providing she's a hardy desert plant. Can grow without tending, thrive on neglect. *(Pries the jaws of the trap apart.)*

HETTIE: Lavinia, your hand is bleeding. Put that damn thing down.

LAVINIA: I'm going to trap a dog.

HETTIE: Whose dog?

LAVINIA: There was a dog in the sheep last night.

HETTIE: There was no dog.

LAVINIA: Maybe it was a coyote. Could have been a wolf.

HETTIE: Put that damned thing down. Please.

LAVINIA: Thought I'd give myself the hydrophobia. Die like Jane.

HETTIE: Come help me plant that garden. It'll be good for you. For me, too. Wear us both out.

LAVINIA: Trap like this can take a dog's leg right off. Wolf's leg too. Man's foot . . .

HETTIE: Lavinia, listen to me. You scrape yourself together. I ain't putting up with you crazy.

LAVINIA . . . That's how T-Legged Tom come to walk the way he does. Stepped in a trap set for a coyote. Snap goes the dragon.

HETTIE: Lavinia, snap out of this.

LAVINIA: Snap.

HETTIE: This ain't even about you.

LAVINIA: Oh no?

HETTIE: You never cared about Ezra, I did. And it ain't your daughter that's marrying him now, it's mine.

LAVINIA: Snap goes the dragon.

HETTIE: You can't ever do nothing small. Always got to make a specimen of yourself.

LAVINIA: Snapping turtles. Snapping dragon.

HETTIE: You and your father both. Live your lives like everything is about you. Most selfish people on the face of the earth. If either one of you ever stopped looking at yourself long enough, you'd find a whole world out there.

LAVINIA: *(Considers what Hettie has said.)* I am not my father.

HETTIE: I said you resemble him.

LAVINIA: I resemble him in stature. Nothing else.

HETTIE: You resemble him in temperament. Act like you're the only one in the house. Yell around in every room.

LAVINIA: My father was insane.

HETTIE: He was not insane. He was never . . . insane.

LAVINIA: He walked head-on into a train.

HETTIE: To make a point.

LAVINIA: That it was stronger than he?

HETTIE: He believed the railroad would corrupt us. He wanted to warn us, to protect us.

LAVINIA: Yes, to protect us. My father walked into a yard full of the children saved from the massacre. They were screaming. Scared. Hungry and hot. Their parents were dead. A toddler, filthy with gore, waddled up to him and hugged his boot. My father pushed her back and walked away. To *protect* the shine on his boot.

HETTIE: Who told you that?

LAVINIA: I saw it.

HETTIE: No.

LAVINIA: He was crazy at the end. That's all I know of justice and all I need to know. *(She twirls the trap by its chain.)*

HETTIE: And what of yourself?

LAVINIA: I'm sane. Sane as the town clock.

HETTIE: What would Jane think of you now?

LAVINIA: She would laugh, stretch out her arms and twirl for the sky. *(Twirls.)* She would laugh and misquote the scriptures. "Behold, these are my beloved buns. See them." *(Twirls and bends over.)* She would laugh, stretch out her arms, and a mourning dove would perch on her hand. *(Reaches for an imaginary dove.)*

HETTIE: No mourning dove ever perched on Jane's hand.

LAVINIA: Of course it did.

HETTIE: Lavinia, it did not.

LAVINIA: I remember it clearly.

HETTIE: You made it up. There's no mourning doves around here. No mourning doves or evening doves or noon day doves. No doves of any sort except you put them there.

LAVINIA: There were flocks of mourning doves back then. They lived in this tree. Jane brought wheat in her apron to feed them. She threw it in the air. The mourning doves would dart from the sky and catch it mid-air.

(The sound of a trap snapping shut. Pause. Hettie freezes, afraid to look.)

HETTIE: Lavinia, are you all right?

LAVINIA: Yes. *(Pause. She is not all right.)* Tell me something about Jane. Something you remember about Jane.

HETTIE: I barely remember Jane.

LAVINIA: I don't know where my mind would go if I didn't remember Jane.

HETTIE: She had that brown skirt and a scarf.

LAVINIA: Green scarf.

HETTIE: Yes, green.

LAVINIA: What did she do in her brown skirt and scarf, green scarf?

HETTIE: I don't know. I don't remember.

LAVINIA: She gave a report on mourning doves. She sat near the alphabet letters — beneath the letter m. M for mourning doves.

HETTIE: You have a remarkable memory.

LAVINIA: I keep in my head every thing she ever said. I quiz Ezra, "Did she say, 'I'm only a child at heart' or did she say, 'I'm only a child in my heart'?" He looks at me sideways. "What difference does it make?" And I guess it doesn't make very much difference, but it seems to make all the difference. All the difference. "No difference," I say, "I'm just thinking." He's never caught on, in all these years, he's never once said, "Why do you care so much about her?" Never said, "Are you in love with Jane?" Because I am so cunning. So intricate. No one has the slightest idea.

HETTIE: I have the slightest idea.

LAVINIA: Of course you do, Hettie. That's why I love you.

(Distant thunder. It starts to rain.)

HETTIE: You still miss her.

LAVINIA: Like the right side of my body. *(Raises her arms out wide. Her hand is in the teeth of the trap. Lights out.)*

SCENE FIVE — TREE HOUSE

DATE: 1897
AGES: 50

This scene takes place in the same back yard ten years later. It is morning. Lavinia is sitting on the steps furiously playing solitaire. She has no right hand. Hettie enters from the side of the house. She watches.

HETTIE: What's got you on the trot?

(Lavinia is still playing furiously.)

LAVINIA: I think I'm losing my beans.

HETTIE: (Studies her.) What's your symptoms?

LAVINIA: Squares of time missing.

HETTIE: (Watches the game.) Seven on the Eight.

(Pause. More card playing.)

LAVINIA: I found myself in that damn box elder tree.

HETTIE: In?

LAVINIA: Up in.

HETTIE: Your fat bottom in that tree. Wish I'd seen it. (She laughs. Lavinia waits for Hettie to stop.)

LAVINIA: When I woke up — came to — it was dark. I couldn't see to get down.

HETTIE: So you had to stay up there the whole night?

LAVINIA: Just till dawn.

(Hettie laughs. Lavinia doesn't.)

LAVINIA: I was that boy at the Massacre. The one who ran into the cedars and climbed a tree to escape. Who had to be shot from the tree like a bob cat. I was *that* boy. In *this* tree.

HETTIE: Oh god.

LAVINIA: Nothing like that ever happened to you, did it!

HETTIE: (Crosses to her.) At this age, we're supposed to lose a little memory. But we gain in creativity.

LAVINIA: I'd rather have memory.

(The game continues.)

HETTIE: Ten on the Jack. Nine upstairs. Is that why you got that gun in your lap?

LAVINIA: If it happens again, I want you to kill me.

HETTIE: Why don't you kill yourself?

LAVINIA: Well, I'll try. But if I miss, I want you to do it.

HETTIE: Lavinia, could you one time, just one time before you die, do something plain? Something kind of regular or ordinary. You always gotta have this big tah-dah about everything.

LAVINIA: I don't want to be a crazy old woman.

HETTIE: Why not? You were a crazy *young* woman.

LAVINIA: (Studies her.) I swear in the next life, you are going to be so much smarter.

HETTIE: (Sits.) I got news for you, dear friend, in the next life, *you* are going to be jolly and comforting. We'll never speak about anything. We'll just have adventures.

LAVINIA: And where will we have these adventures?

HETTIE: *(Thinking, then finally inventing a place.)* Neptune. Three on the Two up above. And so you're gonna carry a gun around for the rest of your days?

LAVINIA: If I have another lapse, I'm afraid I might be too far gone to remember where it is.

HETTIE: Four on the Five. But what if I don't want to shoot you?

LAVINIA: You're the one that's got good sense, remember. That's what my mother always said, "That Hettie, she ain't bright. But she's got good sense."

HETTIE: She didn't say that I wasn't bright. You added that. Your mother was a sweet woman, she would not have said that.

LAVINIA: No, she didn't. But she did say you had good sense and *implied* the rest.

HETTIE: If I didn't have good sense, you wouldn't be here today. And your father would have died in Connecticut.

LAVINIA: That's what Mother *said*.

(The card game proceeds.)

HETTIE: Jack on the Queen and move it over. Now you free your Ace.

LAVINIA: Would you like to play a hand of cards with me? Or do you just want to coach?

HETTIE: You're slipping. I have to help you.

LAVINIA: Either play a hand of your own or be still about mine.

HETTIE: *(Watches, then picks up a card and plays it. Lavinia glowers at her.)* I did not say a word. Well, maybe I'll play just one hand. *(Hettie sits.)*

LAVINIA: The Lord does not approve of cards.

HETTIE: I didn't invite the Lord to play.

(With effort, Lavinia gathers up the cards.)

HETTIE: Here, I'll shuffle. *(Takes the cards from Lavinia.)* It's not against the Word of Wisdom to play with cards. It's just again the Word of Wisdom to *wager* with cards.

LAVINIA: It's against the Word of Wisdom to play with face cards at all.

HETTIE: That's only in the strictest interpretation of that covenant.

(Lavinia's eyes roll to the sky.)

HETTIE: *(Continues to shuffle. She looks around the yard.)* If you had to spend all night with your rear end draped over a branch, this is a lovely place to do it.

LAVINIA: Deal the cards.

HETTIE: *(Still shuffling.)* What kind of climber is that?

LAVINIA: Clematis.

HETTIE: Beautiful.

LAVINIA: It's fertilized with bones.

HETTIE: George Q. Cannon used to say the trees would grow taller and bear more fruit if you buried a few bones at their roots.

LAVINIA: Yes. But he wanted to use the thigh bones of Catholics.

HETTIE: The longer I live, the more I like flowers.

LAVINIA: All right, Hettie.

HETTIE: Every year my garden has fewer vegetables and more flowers.

LAVINIA: The cards, Hettie.

HETTIE: Just planted three bushes of peonies. They're all for your father's grave. He loved peonies.

LAVINIA: Deal-the-cards. *(They play the game of War. It goes on for several seconds.)* Sure you don't want to go down to the freight stop to meet Ezra?

LAVINIA: I'm sure.

HETTIE: I told Tess that would be your answer. But she insisted I invite you to go with us.

LAVINIA: That's like Tess. Very polite.

HETTIE: Yes, she's polite.

LAVINIA: The Commander raised obedient daughters.

HETTIE: The Commander did not raise Tess.

LAVINIA: He didn't raise me, either. *(Pause. The game continues.)*

HETTIE: Don't you want to go for just a few minutes? Do you good.

LAVINIA: I don't want anyone's pity.

HETTIE: It's not pity. It's simple human kindness.

LAVINIA: I will not be pitied!

HETTIE: You are not pitied. That's not a danger for you.

LAVINIA: You go in my place. Make a report.

HETTIE: I'm afraid he'll be embarrassed if you're not there.

LAVINIA: Embarrassed? An emotion unknown to men of the Mormon faith.
(They play for several seconds.)

HETTIE: The baby's going to wear that naming dress you sewed for him.

LAVINIA: In hopes that Ezra will be gratified to see the newest child he's spawned?

HETTIE: I tried to prepare Tess.

LAVINIA: At his age he has no interest in an infant.

HETTIE: Serves him right. Having to live with one now.
(They both chuckle. Pause.)

LAVINIA: You can't imagine how much I do *not* want to see that man.

HETTIE: Aren't you curious?

LAVINIA: Not in the least.

HETTIE: Oh, I am. I'm curious.

LAVINIA: I know what he looks like. Besides, you always found him more interesting than I did.

HETTIE: What was it we found so compelling about him?

LAVINIA: I never found him so compelling.

HETTIE: Oh, I did. I found him thoroughly compelling. Jane too. She found him thoroughly compelling. One year's a long time at his age. Prison is hard on the older ones.

LAVINIA: It's all Tess's problem, not mine.

HETTIE: I gave her some money in case Ezra needed a suit of clothes.

LAVINIA: I already sent him money for a suit of clothes.

HETTIE: Cecil Simpson was sent home in his striped prison garb.

LAVINIA: That's because Cecil Simpson wasn't a good member of the Church.

HETTIE: Ezra's an old man. He deserves respect.

LAVINIA: If you go to prison for polygamy, the Church will buy you a suit of clothes when you get out. That's the deal the Church offers you in exchange for turning you in. Ain't it kindly?

HETTIE: He's got a right to his dignity.

LAVINIA: He's got a right to his dignity. And a six-month-old infant. And a farm in total disrepair. And that semi-officious, all-knowing daughter of yours for a wife.

HETTIE: Tess and you are just alike. That's the reason he married her.

LAVINIA: I wrote him a letter in prison. Told him I did not want him staying here when he got out. Not in this house. I told him he could have the little house at the other end of the lot. It's solid. The rooms are small. The ceilings are low. And it needs a new stove. But it'll be fine for him. And Tess. And the children.

HETTIE: Your generosity of spirit overwhelms us all.

LAVINIA: There's nothing wrong with the little house.

HETTIE: It's a sentence for an unknown crime.

LAVINIA: The crime is known. Cohabitation with plural wives. A crime in the *state* of Utah. Punishable by up to a year in the *state* penitentiary.
(*They nudge each other and grin.*)

HETTIE: Polygamy is dead.

LAVINIA: For time and all eternity.

HETTIE: Your Janie won't even have to worry about it.

LAVINIA: Janie's a mid-wife. Just the profession to give her the right perspective on marriage.

HETTIE: You say the awfullest things.

LAVINIA: She's happy with her life.

ETTIE: But what's she doing with it?

LAVINIA: Living it the best she can.

HETTIE: Well, yes, I suppose she is, poor thing.

LAVINIA: Good Lord, Hettie, neither one of us had the right answer.

HETTIE: I don't know about you, but I'm proud of my life.

LAVINIA: You did all right with what you were given. But god knows, you
wouldn't wish it on anyone else.

HETTIE: No, I suppose not. My mother used to say her life was mirrored in
the migration west. It's beautiful and green in the east when you're young.
There's a large, terrible flat part in the middle. Then the hellish mountains before the children are grown. And after all of it, you end your days
in the desert.

LAVINIA: Hey! Let's lock up the house and go somewhere.

HETTIE: Where shall we go?

LAVINIA: To Neptune.

HETTIE: Let's go up in the tree.

LAVINIA: You're not going to the freight stop, then?

HETTIE: Not if *you're* gonna be in the tree. Besides, I'm not as interested in
Ezra as I once was.

LAVINIA: To the tree!

(They move to the foot of the tree.)

HETTIE: There will be no food or rocks up there.

LAVINIA: None.

HETTIE: Well then, let's go.

(Lavinia starts up the tree, Hettie following. Midway up, Hettie stops.)

HETTIE: Wait a minute. You could fall out of this tree, kill yourself. I want
to know something before you do. What happened to that two-headed calf?

LAVINIA: I told you.

HETTIE: God did not take it back like the Golden Plates.

LAVINIA: Well, no.

HETTIE: It was not stolen by the Indians because they believed it was the
head of God.

LAVINIA: No, I don't think so.

HETTIE: And it was not given to Brigham Young and his last wife for a wedding present.

LAVINIA: I didn't tell you that one. You invented it and I agreed with you.

HETTIE: The truth this time.

LAVINIA: I made it up.

HETTIE: You invented the two-headed calf?

LAVINIA: Ummm-hummm.

HETTIE: God, you're cruel.

LAVINIA: I had no choice, I knew exactly what was in the cellar. Bed clothes, shoes, leather traces for a team. No one could know. Grubbing hoes and pitch forks. A child's coat with bloody mittens. "Speak of this to no one." I mentioned them to no one.

HETTIE: That doesn't explain the two-headed calf.

LAVINIA: Since there was *not* a two-headed calf in the cellar, I *could* speak of that.

HETTIE: Oh. *(Nods. They continue up the tree and stand together on a branch.)* It's right beautiful up here.

LAVINIA: That it is.

HETTIE: You're not going to shoot anyone?

LAVINIA: No.

HETTIE: And you're not going to pelt them with anything.

LAVINIA: No.

HETTIE: How long till they get here?

LAVINIA: I don't know, do I? It doesn't matter, does it?
(They both sit on the branch.)

HETTIE: Things look so small from up here. Look at the washtub. It looks like a cup.

LAVINIA: Shhh. The whole point of being in the tree is silence.

HETTIE: Oh. You can see all the way to Mountain Meadow. *(She turns and looks at Lavinia.)* This where you were.

LAVINIA: *(Indicates a distant point.)* The shooting went on for several minutes. Many people died right away. An equal number did not die — right away. Some of them had to be shot twice, even three times. They watched themselves being killed. *(Long pause.)* Jane, too. She watched herself being killed.

HETTIE: Shhh. Give me your hand.
(Lavinia's "bad" hand is closest. She offers her "good" hand. Hettie takes the "bad" hand. They sit there looking out at the view.)
(Sound of a distant train.)
(Lights fade slowly.)

END OF PLAY

Miracles

By Nina Kossman

For Nadia and Andy

DIRECTOR: Alan Haag
CAST:
LUZ . . . . Marsha Weininger
ANA . . . . Julie O'Hara

ABOUT THE AUTHOR

Nina Kossman, born in Moscow, is the author of four plays, two books of poems in Russian and English, and a collection of short stories, *Behind the Border* (Morrow, 1994, 1996; Japanese translation, 1994), Her dramatic dialogs, short stories and poems have appeared in literary magazines in the United States, Canada, England, New Zealand, Belgium, Russia, and Spain. The U.S. magazines that published her work include *The Threepenny Review, Columbia: A Journal of Literature and Art, P.E.N. International, Confrontation,* and *Michigan Quarterly Review.*

She has translated two books of Marina Tsvetaeva's poetry, *In the Inmost Hour of the Soul* and *Poem of the End.* Her poems and poem translations have appeared in anthologies such as *World Poetry* (Norton, 1998), *Divine Inspiration* (Oxford University Press, 1998), *Gospels in Our Image* (Harcourt Brace, 1995), *Twentieth Century Russian Poetry* (Doubleday, 1993), et cetera. She is the editor of *Gods and Mortals: Modern Poems on Classical Myths,* an anthology published by Oxford University Press in 2001. Her fiction won a UNESCO/PEN Short Story Award in London and was broadcast on the BBC World Service (1995).

Her other awards include grants from the National Endowment for the Arts, Alexander S. Onassis Public Benefit Foundation (OUP), Foundation for Hellenic Culture (OUP), and a residency at Fundaçion Valparaiso, Spain. Two of Kossman's one-act plays have been produced off Broadway.

AUTHOR'S NOTE

Miracles was inspired by a childhood incident, which I first described in a short story published in my collection *Behind the Border.* A first grade teacher in my Moscow school urged us not to accept candy from foreigners, because they hated us Soviet children so much that they would put tiny bombs in their capitalist candy to blow us up. I spent the rest of the week that I heard this in terrible fear, expecting to be blown up, since just a few days before I had accepted candy from a foreigner.

The play is set in Cuba because, while the Soviet Union of my childhood no longer exists, Cuba is still very much a totalitarian state. In *Miracles* I wanted to show the effect of early brainwashing, the early division of the world into "us" and "them," and the way innocent childhood activities, tinged with politics children don't understand, can metamorphose into something big and life-changing, and how family members can be separated, less by the plain fact of state borders than by the collective belief in the sanctity of those borders.

CHARACTERS
LUZ: ten years old
ANA: seven years old

PLACE
An apartment in Havana, Cuba

TIME
The present

MIRACLES

A minimal set. A dinner table and two chairs. On the table are two plates: one plate is clean, the remains of a recent meal are on the other. The walls and the floor in the left half of the stage may be of a different color than in the right half. On the wall in the left half there may be a portrait of Fidel Castro or anything else that would indicate that the action is taking place in Communist Cuba.

In the beginning of the play, both Ana and Luz are in the same ("Cuban") part of the room. Ana is sitting at the table in front of a plate with an unfinished meal. Luz is standing next to her.

LUZ: Finish what's on your plate.

ANA: Don't want to.

LUZ: You must.

ANA: Who said.

LUZ: Mama said.

ANA: What will she do?

LUZ: What will she do if what?

ANA: If I don't. What will she do if I don't finish?

LUZ: She'll spank you.

ANA: No she won't. *(Pause.)* No she won't. She won't spank me. *(Pause)* She never spanks *me. You're* the one she spanks.

LUZ: No she doesn't. I'm the oldest. When Mama isn't here, I get to be Mama. *(Pause.)* Finish what's on your plate.

ANA: What if I don't?

LUZ: You've got to eat. If you don't eat, you won't get big.

ANA: That's not how she says it.

LUZ: Yes it is. Yes it is how she says it.

ANA: Is not!

LUZ: Is too.

ANA: Is not!

LUZ: Is.

ANA: I don't want to play this game. It's a stupid game and I don't want to play it.

LUZ: It's not a game. It's for real. She wants you to eat your food cos you got to be big for real. If you don't get big, nobody will see you. You may be right there with all the rest of them, but they won't see you. They won't even think you're a person. They'll just think you're —

ANA: I don't want to be a person. I like being *me*. What's so great about being a person?

LUZ: I'll be a person cos I eat what they give me.

ANA: I don't want to be that kind of person! I want to be the kind of person that eats what she wants.

LUZ: You won't get to be that kind of person. Cos you won't grow.

ANA: Is the world made up of people who eat what they don't want to?

LUZ: Spit out that gum.

ANA: It's not done yet.

LUZ: It doesn't matter.

ANA: There's still some sweet in it.

LUZ: It doesn't matter.

ANA: I want to chew till the sweet is gone.

LUZ: If you don't spit it out, you'll get blown up.

ANA: Who said?

LUZ: I said.

ANA: What do *you* know? You don't even have some gum. You're just jealous, that's all.

LUZ: I'm not jealous. I'm a teacher.

ANA: No you're not. You're a girl. You're a girl like me. You're my sister.

LUZ: When the teacher isn't here, I get to be her.

ANA: No you're not. *(Pause.)* You're not her. You're you.

LUZ: Spit out your gum or you'll be blown to pieces.

ANA: How come I didn't get blown up yet?

LUZ: It takes time. It may be a slow bomb. In some candy they put a slow bomb.

ANA: Who?

LUZ: Foreigners.

ANA: Why do they pub a bomb in candy?

LUZ: I told you lots of times.

ANA: Tell me again.

LUZ: Tell you what?

ANA: *(Louder.)* Why do they put a bomb in candy?

LUZ: Cos they're foreigners.

ANA: What's that mean?

LUZ: They're not like us.

ANA: So what?

LUZ: Cos they hate us.

ANA: But why do they hate us?

LUZ: Cos they're not like us. They want to be like us but they can't.

ANA: Why?

LUZ: You'll know when you go to school.

ANA: Why do they hate us?

LUZ: Cos we're not foreigners. We're us.

ANA: I'm not us. I'm me.

LUZ: When you go to school they'll tell you. They'll tell you that you are us.

ANA: But why do foreigners hate us?

LUZ: Cos they're capitalists.

ANA: What's that mean?

LUZ: They're capitalists. They only think about themselves.

ANA: They're thinking about us. They're thinking about us when they put bombs in the candy. Ha-ha. Got you!

LUZ: Not funny.

ANA: Is too.

LUZ: Is not.

ANA: Is too.

LUZ: Is not.

ANA: Anyway, this isn't candy. This is gum.

LUZ: So what.

ANA: They can't put a bomb in gum. You'd chew right though it.

LUZ: They have special bombs. They feel like gum. But then three days later —

ANA: It's not true.

LUZ: Is too.

ANA: I don't want to play this game.

LUZ: I know someone who got blown up.

ANA: Do not!

LUZ: Do too.

ANA: I said I don't want to play that.

LUZ: I know someone who chewed American gum.

ANA: Who?

LUZ: A girl.

ANA: What girl?

LUZ: A girl from my class. She chewed American gum and got blown to pieces.

ANA: How many pieces?

LUZ: Doesn't matter.

ANA: Does.

LUZ: Does not.

ANA: I said I don't want to play that game. I said!

LUZ: You started it. *(Pause.)*

ANA: *(Thinks.)* What's her name?

LUZ: She doesn't have a name. She's dead.

ANA: What was her name *then?*

LUZ: It's gone. Your name goes away when you die.

ANA: Not *my* name.

LUZ: Yours too.

ANA: I'll always be me. Even when I die.

LUZ: No you won't. Not when you die you won't.

ANA: How do you know? You're not me.

LUZ: I know cos I go to school.

ANA: So what.

LUZ: They tell us things.

ANA: How do they know? They're not you.

LUZ: That's stupid.

ANA: But how do they know about you? They're not you.

LUZ: Cos they're teachers. They know.

ANA: They know about *them*. They don't know about *you*.

LUZ: When you're a grown-up, you don't know about you. You know about
    other people.

ANA: I don't want to be that kind of grown-up. I want to know about me.

LUZ: You're a capitalist.

ANA: Am not.

LUZ: Are too.

ANA: Don't want to play this game I said.

LUZ: You're a capitalist cos capitalists only think about themselves. They don't
    care about others.

ANA: So what.

LUZ: If you don't think about others, you'll get sent to America.

ANA: So what.

LUZ: You'll never get to see Mama again.

ANA: Mama won't send me away.

LUZ: Yes she will.

ANA: No she won't. I know.

LUZ: She won't want to but she'll have to.

ANA: How do you know?

LUZ: Cos that's what they tell us in school. If you're bad, they send you away to America.

ANA: I won't go.

LUZ: You'll have to.

ANA: I won't go.

LUZ: You will.

ANA: In a little package?

LUZ: What?

ANA: They send you to America in a little package?

LUZ: It's not a package. It's a box. Looks like a shoebox only bigger.

ANA: Maybe it's a coffin.

LUZ: It's not a coffin. It's a box.

ANA: I don't want to sit in a shoebox. I won't have any air.

LUZ: They make special holes for you. So you can breathe until you get there.

ANA: Then what?

LUZ: What?

ANA: What happens when you get there?

LUZ: They take you out of the box and take you to a factory with lots of other kids.

ANA: Then what?

LUZ: *What* what?

ANA: Then what they do?

LUZ: They make you work, that's what, stupid. They make a slave out of you.

ANA: Not out of me.

LUZ: You're not so special.

ANA: Yes I am.

LUZ: If they want to make you into a slave, they will.

ANA: I won't let them. I'll run away.

LUZ: Can't run away from America.

ANA: Yes I can. I can run back home.

LUZ: Can't run away from America, stupid. America's in the middle of a sea.

ANA: I can swim it.

LUZ: No you can't. You don't know how to.

ANA: I'll learn.

LUZ: You'll drown. You'll drown and Mama won't even know where you are.

ANA: I'll dig a tunnel.

LUZ: Can't dig a tunnel from America to here. It's too far.

ANA: So what. I'll dig it all my life. Until I'm big like Mama or your teacher.

LUZ: You won't get to be that big. They won't give you enough food.

ANA: So what.

LUZ: Can't grow without food.

ANA: I hate this food anyway.

LUZ: In America it's even worse.

ANA: Who said?

LUZ: I just know.

ANA: They never sent you there. How do you know?

LUZ: I just know.

ANA: They never sent your teacher to America. How would she know?

LUZ: She knows.

ANA: Does not.

LUZ: Does too.

ANA: Don't want to play this game. *(Pause.)* Maybe I *want* to go to America. Maybe it's not so bad being a slave if they let you chew gum.

LUZ: They won't let you chew it there. They send it from there to here so you chew it and get blown up.

ANA: Maybe over there they make good gum. Without a little bomb inside. So their own kids don't get blown to pieces.

LUZ: No, there's no good gum.

ANA: Yes, there is.

LUZ: You're starting it.

ANA: What?

LUZ: It. You're starting it. You're starting it, and then you say you don't want to play this game.

ANA: Am not.

LUZ: Are too.

ANA: You're the one starting it now.

LUZ: Wasn't me. Was you. *(Pause.)*

ANA: I wish we had a box.

LUZ: What for?

ANA: To put me in.

LUZ: We don't have it yet. Mama will bring it from a store.

ANA: Let's pretend. Let's pretend we're putting me in the box.

LUZ: Okay. You go in.

(Ana lies down in the middle of the room, on the "border" between the "Cuban" part and the "American" part. She brings her knees up to her chin and wraps her arms around her legs.)

LUZ: You in the box yet?

ANA: Yeah.

LUZ: Can't talk if you're in the box. *(Silence.)* You still there? *(Silence.)* Okay. I'm sending you off to America. *(Bends down as though to lift the box, then stands with her arms outstretched, as if carrying something heavy.)* Hold on.

ANA: *(Still crouching.)* Are you sending me by ship?

LUZ: You're not supposed to talk. You're in the box.

ANA: Are you sending me by ship?

LUZ: By truck, by ship, and by airplane.

ANA: All right.

LUZ: *(Pushes the imaginary box away from herself, into the other — American — half of the room.)* There you go. That's where you go if you want to chew gum.

ANA: When do I get to America?

LUZ: Wait five minutes.

(They wait about forty seconds.)

ANA: I see it! I see America.

LUZ: You can't see it. You're in the box.

ANA: I see it through the little holes.

LUZ: The little holes are for air.

ANA: They're for seeing too.

LUZ: That's not right. That's not how you sit in the box.

ANA: That how *I* sit in the box. *(Twists her body out of the imaginary box and stands up in the "American" side of the room.)* Hello! Hello! *(Ana is waving and blowing kisses.)* I see them! I see capitalists and foreigners! Hello!

LUZ: You're not supposed to like them.

ANA: They're giving me whole bags full of chewing gum. Every kind of flavor. Strawberry. Lemon. Chocolate.

LUZ: You're not supposed to take them. You're supposed to say no. Gum is a capitalist thing.

ANA: *(Chewing gum even more passionately than before.)* That's not what *they* say.

LUZ: They lie a lot cause they're foreigners. You're supposed to say no.

ANA: Don't want to say no.

LUZ: Get back in the box.

ANA: Why?

LUZ: They're sending you back. That's why.

ANA: That's not why. It's because you want me to go back.

LUZ: Mama wants to see you. Don't you miss Mama?

ANA: Sure I miss Mama. But I don't want to get back in that box!

LUZ: Well you will.

ANA: No I won't.

LUZ: I'm putting you back in. *(Lifts an imaginary box, puts it down near Ana.)* Get in.

ANA: I won't.

LUZ: I said get in.

ANA: I'm staying where I am. I like it here. I couldn't breathe in the box.

LUZ: You had the little holes for air.

ANA: Not enough air. I need more. *(Makes loud breathing noises.)*

LUZ: But what'll I tell Mama? It's me she'll be angry with.

ANA: You can come here too, you know.

LUZ: I'm not a traitor.

ANA: What's a traitor?

LUZ: Somebody who leaves our country. Like you.

ANA: I didn't leave. You sent me away. So I'm not a traitor.

LUZ: What about Mama?

ANA: She can come here too.

LUZ: This box is too small for Mama.

ANA: It's not. It stretches.

LUZ: Anyway, she won't — she's a mama. Mamas don't go into boxes. *(Pause.)*

ANA: *(Dreamily.)* I like gum . . .

LUZ: So stay there! All by yourself. Stay there for good.

ANA: You should've let me chew it there. *(Worried.)* What'll I do now? All by myself.

LUZ: It's your own fault.

(Ana leaves, at first hesitantly, then decisively.)

(Luz is left alone on the stage. She looks lost, as though she can't understand how it all came about; how come she is alone. She kneels down, picks up one of Ana's toys from the floor.)

LUZ: *(Quietly, as though mumbling to herself — or to the toy.)* They'll send you to a factory. They'll make a slave out of you . . .

(Blackout.)

END OF PLAY

The Butterfly Collection

By Theresa Rebeck

ORIGINAL PRODUCTION

Playwrights Horizons, Inc., World Premiere of *The Butterfly Collection*
Off-Broadway (2000–2001 season)

ARTISTIC DIRECTOR: Tim Sanford
DIRECTOR: Bartlett Sher
SET DESIGN: Andrew Jackness
SOUND: Kurt B. Kellenberger
LIGHTING: Christopher Akerlind
COSTUMES: Ann Hould-Ward
CASTING: James Calleri, C.S.A.
DIRECTOR OF DEVELOPMENT: Jill Garland
PRODUCTION MANAGER: Christopher Boll
STAGE MANAGER: Roy Harris

CAST:
SOPHIE . . . . Maggie Lacey
FRANK . . . . Reed Birney
MARGARET . . . . Marian Seldes
LAURIE . . . . Betsy Aidem
ETHAN . . . . James Colby
PAUL . . . . Brian Murray

Prior to the Playwrights Horizons' production, *The Butterfly Collection* was
seen in readings at the South Coast Repertory's Pacific Playwrights Festival
and at New York Stage and Film Company in association with the Powerhouse
Theatre at Vassar (Summer 2000).

ABOUT THE AUTHOR
Ms. Rebeck's Plays include: *Spike Heels, Loose Knit* and *The Family of Mann*
at Second Stage; *View of the Dome* at New York Theatre Workshop and Vic-
tory Gardens; *Sunday on the Rocks* and *Abstract Expression* at the Longwharf
and *Dollhouse* at Hartford Stage. Other productions include: New Georges,
E.S.T., the Westbank Café, New York Stage and Film, Actor's Theatre of
Louisville, the Source, Alice's Fourth Floor, Manhattan Punchline, Double
Image Theater, Naked Angels, Theatre Geo, Seattle Rep, HB Playwrights Theatre, and the Boston Playwright's Theatre. Rebeck received a N.E.A. grant for

her continuing work on the musical adaptation of the nineteenth century melodrama *The Two Orphans*. A collection of the one-acts, *Rebeck Revisited*, ran for nine months at Theatre Neo in Los Angeles, making the LA weeklies' 10 Best List as one of the 10 best plays of 1999.

Rebeck's plays have been published by Samuel French as well as Smith and Kraus who, in addition to publishing her collected plays, have included her work in the Best Plays by Women series five times. *The Butterfly Collection* was workshopped at South Coast Repertory and New York Stage and Film (Summer 2000) and produced at Playwrights Horizons (Fall 2000). Ms. Rebeck is a member of Naked Angels, New York Theatre Workshops' Usual Suspects and HB Playwright's lab. She has enjoyed residencies at ACT/Hedgebrook and the New Harmony Project, where she workshopped her play *The Bells*. New plays also include *Omnium Gathering* (co-written with Alexandra Gersten) and *Bad Dates*. Theresa is currently working on commissions for South Coast Repertory and City Theatre in Pittsburgh.

In television, Ms. Rebeck has written for the HBO series, *Dream On*, *Brooklyn Bridge*, *L.A. Law*, *Maximum Bob*, *First Wave*, *Third Watch*, and *NYPD Blue*, where she also worked as a producer.

In film, she has written and produced *Kalamazoo*, an independent short, starring Wallace Shawn and Adrienne Shelley. Produced features include: *Harriet the Spy* and *Gossip*.

Awards include: the Mystery Writer's of America's Edgar Award, the Writer's Guild of America Award for Episodic Drama, the Hispanic Images Imagen Award and the Peabody, all for her work on NYPD Blue.

Ms. Rebeck earned her M.F.A. in Dramatic Writing and her Ph.D. in Victorian Literature at Brandeis University, where she met her husband, the stage manager, Jess Lynn. They have a seven-year-old son, Cooper.

AUTHOR'S NOTE & DEDICATION

I would like to dedicate this play to my father, whose father collected butterflies. He lost his father when he was quite young, and then the butterflies were lost. So this play is born of loss; his, and my own as well.

Even so, I do not consider *The Butterfly Collection* to be a sad play. I believe in the wit and courage of these characters, and in their troubled love for each other. I believe that in the depth of our heartbreak, art can and does shed grace on our lives.

It is my hope that this play illuminates some small interstice of that redemptive mystery.

CHARACTERS
SOPHIE: 28
PAUL: early 60s, a novelist
MARGARET: early 60s, Paul's wife
FRANK: 36, Paul and Margaret's son, an antiques dealer
ETHAN: 42, Paul and Margaret's son, an actor
LAURIE: mid 30s, Ethan's girlfriend

SET
The comfortable library/living room of Paul and Margaret's home in upstate Connecticut. A stairway can go up to the second floor, where Paul's office is located. Off left leads to the kitchen and dining room; a doorway to the back porch and yard open directly onto the living room as well.

THE BUTTERFLY COLLECTION

ACT ONE

A woman, Sophie, stands alone and speaks to the audience. She tells her story simply, with matter-of-fact good humor.

SOPHIE: My father's father collected butterflies. This was years ago, in the thirties, and he was quite poor, so he had few resources with which to pursue this elegant hobby, but apparently there was some kind of a network, a network of butterfly-collectors, that spread all over the world. These butterfly collectors would write to each other and trade butterflies through the mail, from exotic locations, Guatemala, South Africa, New Guinea. I don't know more than that, about how it worked, but the fact is, over the years this man collected and preserved many plates of butterflies, beautiful square plates in which he lined the insects up with tiny slips of paper identifying the genus and the species. There were at least a hundred and thirty of these plates; it was an astonishing and exhaustive labor of love. But he died, young, thirty, thirty-two, he caught pneumonia and apparently went very quickly, and as I said, they were poor. So after he died my grandmother took the three children back to her brother's farm in Ohio, where they were equally poor, but at least had family — this brother, and my grandmother's mother, a woman whose legendary meanness is still spoken of, by people who never even met her. The butterflies went with them, but my grandmother had no real idea what to do with them. Huge piles, plates of butterflies, cluttering the barn, or the garage, it must have seemed a strange madness to her. Finally, a neighbor suggested she donate them to the local state university, and one day, someone drove over and picked them up. Years later, when I was fourteen, my mother said to my father, we should go see them, so we drove for hours, to the University of Steubenville, to visit the butterflies. When we got there, no one had any idea what we were talking about, until they found someone who had been there a long time, who said, "Oh yes, those butterflies." He explained that they had been stored in a poorly insulated closet for years, where they were finally badly damaged by water, and tossed.
(Blackout.)

SCENE ONE

The lights shift to reveal the living room of a large, rambling New England country home. Margaret, Ethan, Laurie and Frank are examining a small piece of sculpture.

FRANK: Isn't it amazing?

MARGARET: Oh, Frank, it's absolutely stunning.

LAURIE: What is it doing? That's a snake.

FRANK: Yes, the snake is strangling Laocoon, and eating his children. The original is spectacularly gruesome.

ETHAN: What period is it from?

MARGARET: It's just magnificent, Frank.

FRANK: *(Answering Ethan.)* Which, the original or the copy? Because this, I think this is a copy of the copy.

ETHAN: I don't understand what you just said.

FRANK: There's a copy of the original in the Uffizi, and the original, which nobody knows exactly, it's Roman, maybe sixth century, is in the Vatican museum somewhere, no one will ever let you see it. Anyway, the story is it was dug up in the middle of the fourteenth century, they found it in somebody's garden near Florence, in Florence, Rome maybe, I don't remember, and Michelangelo saw it and was just electrified, it changed his entire — this is why, he realized, it spoke to him. It spoke. And he saw what could be done. What sculpture could be. That painting was not, that he was not, in fact, in his soul, he was a sculptor. That's what the Laocoon taught him.

LAURIE: Oh. *(She reconsiders it with new respect.)*

FRANK: Yes. Which is why, I think, this piece is probably a copy of the copy. Semi-antique, nineteen ten, eleven, Cabrian marble, hand-carved. Whoever did it was a master. Look at the detailing.

ETHAN: And where did you find this? Somebody in the neighborhood had it just hanging around the house?

FRANK: No, I don't, an estate sale over in Barrington. Some old lady died and the kids were just — it was on the lawn, for crying out load. In there with framed pictures of cats, and you know, bad jewelry. Who she was, where she got it, it's a mystery. Twelve dollars.

MARGARET: It's exquisite. Congratulations.

FRANK: *(Pleased.)* Thank you.

MARGARET: Your father has to — *(Calling off.) Paul!* Come see what — *(To Frank.)* If you ever decide to sell it, you must let me know first.

FRANK: Oh no, not now, I'm not —

MARGARET: *Paul!* Come see what Frank found! Where did he — wasn't he out back?

ETHAN: I don't know.

MARGARET: He can't be writing, that girl isn't here yet.

ETHAN: There's a new assistant?

MARGARET: She's coming up this afternoon. Well, I don't know where he is.

LAURIE: Does he live? Does he save his children? *(She looks up from the figurine, hopeful.)*

FRANK: Laocoon? No. The snake is too powerful. His children die, he dies. It's a terrible story. Ovid, I think. Virgil? Herodotus?

MARGARET: *(Looking up stairs.)* I think he's writing. Oh dear. Well, she's late, isn't she? She's late and he started without her, that's not good.

LAURIE: Does Paul always work with assistants?

MARGARET: Well, the past, what is it now, twenty some odd — at the beginning of course no. He didn't work with anyone.

ETHAN: He worked with you at the beginning, Mom.

MARGARET: Yes, I know, but it wasn't the same. I typed for him, mostly. A little bit of spelling and grammar.

LAURIE: So what do these assistants do?

MARGARET: *(Shrugging, a little smile.)* Typing mostly. A little spelling and grammar.

ETHAN: But he has a Nobel now, so it's much more important typing and spelling and grammar. *(A tortured act.)* More elusive, more luminous spelling and grammar. More evocative and rigorous typing and spelling and grammar.

MARGARET: If you think I like it when you make fun of your father you're wrong, you know.

ETHAN: I don't think that.

FRANK: *(To Laurie.)* How long are you here for?

LAURIE: We haven't decided yet. It's so lovely, I can't imagine ever going back to the city. I can't believe how lovely it is here.

FRANK: Well, because I was thinking you should come down to the shop. Because if you don't get out of the city, often, it's what people do here. Of course people do a lot of things, but antique stores is one of — because there are so many things, like this little Laocoon, just treasures, that people have hung onto for so long. And it's a treat, really, to see them. If you wanted to come down.

LAURIE: Of course I want to see your shop. There should be time for that.

MARGARET: Of course there's time. You're staying for at least a week.

ETHAN: Mom.

MARGARET: Ethan, I insist this time. I've only been hounding you for years. How long have you two been, five —

LAURIE: Two —

MARGARET: Two years. I've been hounding you for two years. Two years.

ETHAN: We've been busy.

MARGARET: For two years?

ETHAN: It's been a very active two years.

MARGARET: *(Ignoring him, to Laurie.)* And let me just say right now the guest house is yours. If you wanted to stay all summer, you'd be more than welcome. I wouldn't make that offer if you were here in the house because I think Paul would — well let's face it, we'd all drive each other a bit mad, but the guest house gives us just enough distance. Such a wonderful invention: The guest house. I do like having money.

ETHEN: Laurie works, Mom.

LAURIE: I can take some time. Really, I intended to take some time, I thought we might —

ETHAN: Well, I have auditions.

LAURIE: Yes, but you could run in for those, couldn't you? It's not that far. I'm not saying the whole summer, but —

MARGARET: Why not? You should stay. The guest house is yours. And you have to at least stay for Frank's birthday, that's why you came!

ETHAN: You know very well that even with the guest house, I can't possibly stay for more than three days. Last time we tried, it was a bloodbath. Duchess of Malfi, without the laughs. I think it's very brave, verging on foolhardy, that I've agreed to come at all.

MARGARET: Well, if you would be respectful of your father, and you should, after all, he has a Nobel —

ETHAN: I know about the Nobel, Mom!

MARGARET: Well, you don't act like it, that's all I'm saying.

FRANK: He's been asking about you.

(This more or less stops the conversation cold as Ethan considers this.)

ETHAN: He has not.

MARGARET: Yes, he has. Just, out of nowhere. What you're doing. If you're in a show.

ETHAN: You are both pathetic liars.

FRANK: No, it's true. Last week, he asked Mom where your reviews were.

ETHAN: He read my reviews?

FRANK: Yes!

ETHAN: The good ones or the bad ones?

MARGARET: Oh, please. You know I only save the good ones.

ETHAN: Well, if he did read them, it was largely so he could make fun of the writing style.

MARGARET: Oh Ethan —

(Paul enters. He carries with him a handful of pages from a yellow legal pad. They are covered with a loose scrawl.)

PAUL: Where is she, is she here yet? *(He goes to the back door to look.)*

MARGARET: There you are, Paul. We were just having some iced tea, would you like a glass?

PAUL: She was supposed to be here this morning, right? Was I wrong about that? Roger said he told her the morning.

MARGARET: I didn't speak to him.

PAUL: I spoke to him. That's what he said. This morning. Hours ago.

ETHAN: Hi Dad, great to see you.

MARGARET: Ethan and Laurie are here for the weekend, but I think they should stay longer, don't you? You remember Laurie. You've met, haven't you?

LAURIE: Yes, several times. In the city.

MARGARET: That's right, at that brunch. And at the theater one night. I'm sure.

PAUL: *(Distracted.)* Yes. Hi. Glad to see you. Ethan. You're staying just the weekend?

ETHAN: We don't know yet. Maybe a while. Frank's birthday is coming up. Maybe we'll stay till then.

PAUL: Oh. Good. *(He looks out the window. Ethan rolls his eyes, but Margaret is clearly encouraged.)*

MARGARET: I'm glad you came down, Paul, you'll get to see Frank's little treasure. Frank, show your father the Laocoon.

PAUL: The what?

FRANK: It's not . . .

MARGARET: Look, isn't it fantastic. He found it at an estate sale. *(She indicates the figurine, which Paul considers briefly.)*

PAUL: What is it?

FRANK: It's . . . you know, the Laocoon. Michelangelo . . .

PAUL: Michelangelo didn't do this.

FRANK: No. No. He saw it. At an estate sale . . .

PAUL: *(Impatient.)* What?

FRANK: *(Fighting to stay on top of this.)* He saw it, when he was young. It was, it influenced him, he realized what sculpture . . . *(He starts to disintegrate.)*

MARGARET: *(Helping out.)* He liked it. It made him want to be a sculptor.

PAUL: And what a terrific career choice that was. Couldn't finish anything except a statue of Moses with horns growing out of his head. If it had been up to Michelangelo, there would have been no Sistine Chapel.

FRANK: Well . . .

PAUL: Artists should never be allowed to make their own decisions.

ETHAN: Oh, my God.

MARGARET: Ethan.

ETHAN: What? *(Trying to be nice.)* I'm sorry, I just, uh — artists should never make their own decisions? That's —

PAUL: Yes?

ETHAN: I don't know. It just sounded a little nuts, to me.

PAUL: "Nuts."

ETHAN: Never mind. Sorry. *(He is trying. Margaret jumps in.)*

MARGARET: *(To Laurie.)* He's been writing all morning, with no help. It puts him in a mood.

PAUL: Don't apologize for me. I'm not in a mood, and I'm hardly "nuts." I'm just saying, Michelangelo was no sculptor.

ETHAN: *(Laughing.)* No — what do you call the Pietà?

PAUL: A sentimental homosexual's mother fixation. What do you call it?

ETHAN: A masterpiece.

PAUL: Really? How original.

ETHAN: You just said "I like the Sistine Chapel!" That's not exactly earth shattering.

PAUL: I wasn't trying to be earth shattering, and that's not what I said.

MARGARET: *(Mediating.)* So what are we arguing about now, whether or not the Sistine Chapel is any good?

PAUL: Actually, I think we're arguing about Ethan's manhood, but that's nothing new. How long has it been since you made any money, Ethan? Maybe if you got a job once in a while, you wouldn't have to come up here and take issue with every word I say.

(There is a sudden silence at this.)

PAUL: *(Continuing; knowing he crossed a line.)* Sorry. I'm sorry. I'm . . . this is . . . Christ. Where's that girl? Why isn't that girl here? She was supposed to be here by now.

MARGARET: I'll call Roger, see if he knows anything.

FRANK: I have to go, Mom. *(He collects his statuette and stands to go.)*

PAUL: Oh God, please! There's no need for everyone to start fleeing like frightened rabbits. The monster will go back into his lair. When that girl gets here, just tell her —. You know what to tell her. *(Beat.)* It's good to see you, Ethan. *(He hands Margaret the yellow pages and goes back upstairs. The others sit in silence for a moment.)*

MARGARET: He's much better. He really is. If that girl weren't late —

FRANK: He's been writing about death for twenty years. That would put anyone in a mood.

ETHAN: Why are you defending him? He makes you, you can't even complete a sentence when he's in the room!

MARGARET: Ethan.

FRANK: *(Defending himself.)* I'm, I'm not defending him. I'm just saying, it's not so bad anymore. You don't see him much, really. You know, he's sort of like a nasty old pet, this psychotic cat that comes out once in a while and howls at the moon. Mostly he stays in his den. *(Beat.)* He really did ask to read your reviews.

ETHAN: *(Curt.)* It's fine! I'm not here to see him anyway, and it's a good thing because you know he's just going to hole up there for our entire visit. He's finally finishing the new one, is that the story this time? *(To Laurie.)* These are the reasons one does not have to behave like an actual human being. One: One is starting a novel. Two: One is in the middle of a novel. Three: One is finishing a novel.

FRANK: I don't, it's not clear, actually. Finishing, no. That's not, no.

ETHAN: No? Really? Because I thought —

(Frank shrugs, embarrassed, looks away.)

MARGARET: There's just some pressure. Because he's rather late, this time.

ETHAN: How late?

MARGARET: Writers are always late. Dostoyevski, they were pounding on the door, while he slipped the finished pages under it. That happens sometimes.

ETHAN: So Roger's been coming up, has he, pounding on the door?

MARGARET: He's given him a deadline. *(There is an awkward pause at this. She is clearly embarrassed to admit it. Ethan looks at Frank.)*

ETHAN: A "deadline"? I don't even know what that means.

FRANK: *(Embarrassed.)* He's, it's there's been some concern, the advance.

ETHAN: What about it? *(Beat, laughing.)* Oh come on. He's not being asked to give it back?

MARGARET: Exactly. It's preposterous. Sometimes it just doesn't come, you'd think they'd know that by now, the whole lot of them. He'll have it when he's done, I don't know what else anyone expects.

ETHAN: They did? Wait, you mean, they really did, they did?

LAURIE: How much is it?

MARGARET: Nothing! One-fifty, something like that, complete pocket change to them. Less than pocket change, the whole house got bought up whenever that was, and now they're owned by Rupert Murdoch or someone, you know that if you go through all the channels of this one owning that one, and that one being owed by someone else, Rupert Murdoch is behind it all! And you're going to tell me Rupert Murdoch really needs a hundred and fifty thousand dollars? He doesn't even know it's gone!

ETHAN: Is it? Gone?

MARGARET: That's not the point!

LAURIE: Is he going to give the money back? *(There is a terrible pause at this.)*

LAURIE: *(Continuing; alarmed.)* What? Did I say something wrong?

MARGARET: It is absurd for them to ask for it. It is an insult to a man of Paul's stature. A complete insult. None of them, everyone he worked with for years is gone, and they've all been replaced by twelve-year-old idiots, and they're all obsessed with the Internet and not one of them has a shred of manners anymore. Marcuse was right, capitalism will be the death of all of us, it just sucks the life out of every culture it touches. I blame this whole thing on the fall of the Berlin Wall. They all think it's only money, it's profits and losses and dollars and cents and that damned — fucking — Internet, well, that's not all there is to life! There is art, and culture, and — dignity. Harold Brodkey took eighteen years to write *The Runaway Soul,* and no one ever asked him for the advance back. And needless to say, he did *not* have a Nobel. *(Snapping.)* Where is that girl? He's going to lose an entire day. I'm going to call Roger right now and tell him what I think — this is ridiculous.

(She heads off. Frank, Laurie and Ethan sit, a little stunned.)

FRANK: She's out of her mind. She's so, I don't know, I've never — That's why, I had to, I didn't know what else —

ETHAN: Frank, it's okay. I'm glad you called. She needs me here, of course I want to be here.

FRANK: Him too. I mean, it's true. When they asked for the money back. It shook him up.
LAURIE: How late is he?
FRANK: I don't know. Nine years, ten years.
LAURIE: Whoa. Really?
FRANK: Harold Brodkey took eighteen —
LAURIE: I heard.
ETHAN: Do you think he's lost it, finally?
FRANK: I don't know.
SOPHIE: *(Offstage.)* Hello?
  (All turn toward the door. Through the window, Sophie appears.)
FRANK: I just don't know. *(Blackout.)*

SCENE TWO

Sophie sits on the couch, going through the pages and yellow sheets. Paul comes down the stairs. She jumps, stands, nervous. He looks at her.)

PAUL: Hello.
SOPHIE: Hi. I'm, hi, I'm Sophie Marks.
PAUL: *(Matter of fact.)* I know who you are. *(He holds out his hand. She gives him the pages. He sits to read them with a pencil in his hand.)*
SOPHIE: I didn't, uh, your son gave me the pages you left and said you needed me to type them up and put some shape on them. I wasn't sure, since I hadn't spoken to you directly, I mean, there are places, obviously, where I had to improvise . . .
  (Paul starts to mark on the pages. She watches him, silent, for a moment.)
SOPHIE: *(Continuing.)* I wasn't sure how far to go. What you've done is so — I didn't —
PAUL: I'm sorry, but could you try to finish your sentence? I have a son who does that. It's hard to follow.
SOPHIE: I'm sorry. *(Then.)* Actually, I'm not sorry, I'm nervous. You're making me nervous, a little. That's why I keep interrupting myself.
PAUL: You're doing just fine now.
SOPHIE: Oh good.
  (There is the faintest edge to her response. He raises his eyebrow at her, noting her tone, and goes back to working on the pages. She watches him.)
SOPHIE: *(Continuing.)* It's all right then, what I did?

PAUL: I'll let you know if it's not right.

SOPHIE: *(Laughing a little at this.)* Yeah, yes, of course, Sorry. *(She smiles and sits, not quite knowing what to do now.)*

PAUL: Did you like it? *(He looks up from the pages and indicates them.)*

SOPHIE: Di — oh. Yes. I did. *(Beat. He looks at her.)* What? You want me to tell you what I thought of it? *(He looks at her, waiting.)* I like its . . . tone. The coolness of the surface. There are places where I was having trouble holding onto it, because that glide can, in places, get a little too facile for my taste but overall I liked the elegance. My stuff always seems so, tied, almost, by a chain to the emotional reality that I'm trying to travel, and I know that's a strength, but it's also too earthbound, whereas there's something you do, where it lifts, the language takes it to someplace otherworldly almost and yet connected to the emotion. So the, there is compassion there, I think, and wisdom, without a loss of aesthetics. It's quite . . . *(He's staring at her.)* I'm sorry.

PAUL: No no, you're doing very well. Did you learn that in graduate school?

SOPHIE: No, I've always talked like that. *(She raises an eyebrow a little, wondering if he will smile at this. He doesn't.)*

PAUL: "Facile."

SOPHIE: Facile, I mean, facile in the academic sense. Uh, fluid, easy.

PAUL: I know what facile means.

SOPHIE: *(Rattled.)* No, I'm sure you do, I just, uh . . . *(She stops, unsure.)*

PAUL: Don't stop. Please. What else do you think?

SOPHIE: *(Good-natured, direct, but backing off.)* You know, I don't believe you really want to hear what I think.

PAUL: Why not?

SOPHIE: Well, because I'm a little nobody, and you're — not.

PAUL: How old are you?

SOPHIE: Twenty-eight.

PAUL: Mailer was twenty-five when he wrote *The Naked and the Dead.*

SOPHIE: But he didn't win the Pulitzer until he was in his forties.

(He starts to read again.)

SOPHIE: *(Continuing.)* Um, would you like to read something I've written?

PAUL: What?

SOPHIE: I just thought, we're gong to be working together, and clearly you're going to be relying on my sensibilities, as a writer. So I was thinking you should maybe . . . read something I've written.

PAUL: *(Cold.)* Thank you, but right now, I would like to read something I've written. If it's not too much trouble. Since I've already lost an entire day because you were late.

SOPHIE: *(Embarrassed.)* I had trouble getting out of the city.

PAUL: How fascinating. *(He goes back to the pages.)*

SOPHIE: *(Sits, now miserable.)* Look, could we start over? *(He looks at her.)* I'm sorry. This just started so badly. I'm sure it's my fault. I'm sure it seems that I'm not humble enough. And please believe me, I don't mean for that to come across. I feel humble. I'm so grateful to be here, I know, believe me, what a tremendous thing this is. And Norman Mailer's probably a friend of yours; I'm sorry, I didn't mean to be flip about his Pulitzer.

PAUL: His first Pulitzer.

SOPHIE: Yes, his . . . yes. I see. I do see. I just, I get a little, when I'm nervous, I just . . . But, I want your good opinion. I want to be of service to you. Please let me start again. *(Beat.)* What you've written here is brilliant, it's just brilliant. To be able to work with you, even to be around while you're working is truly a privilege. I'm so grateful. You're such a genius.

(He considers her.)

(Blackout.)

SCENE THREE

Several days later. Ethan is on the phone.

ETHAN: No, absolutely not. He's seen my work — well, then fuck him if he hasn't seen me in something over the last six years, where the hell has he been, running around the regionals? Oh, London. Of course, London, that's so much more impressive, he's probably been over there directing Joseph and the Amazing Technicolor Dreamcoat, and he thinks that makes him the God of Theater. Oh Caryl Churchill, big — whose agent are you? *(Beat. He listens, briefly.)* Fine, that's fine, I understand your point but you need to understand, I'm forty years old and I've done the work that one is supposed to do to get one's self to the point that one is supposed to get to, where one doesn't have to audition anymore. I've gotten the reviews, I've gotten the awards, and not only that, I have the pedigree, my father has a fucking Nobel Prize, I'm a leading man now, I look fantastic, I'm funny. I'm the guy everybody supposedly wants and I still have to audition? For the opportunity to play a part that's going to pay me three hundred dollars a week? Are you joking? No really, are you joking?

(There is a longer pause while he listens to his agent lecture him. Laurie enters, hands him a cup of coffee. He rolls his eyes at her.)

ETHAN: *(Continuing.)* Oh, Sam, God, I understand, on a financial level, why I should have taken that sit-com; God knows the money part makes complete sense. But legitimacy? It would have made me more legitimate? Could you — I don't — I have to go now. No. Goodbye. *(He hangs up. Laurie looks at him.)* Apparently, I am not yet "A" list. This from my agent, a person who works for me, and who I pay. What time is it? Would it be bad for me to have a drink at nine in the morning?

LAURIE: They won't even let you read?

ETHAN: No, they want me to read. They want me to read!

LAURIE: Oh.

ETHAN: Yes, according to Sam, if I agree to humiliate myself one last time, and if the director doesn't find me too *old*, and if I get cast, and if he doesn't botch the production, and if the playwright does some work on the script, and if the critics don't annihilate it, or me, I will finally and irrevocably have made the "A" list. And that's why I should go in and grovel.

LAURIE: It's not groveling.

ETHAN: It's positively, groveling! And I don't care that everyone does it. It doesn't make any sense. Could someone explain to me when groveling became such an attractive quality in a man?

LAURIE: I'm not saying you should grovel. I just, I thought you wanted that part.

ETHAN: I am going to have a drink. *(He goes to the sideboard and pours himself a scotch.)*

LAURIE: Ethan! It's nine in the morning.

ETHAN: Yes. It is.

LAURIE: Okay. I thought we were leaving today. Are we not leaving today?

ETHAN: No. We are not leaving today. *(He downs it.)*

LAURIE: Well, okay. Maybe we should take a drive. I mean, if you don't want to go back to the city, maybe we should take the day and drive over to the mountains, and find some lovely B and B, you know, some place just completely romantic —

ETHAN: There's a great idea. Because if we leave, it will break my mother's heart. You know that. She's only been looking forward to this visit her entire life.

LAURIE: *(Bringing him back.)* Hey, hey — hey.

ETHAN: Sorry. I'm sorry.

LAURIE: (A beat, then.) What is it? Is it your father?

ETHAN: My father? What father? I come up for the first time in two years and don't see him for the entire time I'm here. Why would that bother me? He read my reviews, what more could I possibly want?

LAURIE: We should go.

ETHAN: I am not going back to the city.

LAURIE: We can go anywhere —

ETHAN: *(On a roll now.)* All that crap about making money — you know I didn't, as you know, I did not take that fucking sit-com job because he implied that it was beneath me. More than implied, it was a huge, God, I had to listen ad infinitum to him going on about the death of culture, television being the psychic ruin of us all, and God knows, it is shit. We all know that. Spiritual shit. So I'm not saying he was wrong. But to throw it at me. Within minutes, I hadn't even — how long had we been here? Five minutes?

LAURIE: Ethan, the sit-com, that whole offer, that was years ago —

ETHAN: That's what I'm saying! And then he throws it at me, within instants of our arrival, that I can't make a decent living! I had the chance to make a decent living, and I opted for art instead, so he can just fuck off! *(He turns his back on her, angry. There is a long beat where he sets down the empty glass, and sits at the table. Paws restlessly through a pile of magazines and review books.)*

LAURIE: *(Simple.)* If it makes you so unhappy to be here, we should go. We only meant to stay the weekend anyway.

ETHAN: I don't want to go back to the city, because then I will have no legitimate excuse not to read, is that impossible for you to understand? *(Beat.)* I'm just disappointed, they asked me to read for that part, and I thought it was going to be offered to me. I'm forty years old. I have an Obie, for God's sake, well now I feel stupid even mentioning that, obviously, who gives a shit about an Obie. I'm disappointed. And afraid I won't be able to do it anymore. If I take one more humiliation? All I have to work with is myself. This is the instrument, me, I'm the instrument. If they take that, if I let them take that? I won't be able to act. *(Beat.)* This isn't a speech from Long Day's Journey. This is the truth.

LAURIE: Thanks for the clarification. *(She goes to him; climbs on him and kisses him.)* You are a wonderful actor. You don't have to read for that fucking part. Fuck'em. They can just offer it to you. They don't deserve you. They should be so lucky. And you are a big hunk.

ETHAN: And my penis?

LAURIE: Yes, it's huge.

ETHAN: Thank you.

LAURIE: Actors. You guys are sooo easy.

ETHAN: You know what we should do today? We should go down to Frank's shop. He's desperate to show it to you, and it really is fantastic.

LAURIE: That sounds great.

ETHAN: Absolutely, it's the kind of thing you love. All cluttered and interesting, there is nothing not worth looking at down there. That little statue he had, everything is that fantastic, and he can go on, like that, about all of it. Little icons and artifacts and just pure junk, it's quite spectacular. And he has a little kitchen in back, where he makes sandwiches for anyone who stops by.

LAURIE: *(Laughing.)* Sandwiches.

ETHAN: Yes, little cucumber and egg things. He even trims off the crusts. What can I say, he's a complete fruit, but it's charming. We can spend the whole day there. Go have lunch on the pier.

LAURIE: I'll get my purse. *(They kiss. She goes, passing Sophie in the door, as she does. Sophie carries a stack of papers and books.)* Good morning.

SOPHIE: Hi.

LAURIE: How's it going?

SOPHIE: Excellent. Just, it's so . . .

> *(She can't even say, she's so excited. She disappears up the steps. Laurie goes. Ethan turns, after Laurie's left, and looks after Sophie up the stairs. He goes back to paging through a literary magazine. After a moment, she comes back down.)*

SOPHIE: Have you seen Paul?

ETHAN: No. Oh wait, it's Monday. I think Mom said he'd be going into the city today. Lunch with his agent or something.

SOPHIE: Oh.

ETHAN: He didn't tell you?

SOPHIE: It must've slipped his mind.

ETHAN: That's the advantage of being a genius. You don't have to bother with being polite.

SOPHIE: Did he say when he'd be coming back?

ETHAN: Probably not till late afternoon.

> *(She is clearly disappointed and not certain where to go now.)*

ETHAN: *(Continuing.)* So it's going well, then. The work. You're enjoying it?

SOPHIE: It's amazing. He's — amazing.

ETHAN: Nobel Prize Winner.

SOPHIE: It's not that. It's just such a privilege to be, even, near someone who has such a profound understanding of — everything, he's so —

ETHAN: Oh, everything.

SOPHIE: He has so much at his fingertips. His mind, the way he can just move between Borges and the Bible, Emily Dickinson, Montaigne, Mark Twain, Dante —

ETHAN: Dante. Let me guess. Not the *Inferno* that would be much too commonplace. He quoted — the *Purgatorio*.

SOPHIE: *The Paradiso.*

ETHAN: *The Paradiso!* Of course. Even better. That's perfect. *(He laughs. She bristles, a little embarrassed. Awkward now, she turns to go.)*

SOPHIE: I'm sorry. I must sound like an idiot.

ETHAN: No no, don't go. Please. I'm always complaining about how rude Paul is and I'm no better, it's disgraceful the way I behave, it really is.

SOPHIE: No.

ETHAN: Yes, it is and I, truly, I can do better. Surprisingly enough, wallowing in an informed and gifted bitterness yields interesting nuggets of wisdom. And I promise to stay off the subject of the great man. Or, if you like, I can regale you with hilarious anecdotes that are simultaneously quite respectful of the genius.

SOPHIE: It must be hard, to be his son.

ETHAN: Are you kidding? It's a delight, a complete delight. So much fun. As is, I'm sure, your relationship with your father. *(This makes her laugh.)*

SOPHIE: Oh yes.

ETHAN: What's he like?

SOPHIE: You know . . . I should work.

ETHAN: I completely understand. Very well put. You're writing a novel, is that it? A novella? Short stories? What is it you write?

SOPHIE: I don't know what it is yet. It's fiction. Actually, it's not even pure fiction. It's based on a . . . family story.

ETHAN: Family again.

SOPHIE: No, not actually. It's not about family.

ETHAN: What is it about?

SOPHIE: Butterflies.

(Blackout.)

SCENE FOUR

Paul and Sophie, in light. She scribbles as he speaks.

PAUL: He stands, there's a quality of light, at the window, that he, not peach, or sand —

SOPHIE: The color, or the quality?

PAUL: The quality, the scent —

SOPHIE: The scent? The smell of the light?

PAUL: *(Impatient.)* The texture of something fleet, a hovering sense of loss, just this side of well of course it's death, but that carries such a — you want just the tip of it, the taint without the weariness, the taste of it in the light —

SOPHIE: In the light?

PAUL: Light, change, peach, apricot, it's too heavy — are you writing this down?

SOPHIE: Light, change, peach —

PAUL: Christ, I hate the English language, it's so fucking inadequate — the taste of grief that hovers like a memory, the memory of Venice at dawn appearing like a melody, sorrow, grace, in the smell of the light, not peach —

SOPHIE: Rose?

PAUL: Oh God help us, rose, go back to the taste of grief —

SOPHIE: *(Reading.)* The taste of grief that hovers in the shifting light —

PAUL: That's bullshit —

SOPHIE: No, it's —

PAUL: Facile, huh?

SOPHIE: No, no —

PAUL: *(Grabs the pages and looks at them; shakes his head. He scribbles on them.)* This is complete — what is this —

SOPHIE: Night —

PAUL: Night, night, evening, night is better, evening is so bad Victorian but it does — Venice, what's — fuck, get Venice out of here — Christ, every time someone tries to talk about light Venice comes up — *(He pushes the pages back, she scribbles.)*

SOPHIE: I like the grace.

PAUL: What?

SOPHIE: *(Pointing.)* Melody, sorrow, grace. Grace.

PAUL: You don't think it's too facile?

SOPHIE: No, no, I — there's something subtle about it, grace, something holy without the weight of, the thing we yearn for —

PAUL: Yearning, Christ, God help me, everybody's always yearning, we're always fucking yearning —

SOPHIE: Well, we are!

PAUL: *(Ignoring her.)* Fucking yearning for what, to live forever, I wish I was young again, I wish the human race wasn't so pathetic, I wish sex was not ultimately humiliating — all that fucking yearning. What do you yearn for?

SOPHIE: *(Simple.)* I yearn for grace. *(Beat.)*

PAUL: Christ. Read, read what we got. He stood at the window —

SOPHIE: *(Reading.)* He stood at the window and worried the light. What was it, what is it? Not, peach, or apricot, the words drifted through the night, clumsy, missing entirely; it wasn't a scent, but the taste of grief, the yearning for grace, hovering in the shifting light.
(Blackout.)

SCENE FIVE

A few days later. Margaret is watering the plants as Laurie watches her.

LAURIE: I mean, I'm glad, I really am, I've been trying to get him to take a break for I don't know how long. So I'm relieved, he's finally decided to take some time.

MARGARET: Well, we're delighted. You're more than welcome, weeks and weeks, the whole summer. It's absolutely wonderful to have someone to talk to, when Paul gets writing he's . . . oh dear. Is this a fungus or dust? I hope this isn't some sort of horrible fungus.

LAURIE: *(Looks.)* It's dust.

MARGARET: It is dust? Are you sure? Are you one of those plant people?

LAURIE: Oh God no.

MARGARET: Frank will know. He's a complete genius with this sort of thing. *(She carries the plant to the back door and places it outside.)* There, I don't want it infecting things. You don't think it's infected anything, do you?

LAURIE: I think it's dust.

MARGARET: There, that's a very positive thing to say. You're a very positive person.

LAURIE: I just hope that he and Paul can maintain this truce.

MARGARET: Oh no no. That's really, most of it is in Ethan's head.

LAURIE: Then you do think it will be all right?

MARGARET: Absolutely.

LAURIE: I mean, being here, the whole point would be to take a break, not get involved in something else that's going to make him feel terrible about himself. I mean a real break, out of the city, when we're there he can go for weeks or even months God forbid between jobs, but there's all the auditioning and readings and reading the *Times* and fretting over who's more famous than he is, or who got that part that he wanted — it's hard, I don't have to tell you about it. I just watch it wear on him. And I don't blame him. He's really such a wonderful actor, and I don't think I only think that because I love him, do you?

MARGARET: I always thought he was gifted. Of course, I'm his mother.

LAURIE: And now of course he's turned forty, which hardly helps. He's forty years old, you know, you wonder, you turn forty and you have to wonder what your life is adding up to.

MARGARET: He's what?

LAURIE: I know, it's just a number, and the fact is, you're only one day older than you were the day before, all that, but forty, it's symbolic, it is.

MARGARET: Ethan's not forty. Oh dear, no. He's forty-two.

LAURIE: What?

MARGARET: Oh, actors.

LAURIE: Are you sure?

MARGARET: Am I sure? I'm his mother. Ethan is forty-two, and Frank is forty. I think Frank is forty.

LAURIE: Then you're not sure.

MARGARET: About Ethan I am. The firstborn, you remember everything. It's a curse for everybody. He's forty-two and Frank will be forty.

LAURIE: *(Chagrined.)* I threw a big party for him. Rented a room in a restaurant. It cost a fortune.

MARGARET: Oh, yes, I remember, we couldn't make it down. But you had a good time?

LAURIE: Wonderful. We had a wonderful fortieth birthday party for a man who had just turned forty-two.

MARGARET: Well, that's what's important, isn't it? That you all had fun. And don't worry so much about Ethan. He'll be all right, now that he's got you.

LAURIE: Oh.

MARGARET: No, it's true, it really is. When I see him with you, I know he's going to be just fine.

(Sophie enters from the stairs.)

MARGARET: *(Continuing.)* Ah, someone emerges from the crypt! How's it going up there?

SOPHIE: Wonderful, thank you. *(She heads for the kitchen.)*

MARGARET: Can I help you with anything?

SOPHIE: Thanks, I've got it.

MARGARET: Got what?

SOPHIE: Oh, no, I was just — Paul asked to get him some iced tea.

MARGARET: Well, I can do that. *(She heads for the kitchen herself.)*

SOPHIE: I don't want to bother you.

MARGARET: Don't be ridiculous. I've been getting my husband iced tea for forty-some odd years. It's hardly a bother.

SOPHIE: Yes, but — *(She is uncomfortable.)*

MARGARET: *(Stops.)* Yes?

SOPHIE: It's just, I made it for him yesterday and he said something about, he'd never had it, that way before, and that's why he asked me . . . *(Beat.)*

MARGARET: Surely there are not that many ways to make a glass of iced tea. One goes to the refrigerator. One takes the pitcher out. One pours it into a glass with ice.

SOPHIE: I put lemonade in it.

MARGARET: Well, that would be relevant if Paul liked lemonade.

SOPHIE: No, he did. He liked it very much. So he asked me if I'd make it for him again. *(Beat.)*

MARGARET: *(Short.)* Well, who knew. Forty years of making iced tea, who knew it could be so complicated, so worthy of an extended debate.

SOPHIE: No, I just — well, anyway. It's my job, isn't it? I'm happy to do it.

MARGARET: By all means. *(She gestures to the kitchen. Sophie goes.)* Well, now I feel ridiculous.

LAURIE: No.

MARGARET: Don't patronize me, Laurie. I knew when I'm behaving like an idiot.

LAURIE: It can't be easy, having a total stranger living in your house.

MARGARET: No. It isn't is it? It just never is. *(After a moment, Sophie re-enters, carrying iced tea.)* Well, and there we have it. Iced tea and lemonade, all mixed together. That looks just delicious.

SOPHIE: Would you like me to make one for you?

MARGARET: *(Dry.)* No, I wouldn't, thank you.

(Sophie heads for the stairs.)

MARGARET: *(Continuing.)* So what are you two working on up there?

SOPHIE: Well, um — his novel.

MARGARET: Yes, dear. Which novel?

SOPHIE: Oh — I — there's only one, isn't there?

MARGARET: God, no, he's got six or seven in drawers, half-finished, barely begun, in all states, really. There was one he worked on for four years, he had something upward of six hundred pages, and he finally abandoned it in sheer terror.

SOPHIE: That's terrible.

MARGARET: You have no idea. There were a few years in there, my God, he hadn't a clue what he was doing anymore. It was after his third novel, which was not well-received, really some of the critics were quite cruel and he's never been what you'd call a populist writer, so when the critics abandoned him he did not have the luxury of turning to his audience for comfort. Which made it just that much easier for Dartmouth to deny him tenure. Well, with that temper he's never been exactly embraced by the academy, so we had no money, two small children and he develops what might be called the opposite of writer's block — starting a new project every other week, each one more promising than the last, but none of them growing quite, being given the time to grow before he was onto the next. And heaven forbid I go back to work to help out with the boys, besides whom he needed me around just to keep him sane, I suppose. As sane as he ever gets. We finally got through, he finished his fourth novel and won the National Book Award for his fifth. Smooth sailing ever since. More or less. *(Beat.)*

SOPHIE: I had no idea.

MARGARET: It wasn't that bad. *(Beat.)* The iced tea? He doesn't like to be kept waiting.

SOPHIE: No, of course. Thank you. *(Beat.)* Thank you. *(She goes.)*

MARGARET: *(Watches until she is out of earshot, then.)* I don't like her.

LAURIE: Why did you tell her all that?

MARGARET: Oh please. All that youth and beauty, naïve eagerness, every-thing ahead of her. What does she think is ahead of her? Ask yourself, what does she think? *(Imitating her.)* "Thank you. Thank you." It's enough to make you sick. And you know he's up there just drinking it in, with all that lemonade in his iced tea — *(Sudden, off another plant.)* Where is Frank? Wasn't he supposed to be here by now? This is not dust. This is mildew, this is some disease. Where is he?

LAURIE: He and Ethan were going on some antique hunt. Ethan had some-thing in his head he wanted Frank to find for him.

MARGARET: (*Astonished.*) Ethan?

LAURIE: Yes. (*Almost laughing, in her confusion.*) What is it?

MARGARET: Nothing. I'm sorry. I'm being ridiculous. It's nothing.
(*Blackout.*)

SCENE SIX

Paul and Sophie, in light, in argument.

SOPHIE: I just don't think it's — I mean, have we not seen this, nine thousand —

PAUL: Of course, it's "facile" —

SOPHIE: Oh my God. Are you ever going to —

PAUL: No, I don't think I am —

SOPHIE: Well, then it is facile. It's facile. He's afraid of dying —

PAUL: We're all afraid of dying —

SOPHIE: I'm not.

PAUL: Oh, yes you are.

SOPHIE: All right. Of course I am. But she is a twit. Does he have to fall in love with such a complete — it's just contempt —

PAUL: Contempt?

SOPHIE: For both of them! Isn't it? She's just such —

PAUL: She's beautiful.

SOPHIE: That's not enough!

PAUL: It is for him.

SOPHIE: It's not! My God, this is someone who can stand with his hand on a doorknob for forty pages, thinking about the nature of time and she has no interior life whatsoever —

PAUL: She's young, she hasn't amassed the kind of experience that taints the imagination —

SOPHIE: Oh, "tainting" again, what is wrong with being tainted? All of us are tainted —

PAUL: She's not.

SOPHIE: Then maybe she should be. She's just , if that's it, if this thinly drawn —

PAUL: (*Looks to her.*) Yes?

SOPHIE? (*Beat.*) I think the less of him. He's just projecting onto her. It makes him a narcissist.

PAUL: We are all narcissists, my dear. We are all tainted narcissists.

SOPHIE: Then she is, too. My God, I'm not suggesting anything that hasn't been achieved time and again by the Victorians. Henry James and Edith Wharton, for heaven sake, after Isabel Archer and Lily Bart the fact that male writers now don't even attempt —

PAUL: *(Angrily amused now.)* Excuse me?

SOPHIE: Oh, come on! You know what I'm talking about! John Updike has never written a believable woman in his life. Thomas Wolfe? Hardly. Saul Bellow, Brodkey, your friend Mr. Mailer, let's face it, the whole twentieth century —

PAUL: Oh really?

SOPHIE: Chock full of misogynistic creeps. Conrad, Lawrence, even Fitzgerald, Daisy notwithstanding, surprisingly Hemingway actually does better than he's given credit for, when he takes a shot at it — but overall — not to say they're not geniuses, but really. Half the human race. Don't you think it should be considered a limitation if you can't imagine what it means to be human for half the human race?

PAUL: You who know so much about men.

SOPHIE: But it's not about me, is it, Paul? Let's face it, most of you guys positively brag about the fact you think women are sub-human. It's the last form of bigotry that's still considered hip.

PAUL: I find your mind interesting, Sophie, but in this instance you are full of shit. This has nothing to do with gender studies 101. My novel is about an older man in love with a younger woman, with all the joy and grief that that implies.

SOPHIE: So that's it. You don't have to imagine her life as richly as —

PAUL: *(Cold.)* What? Am I being too facile?

SOPHIE: *(Backing down.)* No. I'm sorry.

PAUL: *(Turning on her.)* Would you like to try it?

SOPHIE: What?

PAUL: Go ahead. You're so fucking sure. Show me what you mean. *(He holds the pages out to her. She takes them. Blackout.)*

SCENE SEVEN

Ethan is on the phone. Margaret moves in and out of the room, setting up for a party.

ETHAN: Absolutely not. No. I told you two weeks ago, two weeks ago, Sam — I am not sabotaging anything! If they want to offer me the part, I will happily accept it, it's a wonderful part even for three hundred fucking dollars a week — No, I'm not going to meet with him, that's ridiculous, either he wants me to do the part, or he doesn't, having a cup of coffee with the man isn't going to convince him that I can act! All he can learn from a meeting is whether or not I look like my headshot, and I'm not driving three hours into the city for that. Yes, it is, three solid hours; they're doing construction on the Cross Bronx. Yes, they are!

What am I — I am relaxing, Sam. That is what I am doing here. I am relaxing in the country with my family.

(Paul appears on the stairs.)

ETHAN: *(Sees Paul, goes back to the phone.) (Continuing.)* Look, it's my brother's birthday and my mother is making a big thing of it, and she disapproves of people who do business on the phone after six, so I've got to go. Yes, I will but I'm not going to change my mind. Seriously, I find it ridiculous that the instant I insist on being treated with the barest pretence of respect, everyone acts like I'm crazy. It's a very sick business we're in. Good-bye. *(He hangs up. Paul stands at the foot of the stairs, uncomfortable.)*

MARGARET: There you are. How's it going up there?

PAUL: Ahhhh.

MARGARET: Well, then it's time you took a break. Here's Ethan, he's been here two weeks already, and you two have barely spoken. Ethan, tell your father about your play.

ETHAN: *(Annoyed.)* There is no play, Mom.

MARGARET: Yes, the one they want you for. Would you like a glass of wine, Paul? *(She goes. Paul and Ethan consider each other for a moment).*

ETHAN: Hello, Dad.

PAUL: Yeah, hi. *(He goes to the table of food and looks at it, clearly unsure about what to do.)*

ETHAN: *(Watches.)* They're hors d'oerves. You eat them.

PAUL: I guess I'm not hungry. *(He moves away from the table, and looks out the back door.)* So, what was that about? You doing another play?

ETHAN: *(Encouraged by his interest.)* Actually, I'm not, this time.

PAUL: It's not any good, huh?

ETHAN: It's fine. It's just not the right circumstances, for me, at the present time.

PAUL: *(Nods, shrugs.)* Why not?

ETHAN: Well — the producers — it's hard to explain. It's a matter of pride, I guess. Not in a bad way. At least I hope not.

PAUL: Sounds kind of — tough.

ETHAN: Yeah, it is, kind of. *(Beat.)*

PAUL: I've never fully understood the appeal of the theater.

ETHAN: *(Beat.)* That's an interesting thought, Dad. Thank you for mentioning it.

PAUL: No, I mean it. It's just — such an emotionally indulgent form. No wonder Henry James couldn't make any sense of it.

ETHAN: Henry James couldn't make sense of it because he was boring, and while one can get away with writing boring novels, it is considerably more difficult to get away with writing boring plays.

PAUL: Henry James couldn't make sense of it because the form doesn't support complexity of language and thought.

ETHAN: Shakespeare notwithstanding.

PAUL: You can't bring in Shakespeare. He was a poet.

ETHAN: *(Irritated now.)* He was a playwright.

PAUL: The genius was in the poetry.

ETHAN: *(Growing anger.)* You can't dissect it. This part of it is genius, that part —

PAUL: I'm not talking about Shakespeare. I was just making an observation about the theater. As a form.

ETHAN: What about it? As a form.

PAUL: Well, it's never really produced a first-rate writer, has it?

LAURIE: *(Enters with a bottle of wine.)* Hello, Paul, how good to see you out of your lair.

ETHAN: *(Losing it.)* What did you say?

PAUL: Okay, here we go.

LAURIE: Oh. I interrupted something.

ETHAN: He just called the theater a second-rate art form!

LAURIE: Oh, Paul. What a thing to say.

PAUL: I didn't say that.

ETHAN: Oh, come on —

PAUL: What I said was, it's never produced a first-rate writer. There is a profound difference.

ETHAN: Not to you!

LAURIE: So Shakespeare —

ETHAN: Doesn't count.

LAURIE: *(Surprised.)* Doesn't count?

PAUL: *(Dismissive.)* Shakespeare, again. You might as well bring up Hitler.

ETHAN: Shakespeare and Hitler, yes, I always talk about them in the same sentence —

PAUL: *(Clarifying.)* People toss around Shakespeare, Einstein, Hitler, fucking Mozart as if they weren't complete anomalies, well guess what? Twenty thousand years of human history, you're going to get the occasional freak of nature.

MARGARET: *(Enters, carrying glasses.)* Did you open the wine, Laurie?

LAURIE: Oh, no, I got a little distracted.

ETHAN: Shakespeare was a freak of nature.

MARGARET: Really? Is that Frank? *(She looks out the door.)*

PAUL: Yes, a freak of nature, obviously genius is a freak of nature or history would see a little more of it, wouldn't we? But instead we're still out here crawling in the mud.

(Frank enters, carrying a package.)

MARGARET: Here's the birthday boy! Happy birthday, sweetheart.

FRANK: Thank you.

ETHAN: That's fascinating, Dad, and as far as I can tell, it has nothing to do with the power of the theater to change men's hearts and minds.

MARGARET: Really, Ethan, Paul, do we have to talk about Art? It won't end well, it never does.

PAUL: Nothing changes men's hearts and minds! If we could change men's hearts and minds, don't you think we would have done it by now?

LAURIE: You brought your own present.

FRANK: No, actually, it's for — Ethan, did you tell her? He didn't tell you, did he?

ETHAN: Then art is what, frivolity? Narcissism? Scribbling nonsense on the walls of a cave?

PAUL: We're not talking about art, we're talking about theater.

ETHAN: *(Angry, direct.)* All right then Dad, what is it? What is it, now, about theater that is so fallen, so corrupt, that no one working in the theater can ever achieve the heights of genius available to, oh, say, a novelist?

FRANK: *(Alarmed.)* He didn't say that.

LAURIE: He kind of did.

PAUL: You want to know what's wrong with the theater? All those people, all those fucking people everywhere, on the stage, in the audience. Wrinkling their candy wrappers. Turning on their hearing aids, talking on their cell phones. You sit there going, where the fuck are the words, you're so drowning in people you can't find the damn words. They're there, they're gone, and no one even notices! Half the actors can't speak, but that's fine, because half the audience can't hear. Or think for that matter. All that emotion. Bad one-liners. Every other word is fuck. Every character's a victim, some battered woman or unhappy homosexual. Don't talk to me about Shakespeare, we're talking about the theater. And remember, you asked. *(Sophie comes down the steps, overhears the whole thing. Paul stops her as she tries to sneak behind him and into the kitchen.)*

PAUL: *(Continuing; to Sophie.)* Where are you going?

SOPHIE: I'm sorry. I didn't want to interrupt.

PAUL: No, stay, it's a party. Somebody give her something to drink. *(Laurie does.)*

FRANK: I disagree. I think theater is — I've had evenings in the theater that I will, I carry them with me, performances, moments, the way someone looks in the, stage light is so pretty, sometimes I just remember, or or . . .

PAUL: Finish your damn sentence.

MARGARET: Paul.

FRANK: *(Sudden.)* "Your name is a golden bell hung in my heart, and when I think of you, I tremble, and the bell swings and rings along my veins. Roxanne, Roxanne, along my veins. Yes, that is love. That fire, that music." *(A beat.)*

PAUL: *(Ironic.)* A golden bell hung in my heart, swinging and ringing, that's good.

FRANK: *(Not backing down.)* It was, just beautiful. I saw it twenty years ago, more than that, and I think about it still.

LAURIE: Cyrano? That's from Cyrano, isn't it?

FRANK: Ethan did it. In high school.

MARGARET: Yes, he was very good in that.

FRANK: I saw it four times. Theater is, theater is —

PAUL: *(Impatient.)* Is what?

ETHAN: It is a form that seeks transcendence.

PAUL: Rostand was a melodramatic hack. Moliere was a comic. Come on, who are the writers? O'Neill, too many Catholic hang-ups, Shaw had his moments, but all that endless droning, who cares. Ibsen, too much moralizing. Strindberg, too much sperm. Who else? Mamet? He's just watered down Pinter, Pinter is watered down Beckett, and Beckett, okay, he could write, but he was a novelist.

ETHAN: Samuel Beckett could write. What a brilliant observation. And for this they award the Nobel Prize.

PAUL: Actually, they award the Nobel for achievement in Literature, Ethan. Not for the quality of debate one has over drinks with one's dissatisfied and disappointed middle-aged children.

ETHAN: That would actually would me, Dad, if I hadn't already heard you dismiss Shakespeare's plays this evening.

PAUL: *(Snapping suddenly.)* That's not what I said! Good God, what I say is outrageous enough, you don't have to twist my words!

MARGARET: *(Sighing.)* Oh really, both of you. We haven't even had dinner yet! How are we ever supposed to make it through dinner?

ETHAN: Fine, let's talk about something else then. How's the book coming, Dad? I heard there was some trouble about the advance. *(Beat.)*

PAUL: You're right. I don't know why I even attempt this bullshit. I'm going back to work.

LAURIE: Oh, no —

MARGARET: Paul, please —

ETHAN: Oh, let him go —

PAUL: Sophie, are you coming? *(He stops on the stairs and looks at her.)*

SOPHIE: *(Sophie stands, embarrassed. All look at her. To the others.)* I'm sorry. *(She starts to go, then stops. She looks at Paul.)* But maybe if we just — thought about all of this, a different way. Because Paul and I, were talking, the other day, about the inadequacies of, of, language, and language, spoken language — maybe — out of context —

PAUL: For God's sake, Sophie, would you finish your Goddamn sentence?

SOPHIE: *(Cowed.)* I just meant, the movement of language, its inability —

PAUL: *(Snapping.)* Finish the damn sentence!

SOPHIE: *(Suddenly snapping back.)* What is the matter with you? You come down here, and tell your son that his life's work is foolish —

PAUL: That is not what I —

SOPHIE: It's close enough. How could he hear something like that from you, from his father, without feeling demeaned, and unloved —

MARGARET: No no no.

ETHAN: That is not what this is about.

MARGARET: They just do this. It's a debate, that's all. A family full of artists, what else do we have to talk about?

SOPHIE: But you're not arguing about — I mean — *(Beat. They all stare at her. Continuing; embarrassed.)* I'm sorry. You're right, I don't seem to be able to finish my sentences. I'm, forgive me. You're having a party. I must go.

FRANK: No, you're right, you . . . It's all right.

ETHAN: Yes, absolutely, we must seem completely insane, there really is no point to arguing with him about anything. He just delights in saying outrageous things. You should hear him on the subject of Michelangelo.

MARGARET: Let's not go back to that, please.

SOPHIE: *(To Paul, very contrite.)* I'm sorry.

PAUL: *(Quiet, kind.)* It's all right, Sophie.

(There is something quite intimate about their exchange. After a moment, Ethan steps forward.)

ETHAN: So, no running off. It's Frank's birthday, there's presents and everything. Look, there's even one for you.

SOPHIE: *(She looks over, startled at this.)* There is?

(Ethan picks up the package that Frank has brought with him. This surprises Frank.)

FRANK: Oh. I thought — *(He looks at Laurie, briefly, as Ethan hands it to Sophie.)*

ETHAN: We looked for days. This wasn't easy. Go ahead, open it.

(Now abashed, Sophie looks around, and obediently opens the present. It is framed plate glass, upon which butterflies have been pressed and labeled. She stares at it, speechless.)

MARGARET: Well, isn't that lovely.

LAURIE: What is it?

FRANK: *(Miserable, confused.)* It's a plate of butterflies. Circa Nineteen Thirty, private collectors, there was actually quite a worldwide subculture of amateur lepidopterists. Nabokov, with his work with the South American blues obviously would be the most famous of these enthusiasts, but there were many, many — who went to extraordinary lengths, apparently, some of the collections are massive. All in private hands, and no one wants to break them up, naturally. Just finding one, it was prohibitive.

ETHAN: Frank finally found a dealer in Ashton, he drove eighty some odd miles —

FRANK: You can get knockoffs on the Internet, now, but they're cobbled together, obviously, just for people to hang on the wall. Not scientifically accurate. Ethan said it had to be the real thing.

ETHAN: Do you like it?

SOPHIE: *(Overwhelmed.)* It's beautiful, I don't — I — I'm sorry. *(To the others, an explanation.)* My grandfather was a butterfly collector. I'm writing about it. *(to Ethan.)* Thank you. *(to Frank.)* Thank you.

(He nods, uncomfortable. Laurie finally steps forward.)

LAURIE: May I?

(Sophie shows it to her.)

LAURIE: Oh, look, all the little white ones. Like a flock. Is that what but-terflies fly in? Flocks?

SOPHIE: I don't know. I still know so little.

ETHAN: That's not true. You should read what she's written. It's fantastic.

LAURIE: Oh. You've read it.

SOPHIE: It's in very rough form.

ETHAN: It's brilliant.

PAUL: *(Dry.)* Maybe you'll let me look at it, sometime.

SOPHIE: Yes, of course, when it's ready, I — I —

PAUL: Well, it's lovely that we're all being civil, but I hope that doesn't mean I have to stand around and wait for her to finish a sentence. Are we ready to eat?

(Blackout.)

SCENE EIGHT

Late that same night. Sophie sits alone on the couch. A single light is on. After a moment, the back door opens. Ethan enters.

ETHAN: I saw the light.

SOPHIE: I couldn't sleep.

ETHAN: Are you all right?

SOPHIE: Yes, I was, I was trying to write, but that room is so small, some-times. Lovely, but small. Sometimes it's hard to think in there.

ETHAN: It's hard to think everywhere in this house.

SOPHIE: No.

ETHAN: Don't be polite.

SOPHIE: I wasn't.

ETHAN: Yes, you were, and there's no one here but me. You can say what-ever you want.

SOPHIE: That's not exactly true.

ETHAN: *(Laughing a little.)* You're very tortured, aren't you? *(He sits next to her.)*

SOPHIE: *(Moves.)* I'm not. Maybe I am. I don't know.

ETHAN: That was fantastic, what you did. Standing up for me like that.

SOPHIE: It was horrifying.

ETHAN: That's what made it so fantastic.

SOPHIE: Oh, God.

ETHAN: Please don't regret it. It was wonderful.

SOPHIE: No, my God, he was so — and when he heard, that I let you —

ETHAN: Let me what?

SOPHIE: You know what. You all, all of you act like you're not aware of what you're doing, and —

ETHAN: Now I don't know what you're talking about, Sophie. You need to be clear. *(He looks at her, uncompromising.)*

SOPHIE: *(Direct.)* Why did you give me that? *(She points to the butterflies.)*

ETHAN: You're so aware of everything, you tell me.

SOPHIE: *(Persistent.)* In front of everyone. Why did it have to be in front of everyone? It was your brother's birthday —

ETHAN: Frank and I have been scouring the entire eastern seaboard for that thing. Was I supposed to wait? Well, I couldn't wait. *(He moves in, takes her hand. She tries to back away. He won't let her.)* What do you think, why do you think I gave you the butterflies?

SOPHIE: Don't play games with me.

ETHAN: I'm not playing games. I've been watching you coming and going, in and out of his lair, you're like a light —

SOPHIE: *(Rebuffing him.)* Please.

ETHAN: I'm sorry. I don't know what I'm saying. I'm at a loss for words.

SOPHIE: No one in this house is ever at a loss for words. *(Beat.)*

ETHAN: Do you want me to take them back? The butterflies?

SOPHIE: *(Beat.)* No. They're the most beautiful things I've ever seen.

(He kisses her. The kiss becomes rather passionate. He leans over and turns out the light. At the window, a figure can be seen, watching.)
(Blackout. End of Act One.)

ACT TWO
SCENE ONE

Laurie and Frank. Frank has set two enamel angels on the coffee table. Laurie is distracted.

FRANK: They're Venetian. I, it's not clear what period, probably late eighteenth century. Enamel on silver. I found them at an auction in Bennington six months ago, and I was convinced that one of my regulars, she's, but she didn't want them.

LAURIE: No? Why not? *(She looks off, toward the kitchen.)*

FRANK: I don't know. Because I thought they were — clearly, because the cast is silver, instead of pewter, they were probably poured for some, well some prince or duke, could've been a bishop perhaps although the enamel suggests a more decorative, private chapel, probably, in one of the palazzos . . .

LAURIE: A palazzo? Where? *(She looks at him fully now.)*

FRANK: Well, they're Venetian. So, a palazzo. On one of the canals.

LAURIE: Have you ever been to Venice?

FRANK: Yes, several times.

LAURIE: I haven't. *(Beat.)* I've wanted to. They say it's so beautiful. But there's never the right time, you know. I'm working, or Ethan's in a show, or has an audition he doesn't want to, you know, it's just the way things happen. You mean to go to Venice, and you never, it never . . . *(Really looking at the angels, almost surprised, suddenly.)* They have wings.

FRANK: Yes, they're angels.

LAURIE: Well, Frank. They are so beautiful. They're exquisite. *(She sits, overwhelmed.)*

FRANK: I thought so.

LAURIE: Is that a lute, she's playing?

FRANK: Yes.

LAURIE: What kind of horn is that? It looks like a clarinet.

FRANK: I don't know, actually. Maybe it is a clarinet.

LAURIE: *(Wipes her eyes.)* Well, look at me, I'm ridiculous. They're so beautiful, they made me cry.

FRANK: I'm glad you like them. They're for you. I want you to have them.

LAURIE: Oh, Frank, I could never afford to buy something like this.

FRANK: No, it's a gift.

LAURIE: Well, but — they must be worth a fortune. Look at them. They're the most beautiful things I've ever seen.

FRANK: I thought so. I thought you would think so. And I felt so stupid, I must apologize, not that, these are not an apology, I, just, I misunderstood. Ethan can be so charming. I don't get to spend time with him. When we were little, I used to follow him around, like a young God, he was . . . well, you can imagine.

LAURIE: Yes.

FRANK: I thought they were for you. The butterflies. But these fly too, you see. Well, they don't literally fly. You know that. Of course, the butterflies don't either. They're dead.

LAURIE: Yes, this is a much better gift because angels don't die, do they? They are never dead. That's important.

FRANK: Well . . .

LAURIE: *(Chattering, brave.)* No, it is. I know about this. Just before Ethan and I met, I'd been with someone for a long time, six years, and he was, he worked at the Brooklyn Museum, and then he went over to the Public Library, he was one of those people who's a curator or something. I could never quite get it completely straight, but it was all quite important, scholarly, knowledgeable. And he was a wonderful, decent person, kind, and interesting, he knew everything about everything, but the fact is, he was just obsessed with death. Literally. It was all we talked about.

FRANK: For six years?

LAURIE: Yes! He knew so much about it. You know, historically how different cultures defined death, what it meant to people, different religions and how they define the afterlife. Anytime we'd go on holiday, wherever we were, we had to stop at the graveyards and study the aesthetics of the local headstones. Because of the Brooklyn Museum, obviously, he knew so much about the Egyptians, so we would have, oh my God, endless, I know so much about mummification, I could do it. I could actually mummify somebody.

FRANK: Really. *(They are both starting to laugh.)*

LAURIE: Yes, but that wasn't even — the field trip aspect of it all was actually kind of entertaining. But the rest of it was just so relentlessly dreary. And I did come to realize, finally, that he may have been fascinating, and honest, and a good person, but he was also completely nuts. I mean, just because you're embracing death does not mean that you're not running away from life. And then I met Ethan, with all that anger and bitterness, and he seemed such a life-force, he . . . *(Catching herself.)* Do you think angels really fly? I mean, you don't ever really see it, in art, paintings and sculpture, and you know, those things in church, the only ones who seem to fly, ever, are those disgusting little fat babies.

FRANK: Putti.

LAURIE: That's such a good word for them, isn't it. Putti. Fat flying babies. But the angels, you know, the titans, they just seem to stand around with those majestic wings and deliver messages, or wield swords or play instruments. Why is that, do you think? Maybe the wings don't work. That would be just like God, wouldn't it, to make something that beautiful that simply doesn't work. Like Ethan. Not like Ethan, not — I don't know what I'm saying. I'm sorry. What's Venice like?

(Frank shifts, uncomfortable, feeling for her.)

FRANK: One morning, the first time I went there, I couldn't sleep, because of the time difference, so I got up at I think four or four-thirty in the morning, and walked around and everything, the piazzas were utterly deserted, and I stood outside Saint Mark's Basilica and there was a nun, sweeping the sidewalk while the sun rose. And then I got lost and found a tiny square, walls and windows rising so simply, archways, children, Marco Polo was born there, this plaque on the wall. It's like that. It's like them. *(He indicates the angels.)*

LAURIE: *(Looks up at him, simple.)* What should I do, Frank?

(Frank looks at her, shakes her head, inarticulate.)

ETHAN: *(Enters, from outside.)* There you are. I've been looking all over for you.

LAURIE: Really? Because I've been looking for you.

ETHAN: Yes, I was afraid you'd be worried. *(To Frank, blithe.)* I couldn't sleep last night so I got up and walked into town. I don't know what's the matter with me. Maybe Paul's right, maybe I am having some sort of midlife crisis, although I would hate to give him credit for any sort of insight about me whatsoever. These are nice. Good God, they weigh a ton. What is this, solid lead? *(He looks at the bottom of one of the angels.)*

FRANK: Silver.

ETHAN: *(Impressed.)* No, really? *(To Laurie, lying easily.)* I should've left a note, I know, but I honestly didn't think it would turn into an all night jaunt. It truly did not even occur to me until I was six miles down the road that you might wake up and worry.

LAURIE: I did wake up.

ETHAN: I'm so sorry. You must have been frantic.

LAURIE: No. I did, actually, I saw a light on, up here, so I thought it might be you. So I came up to see.

ETHAN: You did.

LAURIE: Yes. I stood at the window. The light was on, and then it went out. But it wasn't you, I guess, because you were walking.

ETHAN: Yes. It was quite nostalgic. Frank and I, when we were kids, we used to spend summers with our grandparents over in East Hampton. Sneak out and spend the night howling at the moon. You'll have to come with me, next time. It's fantastic, the moon, stars, smell of dew and wet leaves. *(He is idly playing with one of the angels.)*

FRANK: *(Steps forward and takes it from him.)* Please.

ETHAN: Oh, sorry. It's so solid, you forget, don't you, that it's some sort of unbelievable treasure.

FRANK: I don't. *(He sets it down, not looking at Ethan. Sophie enters from the kitchen. She stops. They all look at each other.)*

SOPHIE: Good morning.

ETHAN: Yes, hello, Off to work?

SOPHIE: Yes. *(Beat, to Frank.)* Thank you. For the butterflies. They mean so much to me.

FRANK: You're welcome.

(Sophie goes. Blackout.)

SCENE TWO

Sophie and Paul, in light.

PAUL: *(Off pages, vaguely surprised.)* Some of this is good. *(He hands it to her.)*

SOPHIE: Thank you.

PAUL: The one phrase, where the sister says "some three years ago," that has a nice sound to it.

SOPHIE: Oh. *(Beat.)* "Some three years ago"?

PAUL: Yes.

SOPHIE: Well, knock yourself out, Paul. *(He doesn't crack a smile.)* I mean, that's all you liked? I wrote ten pages about, well, what you asked. You asked me to write that, I would never, otherwise. I'm sorry. I just — I — I — I know it's ridiculous for me to try and write about one of your characters, but you proposed it, and I — I tried — and — this is as important to me as it is to you. I know I'm a complete neophyte. I know that. But I'm a writer, too.

PAUL: Did you think what you wrote was good? *(Beat.)*

SOPHIE: Yes, I did, actually. I thought some of it was good.

PAUL: Well, that's what I said. Some of it is good. Some of it's facile.

SOPHIE: Yeah, okay.

PAUL: I mean that in the good sense. The academic sense.

SOPHIE: Okay. I said okay. *(She starts to put it away.)*

PAUL: Some of it's good, I said. *(He holds his hand out. She hands him the pages back, confused.)*

SOPHIE: So . . .

PAUL: Some of it's useful.

SOPHIE: *(Surprised.)* You're going to use it?

PAUL: What's this butterfly thing Ethan was talking about?

SOPHIE: *(Reacting, startled at the change of subject.)* Oh. It's nothing. I, it's something I've been working on, based on a family story.

PAUL: What's the story?

SOPHIE: It's not a story, actually; it's just what happened. My father's father collected butterflies, and the butterflies were lost.

PAUL: How were they lost?

SOPHIE: By accident. Someone didn't take care of them, and then . . . they were thrown away.

PAUL: What are you writing about it?

SOPHIE: *(Struggles to articulate this. It is the most open she has ever been with him.)* I'm not sure yet. I'm haunted by it. That someone could spend so much time on something beautiful, that someone else just couldn't see. That someone else would treat so carelessly.

PAUL: What was he like? The butterfly collector.

SOPHIE: I never knew him. He died when my father was very young.

PAUL: What does your father say about him?

SOPHIE: *(Shakes her head, at a loss. After a moment, she gets it together.)* My father actually doesn't speak of him at all.

PAUL: Why not?

SOPHIE: It's not his nature.

PAUL: What is his nature?

SOPHIE: *(Beat.)* I'm not writing about him.

PAUL: Maybe you should be.

SOPHIE: You haven't even read it.

PAUL: Why are you so defensive?

SOPHIE: Why am I — I'm sorry. *(Beat.)* I don't want to talk about this.

PAUL: Why not?

SOPHIE: *(Definitive.)* Because I don't.

PAUL: Why not?

SOPHIE: Paul — you know, Paul — why do you do this? I mean, what are we like bugs to you? We are, you know, you put us in a jar, you shake it up and see what happens. Well, you know, you're — your family may find it amusing, actually, I don't know what they find it, but you're not my father. I don't have to do this. *(She stands, to go.)*

PAUL: I don't want to be your father.

SOPHIE: *(Looks at him.)* I' going, now. I, I don't know —

PAUL: Sentences.

SOPHIE: *(Suddenly really unnerved.)* Would you stop that? Please?

PAUL: Don't go, Sophie. Don't go. Show me what you've written about the butterflies.

SOPHIE: It's terrible. I don't want you to see it. You'll think it's terrible.

PAUL: No. *(He goes to her. She is miserable. After a moment, he reaches over, takes her face and kisses her. She goes along with it for a moment, then pulls away, sudden.)*

SOPHIE: No, no, I can't do this. I'm sorry. Oh. I'm sorry. I can't do this.

PAUL: Yes, you can.

SOPHIE: No. I can't

(Paul reaches for her again, but she absolutely pushes him away.)

SOPHIE: I'm sorry. I have so much respect for you. And I'm so flattered. *(This was the wrong thing to say.)*

PAUL: Oh, you're flattered.

SOPHIE: Please, don't —.

PAUL: Don't? *(Beat.)* No, please, tell me how to feel.

SOPHIE: I'm sorry.

PAUL: Stop apologizing.

(She looks around, helpless, caught.)

PAUL: *(Continuing.)* Those pages? The butterflies? Or would that make you uncomfortable, too? Do I have to beg for that, too?

(She shakes her head. After a moment, she reaches into her folder, takes out a slender manuscript, and hands it to him. Blackout.)

SCENE THREE

Several days later. Margaret is looking through cookbooks. Ethan prowls behind her, alert, looking for Sophie.

MARGARET: How does this sound? "Braised Quail in a Pinot Noir Sauce."

ETHAN: No one really eats quail.

MARGARET: Well, you wouldn't use quail, of course, you'd get those little Cornish game hens.

ETHAN: Then why don't they call it Cornish Game Hens in a Pinot Noir Sauce?

MARGARET: Because it doesn't sound as good, I should think. Braised Duck in Pinot Noir . . . no, that doesn't work either. Oh, how about this? Poached Salmon in a Lime Cilantro Dressing. That sounds very good, but maybe it's too fishy. Do you think it sounds fishy?

ETHAN: Well, "salmon"?

MARGARET: Yes, I see your point. Then again, it could be Orange Roughy, which does not sound a bit fishy, but in fact always is. Salmon isn't always terribly fishy, in fact I find salmon the least fishy of all fish. If only your father would give me some leeway on this fish issue. Fish issue, well, that does not sound good, does it? That's the problem, being married to a writer, you think about things like this.

ETHAN: I think salmon sounds terrific. I vote for the salmon.

MARGARET: You just want it because I reminded you that your father doesn't like it. Really, Ethan, you're ridiculous.

ETHAN: That is a terrible thing for a mother to say to her favorite son.

MARGARET: Who said you were my favorite? You come up here and annoy your father, you're not my favorite son at all. Oh, listen to this! Oysters in Heavy Cream with Sauerkraut, Lemon and Caviar.

ETHAN: That's impossible.

MARGARET: Do you think that sounds good?

ETHAN: It sounds like it will kill you.

MARGARET: It's an appetizer, of course, it's not the sort of thing you could make a whole meal of.

ETHAN: Thank God.

MARGARET: Oysters, heavy cream, sauerkraut, lemon and caviar. I'm trying to figure out what that would taste like.

ETHAN: Russia, before the revolution.

MARGARET: Exactly, I think we have to do it. I could run up to Mystic and get them right off the pier, I haven't done that in years, there's no point, really, since Paul won't eat fish, but oysters. If you and Laurie came with me, we could have lunch. Now this is a plan.

ETHAN: He's gone all day then?

MARGARET: Yes, he had a meeting with Roger to discuss his progress with the book.

ETHAN: Has there been progress?

MARGARET: I guess we'll find out, won't we? If it goes well, I think we might be able to relax, finally. If it doesn't, well then I don't know, I can't think about that. He'll meet with Roger and then lunch with the book review, I think, they want him to do a piece on someone . . . Thomas Mann? Did he already do that?

ETHAN: Somebody did. Somebody always does.

MARGARET: Yes, and I never liked his books. So boring.

ETHAN: Puts Henry James to shame.

MARGARET: Exactly. Books are just like people, aren't they? Some of them are just so worthy, and wonderful and filled with — worthiness, but you just don't like them. And then some of them are just frivolous and entertaining and — I'm not saying romance novels, not like that, but Charles Dickens, for instance. I know he's not as refined as Henry James, but he makes me cry, and laugh, and all those strange sentences. It's life, isn't it? Some books make you feel alive.

ETHAN: Like people.

MARGARET: Some people, yes. For all their faults, you can't help but love them. *(She goes to him, kisses him with real affection.)* You should take that play, you know.

ETHAN: "That play" has not been offered to me, Mom.

MARGARET: Please. Your agent calls about it every day. I know a few things about agents. They don't call like that unless they know you're going to get it.

ETHAN: You may know about agents, but you know nothing about theater.

MARGARET: I may not know anything about the theater, but I know plenty about you, young man. You should go back to the city, do that terrible audition, meet with those horrible play people and charm them, Ethan, I've seen you be charming. Just do whatever you have to do to get that part. And then once you have it, you'll feel better, and you can take Laurie out to a nice dinner in a very nice restaurant and treat her like a queen, because that's what she is, you know.

ETHAN: *(Beat.)* I know. I know, that's what I should do.

MARGARET: *(Gentle.)* I know you know that.

(He kisses her hand, admitting she's right. Sophie comes down the stairs. He looks at her, guilty. She looks away, quickly.)

SOPHIE: Excuse me.

ETHAN: There she is, the elusive Sophie. We've barely caught a glimpse of you all week.

SOPHIE: I'm sorry. I've been so busy. *(She heads for the kitchen.)*

ETHAN: That's no excuse today. I happen to know that Paul is up and gone.

MARGARET: Don't bother her, Ethan. She said she's working.

ETHAN: You just said he was going to be gone all day.

MARGARET: I'm sure she has plenty to do nonetheless. Thank you, Sophie.

(Sophie turns to go.)

ETHAN: She's not a slave.

MARGARET: I didn't say she was.

SOPHIE: I'm fine.

ETHAN: I don't think you are. Look at you, running away like a scared little girl. You are running away, is that right?

SOPHIE: *(Beat, polite.)* I'm afraid I have to.

ETHAN: Well, I won't let you. The ogre is gone for now, and we're just his nice relatives. Come sit and have a coffee with us. All this running away, you can't possibly keep it up forever, it's making all of us extremely tense. *(Sophie does not know how to respond to this. Laurie enters. There is a sudden chill.)*

MARGARET: Oh, there you are, Laurie. We have such a wonderful plan for the afternoon, we're going into Mystic to buy oysters and have lunch. You, me and Ethan.

LAURIE: We are?

MARGARET: Yes, but we have to leave now, I think, because it's a forty-five minute drive, oh, and we can stop and pick up Frank, that will be fun. Let me just find the car keys.

(She goes into the kitchen. Laurie, Sophie and Ethan are alone for a moment.)

SOPHIE: Excuse me. *(She goes. After a beat.)*

ETHAN: I think that Paul may have already ruined that nice girl. Remember when she showed up, how charming she was?

LAURIE: We need to go back to the city, Ethan. *(Beat.)*

ETHAN: Do we? Why?

LAURIE: Please don't do that. Please. The past five days have been hideous, every time I try to talk to you, this — being — is there, you're like a different person and I've been so stunned, I guess, that I've just waited, and

hoped that you'd come back. But I can't keep trying and just getting —
this. This. I've been trying to understand and I can see how it happened
— I can. He's so hard on you, he barely speaks to you, and she's up there,
with him, all the time —

ETHAN: Yes, yes. Okay. Yes. *(Beat.)*

LAURIE: Yes?

ETHAN: *(Ashamed.)* Yes.

LAURIE: Then you admit it. That —

ETHAN: *(Simple.)* Laurie. Don't. You're right. I'm saying you're right, we
should go back. We'll go back. To the city. Today.

LAURIE: Good. *(There is a sad moment. She starts to cry, a bit.)*

ETHAN: Oh, don't — please — I feel terrible enough as it is —

LAURIE: I'm sorry. It's just, I've been so frightened. It's just been terrible, not
being able to talk to you, you've been so —

ETHAN: I know. I know, I know, there's no excuse, I'm not trying to make
one, but you're right, this place works on me, it's him, obviously, you're
right about that, too, not to make excuses, but it's just deeply confusing
for me to be here. I tried to tell you. Before we came.

LAURIE: You did, I just thought you were finally at a place where you could
make your peace with it, and him, you've been so well, so much happier,
lately —

ETHAN: Yes, because of you. You've brought so much sanity into my life,
everything seems possible and you were coming with me, so I thought I
could handle it or I never would have come. You know that, don't you?
If I knew, before, what it would be like, what would happen, I would
never have put us in this situation.

LAURIE: You haven't before? Have you?

ETHAN: What do you mean?

LAURIE: Have you, Ethan? Before. *(Beat.)* Have you cheated on me before.
(Beat.)

ETHAN: No. No, absolutely not, and God knows I've had the opportunity,
but I — you've brought meaning into my life, Laurie, just simple meaning, you know that, I haven't ever needed anyone the way I need you, I
couldn't put that in danger, please tell me I haven't —

LAURIE: I don't want to lose you, Ethan —

ETHAN: Tell me I haven't lost you.

*(There is a terrible, sad moment. She reaches over and takes his hand. He
hugs her, holds her for a long moment, kisses her.)*

LAURIE: Can we go now? Can we just go home right now?

ETHAN: Absolutely. Lunch with Mom, then we go.

LAURIE: No, now. Just now, please.

ETHAN: Laurie. It's fine. We'll be out of the house, we'll be away from it, and then we'll go. Come on, Mom is on pins and needles about Paul's book, we can't just let her suffer all day.

LAURIE: I know, but I just need to heal, now, we need to —

ETHAN: This is what we should do. You go have lunch with Mom. Let me spend the afternoon packing us up —

LAURIE: Ethan —

ETHAN: And then she's got this terrific dinner planned, some kind of oyster extravaganza. Not to be missed, it sounds like. So. We'll say a proper good-bye. And never look back. *(He kisses her hand. She looks at him, devastated.)*

LAURIE: Are you acting?

ETHAN: *(Startled.)* What?

LAURIE: *(Devastated.)* Oh, God. You're acting, aren't you?

ETHAN: No. No! *(He looks at her, beseeching. Laurie looks away.)*

MARGARET: *(Enters.)* Here we go, I'm sorry that took a minute, but I needed to make a list. Are we ready? Oh, we should stop, shouldn't we, and bring Frank his angels, it makes me much too nervous. All week, I can't believe he just left them here. *(She starts to pick up the angels.)*

LAURIE: *(Upset, covering.)* No, he gave them to me.

MARGARET: What?

LAURIE: He brought them, they're for me. They were a gift.

MARGARET: Oh, he couldn't.

LAURIE: Why not?

MARGARET: Well, I — I suppose he could. I just — did he tell you how much they were worth?

LAURIE: No.

MARGARET: They're worth eighteen thousand dollars, at least. That's what he paid for them. I'm sure he could, in this market — well. You're sure he meant to give them to you?

LAURIE: *(Beat.)* Yes.

MARGARET: Well, then we'll just leave them here, won't we? Shall we go?

ETHAN: Laurie and I are taking off tonight, Mom.

MARGARET: *(Pleased.)* Are you?

ETHAN: Yes, I'm going to bow down to the gods of theater, kiss some ass and see if I can resurrect my career.

MARGARET: I think that's wise.

ETHAN: So, she's going to have lunch with you while I take the afternoon to pack.

LAURIE: *(Still.)* You're not coming with us, then.

ETHAN: *(Quiet.)* We just decided, Laurie, to take off right after dinner. You said you wanted to get on the road.

LAURIE: Yes, that's what we decided.

ETHAN: So . . . I just think I should skip lunch. *(A slight, sad pause.)*

MARGARET: Oh, Ethan.

LAURIE: It's fine, Margaret. You and I will have a lovely time, just the two of us. *(She goes to Ethan, decides at the last moment not to kiss him, and goes.)*

MARGARET: *(Looks after her, then turns to Ethan.)* Ethan —

ETHAN: Yes.

> *(Margaret shakes her head, and goes. Ethan sprawls on the couch for a long moment, thinking. Sophie enters, carrying the plate of butterflies. She sees him on the couch and turns to go back immediately.)*

ETHAN: Hello. *(Beat.)*

SOPHIE: *(Stops, speaks with a polite innocence.)* I'm sorry. I thought you had gone. Margaret said you, all of you, were going to lunch.

ETHAN: No, I decided not to go.

SOPHIE: Well. I'm glad you're here. I didn't mean to disturb you. But I wanted to return the butterflies. I didn't realize how valuable they were. I simply can't accept them.

ETHAN: You can't?

SOPHIE: No.

ETHAN: But you thought I was gone. So why bring the butterflies?

SOPHIE: I was going to leave them here. With a note.

ETHAN: Look. I'm sorry I put you in this position. It wasn't my intention. I —

SOPHIE: No, it's fine, I put myself there, I don't blame anyone, I just, it can't happen again.

ETHAN: No.

SOPHIE: No.

ETHAN: I'm going back to the city tonight.

SOPHIE: Good. So, here are the butterflies and, and — that's all.

ETHAN: Please, keep them.

SOPHIE: I can't keep them.

ETHAN: If you're worried about my girlfriend —

SOPHIE: I'm not worried about your girlfriend. Perhaps you should worry about your girlfriend; I don't know your girlfriend. The person I am worried about is . . . *(She stops herself.)*

ETHAN: What?

SOPHIE: Nothing. Please. Just take them back. I need to go. *(She starts to go.)*

ETHAN: He hit on you.

SOPHIE: *(Turns and looks at him.)* What?

ETHAN: My father. Hit on you. Didn't he?

SOPHIE: *(A beat; surprised.)* Yes. He did.

ETHAN: What did you do?

SOPHIE: What did I do?

ETHAN: It's a fair enough question, Sophie. You're not as innocent as you pretend to be, and I suspect you've been hit on before.

SOPHIE: Never with such exquisite complication.

ETHAN: *(Angry.)* Are you going to tell me what happened or not?

SOPHIE: What do you think happened? He kissed me, and — it was — I, I am very confused right now, all right? So —

ETHAN: Did you enjoy it?

SOPHIE: Enjoyed it? I don't — I was overwhelmed —

ETHAN: *(Over.)* Oh, overwhelmed. That's good. He overwhelmed you. So you had nothing to do with it. It was rape, huh, you didn't enjoy it at all, you fought but you know, a sixty-four-year-old guy, he can be pretty overwhelming —

SOPHIE: *(Angry.)* Okay, "overwhelmed" was the wrong word. I was thrilled. It was thrilling —

ETHAN: *(Enraged.)* Thrilling. Which part, the kiss or the rest of it, was it thrilling to have my father feel you up?

SOPHIE: *(Stares at him in shock. He backs down, turns away, knowing he's gone too far.)* Look. I am here to work. This is — I am here to write. I am here to learn.

ETHAN: An aging Nobel laureate and his demonic son have both fallen for you, simultaneously. If you can't learn from that, you're no writer.

SOPHIE: Yes, that's very amusing. Thank you.

ETHAN: Did you sleep with him?

SOPHIE: *(Biting.)* No! I didn't sleep with him!

ETHAN: Are you going to sleep with him? *(She looks at him, enraged by this.)* It's a fair question, Sophie. You came here —

SOPHIE: I came here to work —

ETHAN: Well, other things happened, didn't they? What, am I just his son? Is that all I am to you, "his son," you made a mistake, you slept with the son when you could have had the man himself! Sold yourself short, didn't you? Got to get rid of the son now, 'cause dad's the real prize!

SOPHIE: That is not what I am doing!

ETHAN: It is exactly what you're doing!

SOPHIE: You're leaving anyway, you just said —

ETHAN: Well, that explains your relief. I'm taking off, so you and dad have a clear playing field.

SOPHIE: This is impossible. You see? You must see how impossible this is, already — this entire week has been a nightmare, going in there ten hours a day after I turned him down, believe me, is no fucking picnic, but I do it! And I intend to continue doing it, so I cannot do this! *(She starts for the door.)*

ETHAN: So you're doing this for your art, that's why you've been dodging me all week?

SOPHIE: I'm trying to survive here!

ETHAN: It's going to save you, isn't it? Make you whole. Make you wise. A really great sentence, shows you a corner of insight into the human condition, you think you've seen the face of God. That's why Paul has you. Got to get close to that, he's the lodestone, the magic, you have to touch it, like the hem of Christ's robe — *(Beat.)* It's okay. He's got me, too. All that art, all that approval, all that love, just out of reach. That big hole inside you, he's the only thing that can plug that up. And he's a complete shithead.

SOPHIE: I should have done it. Is that what you're saying?

ETHAN: Quite the opposite, Sophie. I think you know that. *(Beat.)*

SOPHIE: I am drowning here.

ETHAN: I have to know this. If it were just me. If it were you, and me, and nothing else. No one else. What would you be saying to me now?

SOPHIE: *(Lost.)* It's not possible to do that.

ETHAN: It is. He is not here. I am the only one here. *(He is close to her. They kiss. The kiss begins to get involved, but she pulls away.)*

SOPHIE: We can't do this here. *(She takes him out. Blackout.)*

SCENE FOUR

Later that day. Dusk. It is raining. The phone is ringing. Frank and Laurie enter the house, on a run, carrying grocery bags. Margaret runs for the phone.

MARGARET: Ethan, pick up the phone! Ethan, where — oh — *(Getting the phone.)* Hello? Oh, Roger — *(Beat.)* Well, that's wonderful, Roger. I know, we all slow down a bit with age, I'm afraid, so — yes, except for you, it seems, you're a speed-reader, calling so quickly. Paul isn't even back yet, he's still en route. I will, I'll tell him. All right. Bye bye. *(She hangs up.)* Well, Roger loves it!

FRANK: Dad finished? He finished it?

MARGARET: No, he compromised. He gave him half of it. So the advance is off the table, the twelve-year-olds are sated, and the writing is very good, that's what Roger says. Apparently there's some section about a girl, he thinks it's the first time Paul has actually cracked the female psyche. I'm not going to tell him that, of course.

FRANK: That's great, Mom.

MARGARET: Yes, I couldn't be more — just, relieved.

LAURIE: *(Picks a book off the shelf.)* This is the first one?

MARGARET: Yes, but you can't read that, you'll never make it through. It's very beautiful, but a little boring. This one is my favorite. Oh, and this is good. *(Takes the books off the shelves, gives them to Laurie, and goes to the door, looking.)* What time is it? I should start in on those oysters, but I don't see the point of it if no one's going to show up.

FRANK: We're here.

MARGARET: Yes, but there's oysters for six, and they're rather rich. If the three of us ate them all I think it might be a deadly catastrophe. *(To Frank.)* Which ones do you like?

FRANK: They're all good.

MARGARET: Don't listen to him, what does he know. He hasn't read any of them.

LAURIE: *(Surprised.)* Frank. You don't read your father's books?

FRANK: *(Vaguely embarrassed.)* I grew up with it. For a long time I thought that everyone had a father who wrote books. Then when I realized it was something special, I found that I preferred not to know. Sort of like seeing an island off in the distance. If you've never been there, you can pretend there are pirates on it. If you have been there, you know that there are no pirates, there's only a McDonald's.

MARGARET: Well, what a charming image, Frank. I'll be sure to tell Paul, you don't read his books because you don't want to know where the Mc-Donald's is.

FRANK: He doesn't care if I read his books, Mom.

LAURIE: Still, aren't you curious? Not everyone's father has a Nobel.

MARGARET: Oh, dear, yes, but you know they give those things out for all sorts of reasons. Paul's year, apparently the committee was angry because the academics kept shouting about Third World writers and literary racism, things like that, so they were determined that it would go to a First World White Man. Three cheers for the patriarchy, that was the rumor.

LAURIE: That can't be why they gave it to him.

MARGARET: Of course not only that, but you'd be surprised, how things factor in. He's a wonderful stylist, it's true, but some of them slip. When he gets cocky, the surface — frankly, there's nothing underneath.

LAURIE: What should be underneath?

MARGARET: That's an excellent question. You could be a critic.

FRANK: Show her the one you wrote.

LAURIE: What?

MARGARET: Oh Frank, I didn't write it. You've got to stop saying that.

FRANK: You wrote a lot of it. Here it is —

(Laurie looks at them, amazed, as Margaret and Frank fight over the book.)

MARGARET: I drafted a few sections for him. He was having a hard time. I told you about that —

LAURIE: You wrote some of his books?

MARGARET: I contributed to one or two. He reworks everything so many times it doesn't finally amount to more than an idea or two.

FRANK: You wrote big chunks —

MARGAET: I drafted. Drafting is different from writing, and it happens much more than you know. Brecht? It doesn't take away from his genius, mind you, but he didn't write all those plays. No indeed. He slept with some very smart women, that one. *(Beat.)* This is nice, isn't it? Just the three of us. Screw the oysters, we'll have a party just ourselves. Would you like some cheese and crackers? Oo, brie —

FRANK: Yes, thank you.

MARGARET: I'm not taking anything away. Truly. I didn't need any ridiculous Nobel committee to tell me how good he is. And it doesn't matter, the ones that slip. I've lived with the man, and I know what genius is.

Three or four of those really, really stand up. *(Off the book in Laurie's hand.)* And that one is unbelievably good. *(Margaret exits.)*

LAURIE: *(Turns to Frank.)* I can't believe you've never read them.

FRANK: Well, neither have you.

LAURIE: Well, he's not my father, and yes I have.

FRANK: You have?

LAURIE: Yes, of course. When I starting seeing Ethan I read them all. *(Puts the books back on the shelves.)*

FRANK: But you —

LAURIE: I didn't anything. You both just assumed. You have a very strange family, Frank.

FRANK: *(A concession.)* All families are strange, I think.

LAURIE: Mine wasn't.

FRANK: No?

LAURIE: It was just me, and my dad, and my mom. Both of them worked. Sometimes we didn't have enough money, but it always came out all right. And we were all so happy with each other.

FRANK: That sounds — wonderful.

LAURIE: I think it was! Although, maybe it was a little too cozy, is that possible? Clearly, I haven't rushed into marriage, and the men I get involved with. Maybe we weren't really happy. Or maybe I had too much happiness, as a child. Maybe now, I'm looking for unhappiness.

FRANK: Do you really think that?

LAURIE: Well, I spent six years talking about death in what may have been the most ludicrous relationship ever tolerated. And now I've spent an entire week lying next to a man, to a man who the entire time, has been thinking about another woman. The evidence is not in my favor. *(It pains her to admit it.)*

FRANK: *(Thinks, trying to be positive.)* A week, that's not so long, to be unhappy.

LAURIE: *(Brave.)* It is long enough for me. Here, Frank, I hate to do it, but I'm going to have to give these back to you.

FRANK: No, please.

LAURIE: They're much too valuable. I would just worry about them all the time. You keep them. Save them for me. Then come see me, in the city, and tell me how they're doing.

FRANK: *(A brief surprise and disappointment.)* Are you going?

LAURIE: Oh. Yes. I most certainly am.

FRANK: Don't go. Come — *(Struggling.)* There's an extra room. In my apartment. I have the entire building, you know. Above the shop, there's, it's almost like a guest house.

LAURIE: I've had quite my fill of guest houses.

FRANK: Then, it's a room. It has its own bathroom. And the kitchen, it's right there. *(He stops. She looks at him.)*

LAURIE: I don't think I can, Frank.

FRANK: No, of course not. It's foolish. I just hate, after — what, if I hadn't, my God —

LAURIE: Frank, it's not in any way your fault. How could it be?

FRANK: I know, that's not —

LAURIE: What then?

FRANK: It just makes me sad. To think of you alone.

LAURIE: You're alone.

FRANK: Oh. Well. No, it actually, I'm surrounded by so much beauty. The things of culture, the treasures — it's my life's work. People destroy each other. Cultures die. And I'm left with the angels. So. It doesn't seem so bad, really, at all. *(He shrugs, embarrassed.)*

LAURIE: *(After a moment, a statement.)* You're not gay, are you?

FRANK: Me? Oh. No. Why?

LAURIE: Ethan told me you were.

FRANK: Oh. No. *(He laughs a little at the thought.)*

LAURIE: Why does he think that?

FRANK: Oh, Ethan, he — I don't know. *(Beat.)* Listen. I, I wanted to —. If you had met me. First. If you had met me, first, do you think — *(He can't finish. Beat.)*

LAURIE: Oh. I don't know, Frank. There's just no way to know.

FRANK: No, it's fine.

LAURIE: Frank —

FRANK: It's fine. Of course it's fine. Oh, and here he is.

LAURIE: Ethan?

FRANK: My father. Paul.

(Paul appears through the back door, as Margaret returns with the wine.)

MARGARET: Is that Paul? There you are, we've been so worried.

PAUL: Fucking traffic.

MARGARET: Roger called, sweetheart.

PAUL: He called? Already? What did he say?

MARGARET: He loved it. He put everything aside, spent the morning and afternoon reading it, and he loves every word. You have to call him back and hear him, he was raving. You're still a genius, his favorite writer, of course none of us are surprised to hear it.

PAUL: No, that's . . . good news. *(He sits, relieved.)*

MARGARET: *(To Laurie.)* He always worries. And he's always wrong.

PAUL: *(Half to himself.)* Well, you never . . . it shouldn't be a surprise, I suppose, after all this time, but you just never get used to it. There's always that terror, maybe it's not good, maybe you've lost it. Hemingway, Christ, what a fate. He liked it?

MARGARET: Loved it. It's good you let him see some of it. It was a very smart thing to do.

PAUL: *(Shakes his head and moves around, restless.)* I have to get back to work.

MARGARET: Paul, no. It's past six, and I have oysters.

PAUL: Oysters? I don't eat fish.

MARGARET: And oysters are not fish. You like them, you know you do.

PAUL: I have to work.

MARGARET: Really, Paul, I've been looking forward all day to making this strange and wonderful dish —

PAUL: Sophie! Where is she, is she in her room? Go back and get her. *(He heads for the steps.)*

MARGARET: Paul, please. We'll have champagne, it's such good news about the book, Roger says it's really good, as good as anything you've ever done —

PAUL: Then I'd better finish it, hadn't I? Somebody find that girl and send her up.

LAURIE: She's not here. *(Beat.)*

PAUL: *(Turns.)* Well, where is she?

LAURIE: She went off, with Ethan.

PAUL: Where'd they go?

LAURIE: *(Deliberate.)* She's with Ethan, Paul. She's with Ethan.

(Frank looks down. All of them stand for a moment, while Paul figures this out. Blackout.)

SCENE FIVE

Paul, in light. Sophie enters, flustered.

SOPHIE: Hello. Good morning. I'm sorry I'm late.

PAUL: Overslept.

SOPHIE: Yes, I got in late. I was out late, so, I'm sorry. How did it go, yesterday?

PAUL: Sit down. I read your pages.

SOPHIE: You did. I didn't want to ask, I know you've been worried about — how did it go, with Roger?

PAUL: Sophie, I finally read your butterfly story. Do you want to know what I think of it or not?

SOPHIE: *(Beat.)* Yes. *(But she doesn't.)*

PAUL: *(Looks at the pages, then nods.)* They're good. It's good.

SOPHIE: *(Deeply relieved.)* It is.

PAUL: The way you build the internal structure, deepening the tone as the writing goes on, is sophisticated. Beautiful opening sentence, "My father's father collected butterflies," elegiac, evocative — the coldness of the storytelling is maybe a bit off-putting, but it develops into something quite moving. Technique is good overall. There's a warmth at the center of the piece that's terrific, the sort of thing you can't teach, it's either there or it isn't. Kind of old-fashioned, even. Gardner would've liked your stuff.

SOPHIE: Thank you.

PAUL: I have a few reservations about some choices. Images collapse in places, sentences run on a bit. Writing a piece of fiction is like creating a record — does your generation remember records?

SOPHIE: You mean like a phonograph record?

PAUL: God, now I really feel old. Yes, an old phonograph record, the line of the narrative is like a groove on the record and your job as a writer, is to make sure the needle — the needle, right, the reader — doesn't skip out of the groove. So every word is essential. Right? Every image, every comma, exactly in place. Understand?

SOPHIE: Yes.

PAUL: You have an agent?

SOPHIE: No, I —

PAUL: Good. Agents will ruin you; they put young writers on the market years before they're ready and they never develop, or grow into anything. It all becomes hype. Who else have you shown this to?

SOPHIE: No one.

PAUL: *(Correcting her.)* My son.

SOPHIE: Yes. Your, your son, but other than that —

PAUL: No. No one. If it's not ready to be seen, you don't let it out of your hands. When you're young, you get one shot. That's it. No one wants to hear from you. They are not hungrily reading every manuscript looking for the next girl genius. No agents, no editors, no friends of friends who work at the *New Yorker*, none of that nonsense until every sentence lifts off the page.

SOPHIE: Okay.

PAUL: You understand? I'm saying this is good. This is good enough to work on for as many years as it takes. But as it stands, a starting place, you and I need to look at the particulars that are missing as yet. Who is the butterfly collector? What are the facts of his life? All this stuff about you and your family — the writing as I said is a bit plain, good but the larger question is, does it belong there at all.

SOPHIE: Take it out? Altogether?

PAUL: *(Thoughtful.)* He's the center. This paragraph here, that's where the meat of it is. The rest won't get you anywhere, is my bet.

SOPHIE: One paragraph?

PAUL: This paragraph, yes.

SOPHIE: Yes, but it — it's not merely — about — him —

PAUL: Then it should be.

SOPHIE: Why? Why is it always about the man —

PAUL: It's not always about the man, but this time it is. It's your writing, Sophie. You've given him the drive. Everyone else is a mere fact. Including you. This this this — goes — *(Tossing pages aside, he circles one paragraph.)* This is where you start over. *(He shows her. She doesn't reach for it.)* I've lost you.

SOPHIE: No.

PAUL: Don't tell me no, Sophie, for the past three weeks I've spent every waking minute with you sitting two inches away from me. What I've just told you is your dream come true. You're good, you're the real deal, so what's the problem?

SOPHIE: *(Quiet.)* You know I am serious about this.

PAUL: I said, it was good.

SOPHIE: And then you took it away.

PAUL: I merely pointed out that there are six hundred thousand people out there who think they're fiction writers. If you can't do better than this, you're just one of them. I think you can do better than this. That's actually what I said. *(A beat; he sighs.)* What did you think I was going to tell you? That it's perfect, I'm sending it to Roger tomorrow, we're gong to make you a star?

SOPHIE: No, of course not —

PAUL: What I told you is better than that. You're an artist. You're the real thing, and you respond to that with some sort of peevish display of disappointment, what is it you want? You're young, you're pretty, and you're hoping to be the next literary pin-up girl, is that all you want?

SOPHIE: I have to go. *(She stands.)*

PAUL: You respond to criticism the way you respond to life. You run. This impulse will not serve you in the years to come.

SOPHIE: *(Turns, looks at him, suddenly flaring.)* This is not about my character.

PAUL: Isn't it?

SOPHIE: No, Paul, it isn't. This is about the fact that you're angry because I turned you down.

PAUL: I can barely remember the girls I slept with. The ones I didn't don't give me a lot of reasons to think about them.

SOPHIE: Oh, you're not angry? Because that is like only the most hostile thing I have ever heard in my life —

PAUL: Well, you're young.

SOPHIE: And you're mad because I slept with your son, and not you. *(Beat.)*

PAUL: Sex is sex, and writing is writing, and if you can't tell the difference, I can't help you with that. At the end of the summer, you can go back to New York and write a memoir about the three months you spent turning me down. You and Joyce Maynard can tour the country, give a lecture series.

SOPHIE: You're forty years older than me, how was I supposed to — is that what you would have wanted? For me to just sleep with you because — you're old? *(She grabs her manuscript and starts to go.)*

PAUL: Sit down, Sophie. We have work to do.

SOPHIE: You —

PAUL: I don't give a shit who you sleep with. I have a novel to finish. *(He hands her a sheaf of yellow pages.)* We left off, she's in the garden. *(Blackout.)*

SCENE SIX

Later the same day. Frank and Margaret are considering a plant.

FRANK: Okay, Mom: I've studied it, I've worried it, I've considered it, I've tasted it. It's dust.

MARGARET: You're sure.

FRANK: I work with antiques sixteen hours a day, Mom. Dust, I know.

ETHAN: *(Appears in the doorway.)* Ask me what's happened today.

MARGARET: Oh, Ethan, really, I'm angry with you.

ETHAN: Ask me, Mom.

MARGARET: I won't ask. If you've been up to anything worse than what you've done already, I most certainly don't want to know about it.

ETHAN: Frank, ask me.

FRANK: I don't want to know either.

ETHAN: I got the part.

MARGARET: *(Gets Margaret's attention.)* They made you that offer. Oh, Ethan. *(She kisses him.)* See, you should listen to your mother. I told you you would get that.

ETHAN: Apparently they were trying for somebody famous, but everyone's off doing sit-coms. *(Laughing.)* And then I was so absolutely uninterested, they began to panic, they were going to lose me as well. I mean, you always hear that, as soon as you decide you don't want something, or at least give up on getting it, that's when it comes back to you, but I thought that was some sort of idiotic metaphor about love, releasing a bird or something. Who knew it was literally true?

MARGARET: *(Finally laughing with him.)* Where's Laurie? Has she heard? *(She looks out the back door. There's an awkward pause.)*

ETHAN: I haven't told her yet. Sam just called, just this minute. Have you seen her?

FRANK: *(Startled.)* She went back to the city yesterday.

ETHAN: *(Picks up on this, hopeful.)* Oh, she did. That's right, we were going to. I was — so she went ahead?

FRANK: Yes. She did.

ETHAN: Did you talk to her, before she left?

FRANK: *(Chilly.)* Yes, as a matter of fact I did.
(The two brothers consider each other.)

ETHAN: *(Nods, finally.)* Yes, I know, I've been behaving badly. I'll make it up to her. As soon as I get home, I'll apologize, day and night. It'll be fine.

MARGARET: You're leaving too, then?

ETHAN: I have to. Rehearsals don't start for a few weeks but I have absolutely done nothing all summer and my life is a disaster. I've got to put things in order. You know, pay the bills, get the dry cleaning done. It's all just nonsense, but I have to do it now because once the play starts, I'm not going to have time to think of anything.

FRANK: What — that, what?

ETHAN: What?

(There is a brief pause as Frank considers smacking him.)

FRANK: *(Finally angry.)* That's it? That's why? You're leaving now so you can do laundry? So you can give yourself permission to turn into even more of a complete — narcissist, two weeks from now, that's why you want to go back now, when if you had — for weeks you've just been making a ruin, a ruin of people's — and that's why you're going back now? To do laundry?

ETHAN: What are you so mad about?

FRANK: What am I so mad about? You have everything, everything and she's, you run around, taking everything else, as if it's your right, it's not your right! You're not the only person on the planet. You're little! You're as little as the rest of us. Time is going to pass you by, just the way it passes us all. Only not all of us do damage.

ETHAN: You don't live, either.

FRANK: I live.

ETHAN: You sit in your little shop all day, dusting things off, until someone comes by and buys it from you. You don't get out there and act, you don't — do anything! You're a shopkeeper. You collect. And look how happy it's made you. Well, you know what? I am not going to apologize for the damage I cause. And you are not going to make your everyday, damage-free misery my problem.

MARGARET: Ethan.

FRANK: I am the audience, you asshole. The entire human race is the audience to people like you, and you — once in a while, couldn't you try to be worth it?

MARGARET: Frank.

FRANK: Don't talk to me, Mom. *(He sits.)*

ETHAN: *(Raises an eyebrow and turns to Margaret.)* That was a lousy thing to say. Heaven forbid he might actually be happy for me. It's not my fault he's never done anything with his life.

MARGARET: *(Sighs, takes a beat, and puts her plants back in place.)* You know, sweetheart, you can be really — exhausting. *(She looks up as Paul heads down the stairs.)*

PAUL: What's all the yelling? Ethan?

ETHAN: Yeah, hi Dad. I was just telling Mom. I'm taking off.

PAUL: You're going?

ETHAN: Yes, I am. I got offered that play.

PAUL: What play?

ETHAN: The play. We talked about it the other night, at Frank's party, remember? Shakespeare is no playwright, et cetera et cetera?

PAUL: That play?

ETHAN: Yes.

PAUL: I thought you weren't going to do that.

ETHAN: I changed my mind.

PAUL: Why'd you do that?

ETHAN: They offered it to me.

PAUL: So it's only worth doing if you don't have to ask for it, is that how that works? *(Beat.)*

ETHAN: That's right, Dad. Go ahead and fucking demean it.

MARGARET: Oh no. I have had quite enough for one day. Before anyone says another word, I'm making us all cocktails, and we're all going to have a civilized drink. *(She heads for the kitchen, but Paul continues. She stops.)*

PAUL: He's been telling everyone for weeks it was beneath him. Now he wants us to what, congratulate him on getting something he told everyone he didn't want in the first place?

MARGARET: Paul, please. I ask for so little from you. And I am exhausted right now.

ETHAN: *(Overlap.)* Fuck you. You think you're the only fucking person on the planet, everyone in this fucking crazy family —

MARGARET: Ethan! After what was just said between you and Frank, I really think —

FRANK: Don't drag me into this, Mom. I don't say anything, as a rule, but I am not — this is not — you can't —

MARGARET: *(Overlap.)* I know, I'm sorry, you're truly the one person I could ever count on to behave rationally, which is why I'm putting my foot down, now. I'm asking all of you. For me. *(There is a moment of silence.)* Thank you.

ETHAN: It's fine, Mom. It's fine. For you, okay, but him — I'm not getting dragged into his destruction, anymore. Sitting up here, eating people up like some giant toad —

PAUL: Stick to acting, Ethan; simile's not your strong suit.

ETHAN: You can't do it anymore! You're the one who can't finish a sentence, you can't write a goddamn fucking sentence without someone holding your hand! Roger keeps sending these girls to get you through it, rather than admit you've lost it.

MARGARET: *(Dry.)* Well, thank you. I certainly appreciate everyone trying, for my sake —

ETHAN: And he's still trying to fuck them! Ask her, Mom! In your house! He's hitting on her in your house, ask her!

(Sophie stands in the doorway. She is very still. No one sees her. Frank tries to protect Margaret from all this as Paul explodes.)

PAUL: Is this about a woman, Ethan? Is that what this is about? A woman? Because my understanding is that you've been fucking her. Wasn't that enough for you? What is it you want?

ETHAN: *(Shoving him away.)* Nothing. Forget it. You know, the only reason I even came here was because these two were in a complete panic, he's falling apart, he can't write anymore, he's reading your reviews! The old man actually had a half a second of thinking about somebody other than himself, he had a flash of curiosity about his firstborn son, that must mean he's dying —

PAUL: Sorry to disappoint you.

ETHAN: That's all right. I'll be back to see it when it does happen, Dad. Looking forward to it.

PAUL: Wishing your father dead — oh, Ethan, it has a nice sort of Greek ring to it but wouldn't it make more sense to grapple with something a little more subtle, such as your own sense of inadequacy?

ETHAN: Actually, Dad, the only thing that makes sense anymore is leaving.

PAUL: If only you would.

ETHAN: As if I was even here to you! As if I even exist to you. *(Beat.)* Consider it done. We'll just say I sprang out of the earth, full grown, while you sat off in some room somewhere, scribbling bullshit and screwing your students. You had nothing to do with me.

PAUL: I had nothing to do with you? Do you even hear yourself? Go do your play, the theater deserves you. But don't kid yourself into thinking you're your own man. You might have been, if there were more to you. But you're just what I made you. Feels good doesn't it, going off to do your art, you're in the heat of it, I am too, it's all going better and the rest of it is suddenly gone. The self-loathing. The contempt, hating yourself so much that the rest of humanity has to bear the brunt of it, the fear of death or even worse, failure, worse than that even, mediocrity, hovering out there. For half a moment, perhaps, it occurs to you to snap out of it, but change is a fleet thought, isn't it, fuck the chance to find something in yourself, so that when you die you're not just looking at the end with terror in your bones, trying to figure out why all of it, fame, awards, the luck even just to do it, every day, why that just didn't add up to more. Why the sheer beauty of just being alive never lifted your heart beyond — this. *(Pause.)*

ETHAN: That's it? That's what I get after forty years? You'd be a better person if you weren't so much like me? That's your fatherly wisdom?

PAUL: If that's what you heard, that's what you get. *(To Margaret.)* Are we having those oysters?

MARGARET: *(Startled.)* Well, they're still in the refrigerator, not quite as fresh as they would have been last night but still very fresh, if you're really interested.

PAUL: You said you had some recipe.

MARGARET: Spectacularly decadent, yes.

PAUL: That sounds good. You still want that cocktail?

MARGARET: I think I could use one, frankly.

PAUL: A Rob Roy, right?

MARGARET: *(Looks at him, even more startled.)* If it's not too much trouble.

PAUL: I hope I can remember how. *(He heads for the kitchen.)*

ETHAN: *(Yelling after him.)* Hey, it's been great! Huh? Fun visit! Because you know, I was nowhere near scarred enough!

MARGARET: *(Sighs.)* Well.

ETHAN: It's okay, Mom. I'm leaving. I wish I'd never come. *(As he gets to the door, it occurs to him what he's said. He stops, frustrated with himself.)* I didn't mean that. I'm sorry, Mom. It's been great to see you, at least. *(He tries to kiss her.)*

MARGARET: *(Turns on him.)* There is a cost to things, Ethan. Are you even aware of that? Are you aware of what this past week has cost us all? Are you aware of what it's cost you? *(She looks away.)*

ETHAN: *(He glances over to Sophie, who is trying to quietly sneak out of the room.)* *(to Sophie, awkward.)* You'll come to see me, won't you? This fall. As you may have guessed, I'm doing that play after all. I'm not sure when we open, mid-September, I think. I hope you'll come.

SOPHIE: Come see your play?

ETHAN: I think it's going to be pretty good.

SOPHIE: *(Beat.)* Of course. Thank you.

(Ethan goes.)

MARGARET: *(After a moment, Margaret looks up at Sophie, polite.)* So it's going well? The writing?

SOPHIE: *(Short.)* Yes.

MARGARET: I could tell. I think it's been twenty years since he last offered to make me a drink.

SOPHIE: The writing is going very well.

MARGARET: Good. And as the rest of it — I hope that you don't take any of that personally. I certainly don't. Although I suspect that's a sort of trick that comes with age. Oh, dear. You know at times like this, one can't help think about Tolstoy, can one? All that nonsense about happy families, and unhappy ones. He was a very good writer, but really, as if we could separate it out. This family is happy, and this one — isn't. I hardly think it's all that simple. *(Checking her watch.)* Will you be having dinner with us? I think it's just Paul and I, tonight, I don't know if Frank's staying.

FRANK: No.

SOPHIE: No, I don't think I will join you, either.

MARGARET: All right.

(Margaret goes. After a moment, Sophie continues down the steps. She sees the butterflies, where she left them. She goes to them, looks at them for a moment, picks them up and sets them on the coffee table. She picks up one of the angels and brings it down with real force on top of the butterflies. The glass breaks. Frank jumps out of his chair, totally startled by what she's done.)

FRANK: No, please!

SOPHIE: *(Stops, looks at him.)* Why, is it very valuable?

FRANK: It's not that. It's just — if you use the angel, the gesture is much too baroque. *(He takes the angel from her.)*

SOPHIE: *(Looks at the shattered frame.)* It felt good, actually. It meant so much to me. But it felt quite good, to destroy it. I guess that's no surprise.

FRANK: No — no — listen. My mother is right. You shouldn't — it's not . . . personal.

SOPHIE: Yes, I understand that. I do. It's just funny. For the past three weeks, both of them have been trying to sleep with me, and I was never even in the room. That is funny, isn't it?

FRANK: Hilarious.

SOPHIE: And I went along with it. It was like someone just said, here, I'm gonna hit you in the head with a hammer, and I said, okay. And then they hit me in the head with a hammer. And now, my head hurts. *(She starts to go.)*

FRANK: *(Sees that she's left her butterfly story, which is now a bit crumpled. He picks it up, looks at it.)* Don't you want this?

SOPHIE: No. I don't.

FRANK: This is the butterfly story? *(She doesn't answer.) (He looks at it, briefly.)* Ethan said it was really good.

SOPHIE: Ethan was trying to seduce me.

FRANK: If it wasn't any good, he wouldn't have tried.

SOPHIE: Well, I don't need it anymore, do I? It's poisoned, now, isn't it? Well?

FRANK: I don't . . . I can't tell you that. *(Then.)* Would you like to know, you never asked me, about the plate?

SOPHIE: *(Turns, surprised and somewhat curious at this change in subject.)* What about it?

FRANK: I met the man who made it.

SOPHIE: You did?

FRANK: Yes, he's very old. Ninety-six. Mean as a snake.

SOPHIE: Of course.

FRANK: His favorite part was, uh, killing the butterflies. He liked to watch them beat their wings in agony and then go limp. He's got hundreds of plates, stacked in a room in the back of his son's house. The son is seventy-two. It's just the two of them, and they don't seem to talk to each other. The old man sits in the back room, killing butterflies, and the son sits in the front, watching television. They seem to live off packets of frozen food, and there was this odd moment when the son went to the freezer, took out a sort of solid wedge of something frozen, went into the garage, and cut it in half with a power saw. I don't know what that was about.

SOPHIE: Is this supposed to make me feel better?

FRANK: It's just facts. They don't take away from the plate. They're different things, life and art; you shouldn't get them confused. It's hard, because they lie right next to each other, don't they, hovering behind each other, all the time. All the dark and the light that is life. And the art that we make of it. But really. Try not to get them confused. *(Melancholy, he hands her the story and goes. After a long moment, the lights dim down to a spot on Sophie.)*

SOPHIE: In the room next to him, Katie was scolding the boys to sleep. He raised his head at the interruption, rubbing his eyes beneath the spectacles, tired tonight, some nights his eyes stung with the delicacy of the work. Through the thin walls her voice rose, shrill, with exhaustion, as the boys foolishly protested their innocence. It was their nightly ritual, her anger, their half-hearted rebellion, roles acted almost unknowingly, played out within the ether of their love for each other. He felt flushed, a cold coming on, and he knew Katie would be in soon, to scold him into bed as well, although both of them were still unaware of the pneumonia already nestled in his lungs. He was nearly finished. His final specimen, a tiny peacock pansy, fluttered anxiously in its jar, as it fought the effects of the anesthesia, which would render it finally inert. When just a child, the specter of death in the form of a terrified insect caused him inordinate delight, but over time his response changed, as he grew by degrees un-nerved, then horrified, then fascinated, then philosophical, as he proceeded year after year to murder these stunning creatures in the name of love. For what was it if not love that kept him awake night after night, hum-bled by his own devotion to them? There was a time, he knew, when tribal peoples had carved butterflies into stone, had reckoned them messengers from the gods. In the deepest part of him, he understood these ancient beliefs. And so as his own death bloomed within him, the butterfly col-lector watched as the wings went still, one more specimen of doom and beauty surrendering itself to his care. *(Blackout.)*

END OF PLAY

¡Curanderas!
Serpents of the Clouds

By Elaine Romero

For George and Irene Romero

WORLD PREMIERE PRODUCTION
The Invisible Theatre

DIRECTOR: Deborah Dickey
PRODUCER: Susan Claassen
TECHNICAL DIRECTOR: James Blair
SET DESIGN: Susan Claassen and James Blair
LIGHT DESIGN: James Blair
COSTUME DESIGN: Stephanie Maus
PROP DESIGN: Thomas Ryan
STAGE MANAGER: Angela Carter
EQUITY STAGE MANAGER: Susan Claassen
SOUND OPERATOR: Mark Johnson

THE CAST:
PALOMA.................................... Norma Medina
VICTORIA .... Jennifer Fisk-Wilken
AZTEC WOMAN .... Rosanne Couston
MAN .... Roberto Garcia

WORKSHOP PRODUCTION
Guadalupe Cultural Arts Center

THEATRE PROGRAM DIRECTOR: Jorge Piña
DIRECTOR: José Manuel Galván
COMPOSER: Alice Gomez
CHOREOGRAPHER: Javier Romero

THE CAST:
PALOMA .... Lisa Suarez
VICTORIA .... Leticia Soza
AZTEC WOMAN............................. Lina del Roble
MAN... Johnny Dimas

ADDITIONAL CREDITS

The playwright offers thanks to all the theaters involved in the development of this play. *¡Curanderas! Serpents of the Clouds* received a workshop production at the Guadalupe Cultural Arts Center with major support from the Ford Foundation in San Antonio, Texas (1996). It received further staged readings at Kitchen Dog Theatre's New Works Festival 2001 in Dallas, TX, Invisible Theatre in Tucson, AZ (2000), Ensemble Theatre in Phoenix, AZ (as part of the New Plays Marathon 2000), the Southwest Festival of New Plays (Women's Playwrights' Division), at Stages Repertory Theatre in Houston, TX (1998) where the play won First Prize; and the José Galvez Gallery in Tucson, AZ (1997). Special thanks to Susan Claassen of the Invisible Theatre.

ABOUT AUTHOR

Elaine Romero has been named the winner of the 2002 Arizona Commission on the Arts Playwriting Fellowship (AZ), the 2002 Sprenger-Lang New History Play Contest (DC) and the 2001 Arizona Playwrights Award (AZ), for her play *Before Death Comes for the Archbishop*. She has received a 2002 Arizona Commission on the Arts Project Grant to write a new play about the life of Catalina de Erauso. In 1998, the Arizona Theatre Company (ATC; AZ) and Romero received a $100,000 TCG/Pew National Theatre Artist in Residence grant (NY) to develop two new plays:

Before Death Comes for the Archbishop and *Secret Things* both received workshop production at ATC. *Before Death Comes for the Archbishop* received readings at PlayBrokers in San Francisco (CA), the Sprenger-Lang Foundation at the Warehouse Theatre (DC) and Arizona State University (AZ). *Secret Things* received further development at Actors Theatre of Phoenix (AZ) and at the Bay Area Playwrights Festival in San Francisco (CA). As Playwright-in-Residence, Romero runs ATC's National Latino Playwrights Contest and the Latino/Native American Playwrights Mentorship Program.

Romero's works have appeared across the country at Actors Theatre of Louisville (KY), Urban Stages (NY), San Diego Repertory Theatre (CA), Arizona Theatre Company (AZ), Kitchen Dog Theatre (TX), Theatre By the Blind (NY), Planet Earth Multi-Cultural Theatre (AZ), Jump-Start Performance Company (TX), Miracle Theatre (OR), El Centro Su Teatro (CO), City Theatre (FL), Le Petit Theatre (LA), the University of California at Davis (CA), and The Working Theatre (NY) among others. She is a winner of many awards, including the NEA/TCG Theatre Residency Program for Playwrights (NY) with San Diego Repertory (CA) where she developed *Barrio Hollywood*, the

Invisible Theatre's Play Contest (AZ), the Chicano-Latino Literary Award (CA), the Tennessee Williams One-Act Play Contest (LA), and the Old Pueblo Playwrights' "2002 Play in a Night Contest" (AZ) for her co-written play, *Watching*.

Romero's published plays have appeared in *More Ten Minute Plays from Actors Theatre of Louisville, Volume 4* (Samuel French), *The Best Stage Scenes 1998* (Smith & Kraus), *Poems & Plays, More Monologues for Women, by Women* (Heinemann Press), *Ollantay Theatre Magazine, Puro Teatro: a Latina Anthology* (University of Arizona Press), and *30 Ten-Minute Plays for 4, 5, and 6 Actors* (Smith & Kraus). *Walking Home* will be excerpted in an upcoming anthology by Arte Público Press, Houston, TX (2002). Her award-winning fiction appears in *The Alaska Quarterly Review, Rosebud Magazine* and *Tucson Guide Quarterly*.

¡Curanderas! Serpents of the Clouds received its World Premiere at the Invisible Theatre in 2000. The play received its initial workshop production at the Guadalupe Cultural Arts Center (TX). It won a First Prize in the Stages Repertory Theatre's Women's Playwrights Festival (TX) where it received a reading. It will be produced in 2002 at Aurora Theatre in Duluth, GA and 2003 at Kitchen Dog Theatre in Dallas.

Her film, *Dream Friend*, screened at the Arizona International Film Festival (AZ), the National Association of Latino Independent Producers (NALIP) Conference (CA), the Pacific Coast Film Festival (CA) and 2002 CineFestival (TX). A finalist for the Humana Festival and the Heideman Award (KY), Elaine's commissioned play, *Day of Our Dead*, received its World Premiere Off-Broadway last year at the Working Theatre (NY). A member of the Dramatists Guild, Elaine has taught playwriting and screenwriting at the University of Arizona. She holds her MFA in Playwriting from UC Davis.

AUTHOR'S NOTE

I grew up on vivid stories of my Great-Great Grandmother Marita. Grandma Marita had long since died, but legend held her as a family saint. I knew four things about her: (1) she was short, (2) she had a dog-eared prayer book that she recited from nightly, (3) she was a veritable dictionary of dichos (rhymed Spanish sayings) and (4) she would go about Northern New Mexico collecting plants, roots, and herbs to be used for medicinal healing. She was so renowned for her knowledge of plants that "the doctors would come to her as a last resort" after their allopathic methods had failed. Her remedies were sometimes unorthodox. One time she had my grandparents leave my three-month-old mother outside on the porch in freezing Albuquerque weather to rid her of pneumonia. It worked. My mother says that our humble grandmother never called herself a curandera (folk healer), but she did practice curanderismo. Among definitions of curanderas (it has its own branches like other types of medicine), our grandmother would be categorized as an herbalist. Interest in healing skipped a few generations; love of medicine trickled down to a nurse here (a cousin), a paramedic there (my brother), and finally to me. I am known to espouse my own herbal remedies, but I'm certainly not a curandera.

¡Curanderas! Serpents of the Clouds had an odd birth. It began as a multidisciplinary collaboration at the Guadalupe Cultural Arts Center in San Antonio, Texas funded by the Ford Foundation. I collaborated with Javier Romero, a choreographer from Mexico City, who had brought an Aztec drawing, the Codex Boturini, literally to our table. He had painstakingly photocopied and taped the long scroll into one unwieldy, intimidating document. The scroll represents the journey of the Aztecs from Aztlan (their homeland) to the founding of Tenochtitlan (Mexico City). In conjunction with our other collaborators, Chicana composer Alice Gomez and Mexican director, José Manuel Galván, we had agreed to use the codex as our map to the play, topographically, structurally, and spiritually. Our characters would literally follow the journey of the Aztecs from Aztlan, now the American Southwest, to Mexico City. Alice wanted me to include the idea of curanderos. Though I stayed up late many nights staring at the primitive images of the codex, I could not see a play nor even a curandero there.

I decided to look at the scroll from a new perspective. I had been expecting the scroll to hand me the entire story, but the scroll felt too linear, too confining. Instead, I saw a figure sitting on a rock, somewhere on her journey, crying from a deep place inside herself. The scroll had become a place to start asking questions. I decided the figure could be a woman, but what was she crying about? The figure's pain became a window into my young Chicana doctor, Victoria. Then, I saw a tree broken in half, but with human hands and feet. The tree could represent something that had to do with the *curandera*. Her marriage might seem dead, but be very much alive. Image after image began to welcome me into a very different play than I had ever written — some of it felt like dream, some of it felt like souls exchanging something quite profound. Suddenly, the codex and the curanderas seemed inextricably linked. The real world melted away in favor of the ancestral world and the subconscious. In this newly created world, I could move the text anywhere at any moment. My characters communicated beyond the limits of reality, death and space. Structurally, I'd never felt so free. Thus, *¡Curanderas! Serpents of the Clouds,* was born.

CHARACTERS

PALOMA: A Chicana curandera, a folk healer, in her early forties.

VICTORIA: A pocha (a Mexican-American who does not speak Spanish). A young doctor in her twenties.

MAN: An everyman. At times, he appears as neutral man. At other times, he transforms into Victoria's thirtyish fiancé, Jesus, and Paloma's husband, who is in his early forties.

WOMAN: Aztec Woman. She appears in full Aztec regalia. She is Paloma's spiritual guide. She appears under a number of disguises — an announcer, a hotel clerk, a tour guide and dream woman — always remaining Aztec Woman.

TIME

The ancient and recent past. The present.

PLACE

On the road from Aztlan (San Antonio/American Southwest). In and around Mexico City. Physical and spiritual worlds (The bellybutton of the moon). Dreams, visions and nightmares.

SETTING

The stage is a flexible space, with an implied set, where the scenes transpire. ACT ONE: Prologue, Train, Hotel, Museum, Beach. ACT TWO: Bellybutton of the moon, Hotel, Dream, Hotel, Bellybutton of the moon, Hotel.

NOTES

In Nahautl, Serpents of the Clouds refers to curanderos (healers). The *Mexica* were an Aztec tribe who were in power at the time of Cortez.

¡CURANDERAS! SERPENTS OF THE CLOUDS

PROLOGUE

Victoria, a Chicana in her twenties, moves alone on stage. She carries a satchel of books in one hand. She circles around, leaves the satchel behind her. Man, dressed in dark colors, enters. He is Jesús. The more he moves around her, the more disoriented she becomes, turning in circles. She cries into one hand. As Jesús exits opposite her, she keeps her eyes covered with her hand. Victoria ends up prone on the floor. In this final moment of susto — her soul leaves her body in her grief.

Paloma, a curandera (a healer) in her early forties, enters, carrying two overstuffed suitcases. She looks like a little girl running away from home, distraught and scared.

Woman, Paloma's guide, appears behind the scrim in full Aztec regalia. She watches Paloma, but Paloma does not see her. Woman gestures for the revels to begin.

ACT ONE

Woman transforms into train announcer. The sound of a train whistle. Victoria sits in a window seat, leaning against the window somewhat dreamily. She hears the sound of rain splashing against the window. Woman enters.

WOMAN: Pasajeros con destino a la Ciudad de México favor de abordar el tren. Ultima llamada.
(Paloma enters, carrying her oversized suitcases. She lifts them overhead as if pushing through a crowd of people. She plops down into the seat next to Victoria, placing one of the suitcases momentarily on Victoria's lap. Victoria tries to help Paloma lift the suitcase up. Victoria hurts her finger.)
VICTORIA: Ouch. *(Victoria shakes her finger in pain. Paloma quickly grabs Victoria's finger and does a quick little soba — a massage to heal the finger. It is a magical moment. Victoria looks at her finger, surprised and relieved.)* What'd you do? *(Denying the magic.)* It must not have been that bad.
PALOMA: *(Belated.)* Perdóneme.
(Victoria nods, moves closer to the window.)

PALOMA: Mire nomás a todos esos tontos empapándose. Tengo el último boleto.

VICTORIA: *(Bad Spanish.)* No entiendo. *(Victoria gives Paloma a blank look.)* *(Paloma excitedly taps her feet on the ground; she energetically leans back, arms outstretched, drinking in the joy of her seat. This woman causes a tornado wherever she goes.)*

PALOMA: A veces la gente no sabe cuando deben moverse.

VICTORIA: I know you people have different space bubbles, but Christ.

PALOMA: Perdone usted. Aren't you a Mexican?

VICTORIA: *(Embarrassed.)* You speak English.

PALOMA: I don't know nothing about no space bubbles, and all that fancy stuff, but I do know when you have to get going, you have to go.

VICTORIA: Yeah, right. Well, I'm just gonna drift off here for a second.

PALOMA: Where are you gonna drift off to?

VICTORIA: So, if you could refrain from engaging me in conversation, I'd appreciate it.

(Paloma shakes her hand as if to say this woman thinks she is too big a deal.)

PALOMA: I won't say a word. Shhh. *(Paloma zips her mouth shut.)*

(Victoria closes her eyes, enjoying a moment of peace.)

PALOMA: Didn't your parents teach you Spanish?

(Victoria is startled.)

VICTORIA: *(To herself, reflective.)* My Spanish is lost somewhere in my cells.

(Paloma starts munching down a bag of chicharrones, fried pork rinds.)

VICTORIA: Would you mind?

PALOMA: I don't know. It's a public place, public train, public bathroom . . .

VICTORIA: I came here to think. I just need some peace and quiet.

PALOMA: You came to México for peace and quiet? Mija, buscate otra agencia de viajes.

VICTORIA: Be careful. I understand some Spanish.

PALOMA: *(Continuing.)* Between all the babies crying, mariachis playing and little old ladies gossiping until their teeth fall out, I don't think you're gonna find no peace and quiet here.

VICTORIA: You don't understand. I'm going through a hard time. I just finished medical school.

PALOMA: You finished medical school, but you can't learn Spanish?

VICTORIA: It's very stressful.

PALOMA: Excuse me for being born. If you don't want to share no air . . .

VICTORIA: I don't mean that.

(Paloma blows on her. Victoria smells the stench. She brushes Paloma's breath out of her face.)

VICTORIA: Christ, what'd you eat for breakfast?

PALOMA: Garlic cloves and rattlesnake pills. They're good for the blood.

VICTORIA: *(Doubling over.)* My God, I think I'm gonna be sick.

PALOMA: They drive away all sorts of nasty and creepy witch doctors. Have you ever smelled a brujo up close? ¡Híjole!

VICTORIA: Can't say that I have.

PALOMA: They make pigs smell like perfume. And they're always trying to kiss me with their pinche bad breath. But I know what they really want. They want to steal my power.

VICTORIA: Are you a witch or something?

(Paloma takes a map out of her bag.)

PALOMA: Where are we anyways? *(Paloma in a quick few seconds has entangled herself in the map, even ripping it in a few places.)*

VICTORIA: Here, let me see that. What are you looking for?

PALOMA: I always find where I am anyways. Or people find me. They just drive up and ask me, "May I help you"? See, the power draws them. The world takes care of curanderos, healers, because we take care of the world. *(With a tinge of sadness.)* That's what the people say. *(After a second.)* One man gave me a ride all the way to Houston, and it was four hours out of his way. For nothing more than for me to cure a viejita, a little old lady. And she lived for four more years to the date, one year for every hour he went out of his way.

VICTORIA: Charming story.

PALOMA: God helps us when we're willing to make a sacrifice. Like that stranger made a sacrifice and he didn't even know it. Most sacrifices are like that. They don't happen in the mind. They happen in the heart. *(Another tinge of sadness.)* Los dioses listen to the heart.

VICTORIA: Did you say gods?

PALOMA: I meant God. *(Paloma makes a quick sign of the cross, and then she chews her finger.)*

VICTORIA: I was beginning to think you weren't even Catholic.

PALOMA: Have these things happened to you? People coming to you when you needed them? Even when you didn't want them to?

VICTORIA: No one's ever driven me to Houston for no reason.

(Paloma motions her disapproval.)

PALOMA: I had a reason.

VICTORIA: Oh, that's right. You were going to heal somebody.

PALOMA: Yes, I was.

VICTORIA: You can't heal anybody. Well, not unless it's some trumped up folk disease like the evil eye.

PALOMA: Mal ojo.

VICTORIA: I read an article about that in medical school. Do you really think a baby will get sick if someone admires it too much? C'mon.

PALOMA: Or susto, illness from fright. I bet you don't believe in susto either. *(Paloma looks Victoria straight in the eye as if she is peering into her.)*

PALOMA: It's when something so upsetting happens to a person that their soul leaves their body. It can even lead to death. You can tell if someone has susto because their nose feels soft como algodón, like cotton. *(Paloma does the susto diagnosis on Victoria's nose. Victoria recoils.)* And to bring the soul back, you have to say the Apostle's Creed three times, clap your hands, and say that person's name. *(Paloma releases one very haunting cupped clap.)* Victoria!

VICTORIA: *(Defensive.)* How'd you know my name?

PALOMA: It's carved in your eyes. *(Paloma snaps her fingers. Paloma drops her hand, frustrated.)* It didn't work. You have to believe in it first. *(Hypnotized, Victoria does not move.)*

VICTORIA: One time though something really strange happened. A stranger came to me. He asked me if I'd heal — oh, forget it.

PALOMA: What was it?

VICTORIA: Nothing.

PALOMA: You've had these experiences. You just don't want to admit it.

VICTORIA: I haven't.

PALOMA: *(Teasingly.)* Liar.

VICTORIA: Hey, I haven't.

PALOMA: Okay, I'll believe you.

VICTORIA: It's just I don't believe in all that spiritual stuff.

PALOMA: ¿No?

VICTORIA: It not rational.

PALOMA: ¿No?

VICTORIA: All these wacky beliefs — like thinking dead people hang around us all the time. It's spooky.

PALOMA: Who am I to fight with a medical doctor?

VICTORIA: I'm gonna be an emergency room doctor. After my residency.

PALOMA: Stressful.

VICTORIA: I like buckets of blood.

PALOMA: Really?

VICTORIA: A little medical humor.

PALOMA: It wasn't funny.

VICTORIA: *(Short beat.)* Blood spurting out of jugular veins, gun shot wounds, severed limbs — that visceral stuff doesn't bother me. I'm tough. Tough as nails.

PALOMA: It should bother you.

VICTORIA: I guess, I'm just like you. I'm special. *(Victoria leans back self-satisfied.)*

(Paloma takes the map back.)

PALOMA: It's just some pyramids or something. I'm sure we'll find them when we get there. They should be standing up into the clouds.

(Victoria twists her engagement ring, gazing out the window. Silence.)

VICTORIA: *(Dreamily.)* The pyramids. He wanted to see them.

PALOMA: Who?

VICTORIA: Oh, my boyfriend. I mean, my fiancé. He wanted to come, but . . .

PALOMA: He had to work.

VICTORIA: Yeah, he was working.

PALOMA: So, when's your last day of freedom?

VICTORIA: I don't see it that way. He isn't like that. He's very open.

PALOMA: A feminista?

VICTORIA: And a communist.

PALOMA: Doesn't seem your type.

VICTORIA: *(Defensive.)* He is. He is exactly my type.

PALOMA: Are you sure what you're getting into? People can't always live up to what they say they are.

VICTORIA: He is who he says he is. I'm sure of that.

PALOMA: So, when's the big day?

VICTORIA: I'm not telling you. You're not being supportive.

PALOMA: I don't care whether you tell me or not. I was just asking to be po-lite. I'll just take a nap right here. *(She closes her eyes, leans back, feigning a lack of interest.)*

VICTORIA: *(Beat.)* The wedding's in June.

PALOMA: Nice. June wedding. You don't have much time left to get ready, muchachita. ¿Qué haces por aqui?

VICTORIA: *(Getting worked up.)* Don't make me nervous. I've got it all planned.

PALOMA: Sure you didn't miss any little details?

(Victoria glares at her.)

PALOMA: Just checking *(Short beat.)* Now, you're sure about this man?

VICTORIA: He's the most wonderful man in the world.

PALOMA: *(Simultaneously.)* . . . wonderful man in the world.

(Man appears behind the scrim as neutral man.)

VICTORIA: How'd you know?

PALOMA: It's what all young brides say.

VICTORIA: *(Sad.)* He is though. He really is. He's different.

PALOMA: I believe you. I'm sure your man is great. *(Man transforms into Jesus.)*

VICTORIA: Jesus. His name is Jesus. *(Beat.)* What about you? You married?

(Man transforms into Husband and disappears.)

PALOMA: Do you know what time we're supposed to get there?

VICTORIA: In a hurry?

PALOMA: Just want to get there. I wanna know what it's like to stand on top of a pyramid and talk to the gods.

VICTORIA: Oh, yeah?

PALOMA: You?

VICTORIA: The beach.

PALOMA: In Mexico City?

VICTORIA: It isn't on the beach? I'm an idiot.

PALOMA: The word is pendeja, mi amor.

VICTORIA: My travel agent said they had white sandy beaches that stretch for miles. *(Slightly defensive.)* A simple vacation. That's all I'm here for. Nothing more.

PALOMA: *(Beat.)* You're going to be a lovely bride.

VICTORIA: *(Touched.)* You think so?

PALOMA: And him, do you have a picture?

(Victoria takes a picture out of her wallet. When Paloma looks at the picture, she looks concerned.)

VICTORIA: That was taken last year. *(No response.)* That's my favorite one.

PALOMA: Is he ill? Your fiancé?

VICTORIA: Why do you say that? He's perfectly fine. *(Victoria quickly puts the picture away.)*

PALOMA: It's just — in that picture I sensed he was ill.

VICTORIA: He did not look ill.

PALOMA: Okay, he looked fine. Healthy and strong.

VICTORIA: I'm a doctor. I should know about things like that.

PALOMA: You should. You should see things coming, but you don't always trust that feeling inside.

VICTORIA: You think you know everything. How do you know what I feel and don't feel?

PALOMA: You can see more than other doctors do if you try. Illness isn't just in the body, you know. It invades the mind. It infects the spirit. Sometimes you can see it like a cloud over people, stealing their breath out of the tops of their heads. We can snatch that illness away with the force of our hands. We're that powerful.

VICTORIA: I've always found antibiotics to be effective myself.

PALOMA: We, curanderos, don't live long, you know, because we're willing to fight that thing — that unseen thing. Doctors don't see nothing like that. Can't stand the cabrones myself.

VICTORIA: You're going to insult me to my face?

PALOMA: You're one of them, but you're also one of us.

VICTORIA: It's research and experience in the medical community that count, not voodoo and shit. I have too much tangible information to be one of you.

PALOMA: Oh, education can cause trouble for the young.

VICTORIA: I'm very proud of my education.

PALOMA: Your education has made you proud. *(Short beat.)* Believe me, mija, human beings knew something about medicine before they discovered penicillin. *(Paloma takes out her lipstick and draws a line between herself and Victoria.)*

VICTORIA: Excuse me? What're you doing?

PALOMA: Making it bigger — this space bubble.

VICTORIA: Fine. Don't call me if you're ever bleeding to death.

PALOMA: Don't call me if you ever get susto. If something traumatic happens to you and your soul leaves your body, I'll just stand here on earth and wave good-bye. Have a good trip!

VICTORIA: Nothing traumatic has ever happened to me. *(Ignoring Paloma, Victoria gazes out the window.)*

PALOMA: You keep looking out the window, but it's like you're not even here. It's like you left your soul in a field two farms back.

VICTORIA: I'm here. I'm here.

PALOMA: You walk this land, you learn things. You got plants that talk to you. Waters that heal when they kiss your skin. And people walking around con el don — the gift — carved into their hands. They don't know it, but it's there.

VICTORIA: You some kind of palm reader or something?

(Paloma shows her own palm to Victoria.)

PALOMA: See, a star. It's proof. I didn't have a choice about who I was going to become.

(Victoria looks at her own palm, discovers a star, and traces it with her finger.)

VICTORIA: That star doesn't mean anything. I've got one of those. Look.

(The sound of the train stopping. Woman enters as the train announcer, late for her announcement. She rubs her eyes as if she just woke up.)

WOMAN: Dos minutos para llegar a la Ciudad de México.

PALOMA: Two minutes? But we're already here. Ay, mi gente.

WOMAN: Señores pasajeros, última parada.

VICTORIA: Wish I could say it's been a pleasure.

(As they shuffle off the train.)

PALOMA: Study your hand. It will show you where to go.

VICTORIA: That star business is a bunch of bull.

PALOMA: That picture you showed me. You as the happy couple? It doesn't tell the whole truth.

VICTORIA: Are you calling me a liar?

PALOMA: You are a woman who is alone in this world.

VICTORIA: I have a fiancé. We're getting married at Mission San José in San Antonio.

PALOMA: You are a woman who is alone in this world and you don't like it very much.

VICTORIA: You're probably just one of those bitter divorced women who wants to infect others with your unhappiness. You've all been trying to ruin my wedding. I just came here to get some peace and quiet.

PALOMA: *(Simultaneously.)* Peace and quiet.

VICTORIA: Don't taunt me.

PALOMA: There's only one problem with the truth. If follows you like a snake.

VICTORIA: Me? A problem with the truth. *(Raising her voice.)* I am the most honest — *(Suddenly self-conscious; people are looking. A hush.)* The most honest person I've ever met. And I've met a lot of people.

PALOMA: I'm sure you have. *(Pointing at the train exit.)* Your exit.

VICTORIA: *(With an edge.)* Good luck crawling on top of that pyramid.

PALOMA: *(Mismatched sincerity.)* Thank you.

(Victoria pushes ahead.)

PALOMA: It's like that with all of us. It's written in our hands. *(Paloma looks at her own hand, touches her star. Lights shift.)*

(Woman, now a hotel clerk, accepts money from Paloma at a hotel reception desk. Victoria enters, frazzled. She does not see Paloma. Paloma occupies herself with her bulging bags. Perhaps one has popped open and she is stuffing the contents back into her suitcase.)

VICTORIA: *(Struggling with her Spanish.)* Perdóneme, Señora. *(A mistake.)* ¿Hay cuartas por noche? Hoy.

WOMAN: *(Correcting her.)* Cuartos. Cuartos.

VICTORIA: *(Frustrated.)* God, I hate this language.

(Woman shoots Victoria a nasty look. She understood that.)

WOMAN: I already rented the last one.

VICTORIA: You're kidding me.

WOMAN: I'm not. We don't have nothing.

VICTORIA: I really need a room. I don't take a lot of space. Don't you have something?

WOMAN: I have a broom closet.

VICTORIA: I'll take it.

WOMAN: That was a joke. *(To herself.)* Muchacha pendeja.

VICTORIA: What are you saying? I really need a place to spend the night. I went to eight hotels already. No rooms.

WOMAN: Do I look like the kind of person that can just snap my fingers, and voilà, there's a room. Do I look like a magician or what?

VICTORIA: What am I supposed to do?

WOMAN: This lady got the last one. Live with it.

VICTORIA: You're right. It's not your problem. It's my problem.

(Paloma turns. Victoria realizes it is Paloma.)

PALOMA: If you're nice, I'll rent you the other bed.

VICTORIA: Christ.

PALOMA: Christ doesn't like it when you say that.

VICTORIA: I just want to be alone.

PALOMA: You don't look like you'd make it on the street, princesa. What do you say?

VICTORIA: *(Without enthusiasm.)* Thanks.

PALOMA: I'll stay out of your hair if you stay out of mine. We can just ignore each other.

WOMAN: Gringas locas. Sharing rooms with people you don't even know. *(To Paloma.)* Don't come crying to me if she robs you blind. First your money, then your man. Cuídate. Some cabrona did it to me. And now I've got to work this maldito trabajo to support my five kids. *(Beat.)* I guess, you don't want to hear about it. Nobody wants to hear about my pinche life.

(Woman shows them to the room and exits. There are two single beds and two nightstands. Stone silence as Paloma and Victoria go about their business, setting up, claiming space without exchanging words. Victoria pulls out

Lysol and Paloma pulls out rose-scented Virgin of Guadalupe spray. Each woman sprays her own side of the room until she turns and sees the other.)
(Paloma hums relentlessly. She whips out her portable altar, installed in an old hard-cover suitcase. Religious candles, crosses, statues of saints — like the Infant of Prague — are all glued into place. This should be a visual gag. Her humming gets louder.)

VICTORIA: Are you going to hum the whole time because that's going to drive me nuts?
(Paloma blesses the space with copal and lights religious candles. She has brought San Antonio, the Virgin de Guadalupe, Don Pedrito Jaramillo and San Martin de Porres. Paloma hums to herself. She kisses Don Pedrito Jaramillo on the forehead. She says the following in a loud whisper as not to disturb Victoria.)

PALOMA: My favorite Saint. *(Fearful that she might have slighted San Antonio, she kisses San Antonio on the forehead.)* Oh, you're my favorite, too. Ah, there's enough love in my heart for the both of you.
(Victoria, on the other hand, takes an obscene number of books out of her suitcase. No clothes.)

VICTORIA: Damn. *(No response.)* I forgot one of my books. I've got a lot of reading to do. It has to be absolutely quiet for me to concentrate. You people know nothing of privacy. Talk to each other through the bathroom door. Read each other's diaries. Can't keep a secret if your lives depended on it. Gossip, gossip, gossip. I hate it. Oh, candles. Candles. You remind me of my grandmother. A candle for this. A candle for that. You think the whole world's going to turn around for the better if you just light a damn candle. Well, it's not. A candle can't do a damn thing. It is not a magical object. Nothing is.

PALOMA: I'm trying to pray.

VICTORIA: Praying isn't going to do a damn thing either. I know. I've tried. I've prayed really hard. Really hard on my knees until they bled and it didn't do a damn thing. It's just all this superstition and bullshit. How did I come from people like you? From bullshit?

PALOMA: Maybe you didn't come from people like me.

VICTORIA: Maybe I didn't. *(Silence falls.)* You're being very quiet, but it's like you're listening. It's like you're hearing everything. And that's what it's like to be in my family. They hear things you don't say and then they act on them. I just wish people would say what they think sometimes. Say what they think. Get it all out there. None of this communication non-communication bullshit.

PALOMA: Where are your clothes?

VICTORIA: What?

PALOMA: You didn't bring any clothes?

VICTORIA: I've got a lot of reading to do. You can pack these things full of clothes and there's no room for the books.

PALOMA: I see.

VICTORIA: I'm not one of those fashion girls. I don't have to look different every morning. I brought a few changes of underwear. I've got good hygiene, all right?

PALOMA: I can't heal right now.

VICTORIA: Right now? How 'bout never?

PALOMA: I can't heal you.

VICTORIA: Well, I think I'll survive. I don't need you. I don't need your strange powers and your hocus pocus.

PALOMA: Didn't your mother teach you respect?

VICTORIA: She did. I don't learn very fast. Facts, I do. It's just the other part, the people part, takes a little longer.

PALOMA: Is that an apology?

VICTORIA: Sort of. Kind of. Supposed to be.

PALOMA: I accept.

VICTORIA: And I came here not to talk to anyone, so let's not talk.

PALOMA: Yeah, I came here for that, too.

VICTORIA: You?

PALOMA: For peace.

VICTORIA: The thing about peace is — when you chase it, it always runs away.

PALOMA: That's the thing about peace.

VICTORIA: And love's like that. And hate.

PALOMA: It all just runs away.

VICTORIA: And I –

PALOMA: I can't heal you right now.

VICTORIA: You said. *(Beat.)* Something really bad happened to me before I came here.

PALOMA: I'm sure you'll get through it.

VICTORIA: I will. Maybe someday I'll be able to tell you — maybe someday I'll be able to tell another living person.

PALOMA: And when that time comes, you'll tell me. When you're ready.

VICTORIA: I will think happy thoughts. I will focus on smiling things. I will make myself forget.

PALOMA: Good.

VICTORIA: Good?

> Once upon a time there was this man and this woman who didn't have much in common, except he reminded her of who she used to be and she made him think of who he could become. And when they met on that path at the crossroads of past and present, which is situated by a very pretty lake, they decided to swap places with each other for a moment. And at this moment of exchanging places, they fell desperately in love. Like a crevice, like a great big hole the earth makes when it splits apart. They fell in there. And when they looked up, they were holding hands because they'd grabbed onto each other to break the fall. And when the woman looked away, she saw the lake. So she took him down by the lake and sat him on the grass. They both knew that this talking and sitting would lead to their first kiss. And she liked him because he seemed scared. He was beautiful but he was scared. And she was so certain of his growing love for her that she promised him that she would kiss him only if he ate the tiny spider that had started to crawl up her arm. She didn't mean it, but he didn't know that, so he did it. *(Victoria is suddenly sad.)* He did that for me. And I kissed him — hmm. *(A hum.)* That was the first time.

PALOMA: With the spider in his mouth? *(Beat.)* Too bad he couldn't come with you.

VICTORIA Yeah. But he comes to Mexico a lot. Some political thing.

PALOMA: You're angry?

VICTORIA: No, I try to understand.

PALOMA: I'm sure you'll come to know him as the years go on.

VICTORIA: *(Defensively.)* I will. He won't hide anything from me. He won't hide his heart.

PALOMA: Nor you from him.

VICTORIA: That's right. We aren't going to be that kind of couple. I refuse it.

PALOMA: *(Self-irony.)* You can't always control what kind of couple you'll become.

VICTORIA: How do you know? You're not even married.

PALOMA: ¿Oh sí?

VICTORIA: You're not the kind of woman that would ever marry.

PALOMA: What kind of woman is that?

VICTORIA: Strong. You are strong. Stronger than me.

PALOMA: *(Hears her, considers.)* You'll be okay. *(Paloma pats Victoria on the back. It is a magical healing moment; something transpires between them even against Paloma's will. Victoria senses something.)*

VICTORIA: What'd you do?

PALOMA: Nothing.

VICTORIA: I felt something.

PALOMA: I thought you didn't believe in me.

VICTORIA: You did something; I felt it.

PALOMA: I wasn't trying to.

VICTORIA: *(Touching her chest.)* Ouch, my heart. Why'd you have to do that? It's making me want to cry.

PALOMA: Be strong, mija. You must look into the past and not be afraid.
(Man, as Jesús, moves onto the stage around Victoria. Victoria breaks into a scene with him. The past.)

VICTORIA: I wish you wouldn't go.

MAN: You know our agreement.

VICTORIA *(Ambivalent.)* Perfect freedom?

MAN: It works. *(Man coughs lightly.)*

VICTORIA: I wish you'd at least quit smoking.

MAN: It's that mother thing again. You've got to stop that.

VICTORIA: I will, after we're married.

MAN: Promises, promises.

VICTORIA: It's just with your asthma.

MAN: *(Beat.)* I'll quit for you. After my next birthday, okay?

VICTORIA: Okay. Kiss me then.

MAN: I'll taste like spiders.

VICTORIA: You've got to forgive me for that. *(They kiss.)* Don't go this time.

MAN: *(Pulls back.)* They're expecting me.

VICTORIA: What are you trying to prove? People know you care.

MAN: Maybe if you went with me. I know you can't, but someday school's gonna end, and I just wonder if you're gonna be up for this.

VICTORIA: *(Unsure.)* I am.

MAN: *(Beat.)* How can you make people better if you don't feel their pain?

VICTORIA: I know what I'm doing.

MAN: Is there anybody you'd die for, Vicky?

VICTORIA: *(Beat.)* I don't know.

MAN: Would you die for me?
(Victoria is unable to answer. Man disappears.)

VICTORIA: *(To Paloma.)* You don't know how hard I tried to understand.

PALOMA: You've got to break yourself open and see what's inside. You've got to peel away some skin, and let someone touch underneath.

VICTORIA: I can't. You know I can't.

PALOMA: It hurts when they touch you, but you know they feel something, too.

VICTORIA: What makes you such an expert on love?

PALOMA: Nothing. I watch people. I sense them, and sometimes I know what they're feeling. My mother when I was a child told me that was a gift, so I watched and watched. Always on the outside, never on the inside. Then, I stepped through that invisible wall I used to guard my heart. I touched under somebody's flesh and let him touch under mine. It hurt. That was a long time ago.

VICTORIA: And you really do that? You let people touch you all the way to your heart?

PALOMA: Something happens when people like us love people like them.

VICTORIA: What happens?

PALOMA: You should get some rest.

VICTORIA: *(Ironically.)* Me? Right.

PALOMA: Why not?

VICTORIA: I don't sleep anymore. Nightmares.

PALOMA: What kind?

VICTORIA: The kind you think about all day. The kind that chew on your stomach and you can't let go.

(Paloma touches Victoria's head.)

PALOMA: I guess, they're there to teach you something. *(Paloma withdraws.)*

VICTORIA: You can't do anything about them anyway. You can't cure anything.

PALOMA: I can, but it isn't time.

VICTORIA: *(Angry.)* What about cancer? Can you cure lung cancer? Can you cure lung in a young person when it's metastasizing out of control?

PALOMA: I don't cure. God cures through me.

VICTORIA: Well, God's asleep or comatose, isn't He?

(Paloma makes a quick sign of the cross.)

PALOMA: Watch your tongue. He might take you away for speaking that way about Him.

VICTORIA: He can have me.

PALOMA: You want to die?

VICTORIA: I don't want to feel love anymore.

PALOMA: But you love your fiancé.

VICTORIA: Right. I love him. *(Beat.)* I wish he were here. Mexico City. He would like this. All of it.

PALOMA: *(Beat.)* Maybe he can come someday.

VICTORIA: Maybe.

PALOMA: Maybe for your honeymoon.

VICTORIA: He'll probably want to go to southern Mexico again. He was very upset that I didn't have time to go with him.

PALOMA: What's there?

VICTORIA: Indians. That's the way he is. He can't just go somewhere for fun. He has to have a reason — he has to chase a cause.

PALOMA: He believes with his heart.

VICTORIA: He just wants people to admire him. He would die, you know. He would die for the people down there if somebody'd let him. *(Light laugh.)* I don't know why I love him, but I do. *(Beat.)* I always tell him, if you don't shut up, I'm gonna nail you to a crucifix, so you can know what the real Jesús felt like.

PALOMA: You're in love with a martyr.

VICTORIA: Can we shut up about my heart already? It's starting to beat harder and I don't like that feeling.

(Lights change and light up the codex. Paloma and Victoria are tourists, visiting the Museo Nacional de Antropologia e Historia, the National Anthropological Museum, the site of the ancient codex. Victoria leads the way.)

VICTORIA: What the hell time is it? I'm on vacation.

PALOMA: We had to get here first. They say you could spend your entire life trying to see the whole thing.

VICTORIA: Yeah, right. *(They step further into the museum.)* This place is huge.

PALOMA: Where shall we start?

VICTORIA: Do they have a café or something? Maybe we could get a cappuccino.

PALOMA: You wouldn't need that if you weren't up half the night — reading.

VICTORIA: Did the light bother you?

PALOMA: No, I like sleeping with the lights on. *(Beat.)* Don't you want to look at the art? I thought you were addicted to learning.

VICTORIA: I am.

PALOMA: Prove it.

VICTORIA: It's just this problem I'm trying to solve. It's like an equation or something. Every problem has a solution. That's what makes sense, right? That's the logical thing.

PALOMA: You're such a hostage of everything you know.

VICTORIA: I'm not a hostage.

PALOMA: You're like your own little prison guard — trapped inside your own little brain.

VICTORIA: I'm not my own little prison guard.

PALOMA: The mind wants to fly, be free.

VICTORIA: The mind wants to conquer the truth.

PALOMA: Like Cortez got the Indians. So you came all the way here to connect to your Spanish roots?

VICTORIA: I'm going back to the room.

PALOMA: *(Beat.)* Do what you want. You're on your own.

VICTORIA: Well, since you pulled me away from my reading. Since you compare me to some ruthless killer of the Aztecs. Since you make me feel all warm and cozy like that —

PALOMA: Fine. Stay. I don't care.

VICTORIA: I don't care either.

(Paloma gets instantly entangled in the map.)

PALOMA: *(Looking at the map.)* I don't know why I read these things.

VICTORIA: *(Taking the map.)* Let's try this room. Ancient cultures. Aztecs and stuff.

PALOMA: Are you coming?

(Victoria follows Paloma.)

VICTORIA: You'd never make it back to the hotel on your own. I don't want to get stuck with the bill. In case someone doesn't find you and point you in the right direction.

PALOMA: Suit yourself. *(Paloma anoints herself with a dab of holy water that she stores in a pendant that she wears around her neck. Victoria watches her with disapproval.)*

VICTORIA: What're you doing?

PALOMA: Preparing.

VICTORIA: You're embarrassing me.

PALOMA: Okay, we can go our separate ways. You go to that side of the room, and I'll go over there.

(Victoria does not seem entirely comfortable with the slight parting. Paloma whips out a bright colored fan and fans herself for emphasis. Victoria goes her own way. While Victoria wanders around looking for something interesting, Paloma finds La Gran Coatlicue. The engraved stone image appears of La Gran Coatlicue.)

PALOMA: ¡Madre Santísima!

(Victoria tries to act disinterested.)

PALOMA: The Grand Coatlicue. Serpent Skirt. Earth Goddess. The Goddess of life and death.

(Fighting her interest, Victoria tries to occupy herself with something else.)

PALOMA: *(Too loudly.)* But she has lost her head. La madre tierra is decapitated.

VICTORIA: Shh!

PALOMA: This isn't a library, a church, or . . .

VICTORIA: I'm looking at a very interesting pole, okay.

(Paloma bows her head in respect. Woman enters as the tour guide. Victoria has taken interest in something else.)

WOMAN: Here, we have the Codex Boturini, an ancient Aztec scroll, depicting the journey of the Aztecs from their homeland in Aztlan to the founding of Tenochtitlan — México City. Painted on paper made from fig bark, we classify this document as a Pre-Columbian Historial Pictography of the Mexica Civilization. And in our next room. *(Woman leaves.)*

VICTORIA: Come here.

PALOMA: No, you come here.

VICTORIA: No, you come here.

(Paloma whips out a sage smudge stick. She smudges herself with sage, taking the smoke in from La Gran Coatlicue. Victoria gestures for Paloma to come over.)

VICTORIA: What's that?

PALOMA: Sage.

VICTORIA: You're not supposed to mess with the artifacts. *(Victoria grabs Paloma by the hand.)* Come over and see this. There're a whole bunch of little angels with wings. *(Victoria leads Paloma to the codex. Paloma and Victoria study the images from the codex. The image of the broken tree appears.)* Do you see anything?

(Paloma looks uneasy, like she wants to flee.)

PALOMA: Let's go.

VICTORIA: You're the one who rousted me out of bed. The least you can do is look at the damn thing.

PALOMA: I've got some other things to do.

VICTORIA: Don't give me that. I want a better look. Here's some barbecued brains. Yum.

PALOMA: You have to respect these things. These ancient things.

VICTORIA: But you want to leave?

PALOMA: Sometimes. Sometimes I do.

VICTORIA: What'd you see?

PALOMA: I saw nothing.

VICTORIA: Look, at this tree. It's broken.

PALOMA: I saw that.

VICTORIA: See, all these people with headdresses. They're silly.
(Paloma has turned away from the codex but Victoria has gotten that much more into it. Seated, Paloma takes deep breaths.)

VICTORIA: Hey, what's this? It's like a hand with leaves for fingers. *(Victoria reads the image of the Malinalca — the twisters.)* It's turning and twisting. *(Victoria sinks to the floor, twisting her hair.)*
(Woman enters and stands behind Paloma.)

WOMAN: *(Warmly.)* Think about it, Paloma. How did your tree break?

PALOMA: *(Beat.)* The wood rotted from the inside out. The wind came and it cracked in two. Dead.

WOMAN: It isn't easy to be your guide.

PALOMA: I imagine that's true.

WOMAN: Truthfully though.

PALOMA: Truthfully.

WOMAN: It takes a lot of strength to break a tree.

PALOMA: It takes a lot of strength to heal a person.

WOMAN: Do you think you know everything?

PALOMA: More than that little girl. I'm not going to heal her.

WOMAN: Once you let yourself feel something you might. It isn't just in the head, you know. You feel it in your body and then you can't —

PALOMA: Help myself? I'm looking at this tree. I've seen a lot, but . . .

WOMAN: Nothing like this?

PALOMA: No, not in me.

WOMAN: When somebody breaks apart a wise old tree, the world stops, because in its broken trunk, there is still life. *(Beat.)* The sap falls to the earth like blood. *(Beat.)* There's a reason to cry. *(Beat.)* There's a reason to mourn the death of a brave and aged tree. *(Beat.)* You know these things. I've taught them to you. *(Woman exits. Man enters as Paloma's husband. A vision where their spirits speak to each other across time.)*

MAN: If you just — if you just —

PALOMA: I'm waiting.

MAN: Needed me more. My God, you're like stone inside.

PALOMA: I'm not. I love people.

MAN: You love the world, but you don't think about us. You go out and fight with spirits, and come back with a bloodied face and scratches this close to your eye. *(Man demonstrates with his fingers how close to her eye he means.)* And here I am, your husband, lying next to you in bed, and I'm not supposed to want to protect you?

PALOMA: You don't have the power.

MAN: You remind me again and again.

PALOMA: I didn't create your spirit.

MAN: You didn't create it, but —

PALOMA: You never finish your sentences.

MAN: You steal my words.

PALOMA: I don't take them. You forget them. *(Beat.)* I just want to know why you did it.

MAN: You destroy me.

PALOMA: I loved you.

MAN: You don't care if you tear me apart.

PALOMA: Why wouldn't I care?

MAN: I don't matter to you.

PALOMA: ¿O . . . no?

MAN: I spend everyday in the same house with you and I don't feel any better. Maybe you're not a curandera.

PALOMA: Maybe you're not my husband. Maybe you're just some vato — some vato who doesn't give a shit.

MAN: You never needed me. It's true.

PALOMA: You're right. I never needed you. *(Beat.)* But, viejo, I chose you.

MAN: Lucky me. Thanks a lot.

PALOMA: You're welcome. *(The silliness of the last exchange cracks Paloma up for a second. Man tries to move in on the moment.)*

MAN: Paloma, you can love me again. I know you can.

PALOMA: *(A burst of disgust.)* Why with her? Just go away. *(She whisks him off. Man transforms into Jesús. Victoria gets up. Vision begins. It spans across worlds, linking the spiritual world and the physical world. Victoria sees him, but she keeps trying to block him out.)*

MAN: *(Calmly.)* Victoria.

VICTORIA: Logic tells me that there is no way you could be here. Logic tells me that when a person dies, they die forever, that's the hard fast truth of our wretched existence.

MAN: *(A little louder.)* Victoria.

VICTORIA: *(Breaking.)* Logic tells me. It tells me things I don't want to believe anymore. That I can't believe.

MAN: *(Louder.)* Victoria.

VICTORIA: *(Beat; to him.)* I break down crying most days. That is, on good days I cry. On bad days I sit in the dark with the lights off. I leave her there. Over there. On the couch, and I hang up in the corner of the ceiling looking down at her. I feel sorry for her, I do, but I'm not her. I can't be her. I can't be a person whose fiancé died. I cannot be that unfortunate person. Bad things don't happen to me. I'm good. I'm smart. *(An example; proudly.)* I could wrap my words around his brain and make him dizzy. That's what I used to do when we fought. Me and my love. That's what I used to do to you.

MAN: You did.

VICTORIA: *(Beat.)* You're not here. You can't be here. I deny your existence. I obliterate you.

(Man just stares at her. It is difficult to deny his presence.)

VICTORIA: I'll speak with you. I will. I won't believe you are real, not until that thing moves inside me — that continental drift — when the world — the worlds shift and reorganize and I realize that I'm somewhere else and somebody else, not the woman who loved you at all, but someone better.

MAN: You had something you wanted to say to me.

VICTORIA: You and your notebook. You and your camera. Did you really think you were going to change the world?

MAN: I thought there was a chance. If we got the right exposure. The right newspaper.

VICTORIA: You are so naïve. You're like a child.

MAN: I love these people. They matter to me.

(Victoria takes offense.)

MAN: Well, you matter to me, too. *(Beat.)* I couldn't foresee the future.

VICTORIA: There's so much they can do nowadays. When they know in time.

MAN: You want to make hope where there is none.

VICTORIA: That spot on your lung was probably nothing when you left for Mexico.

MAN: You don't know that.

VICTORIA: You didn't have to die.

MAN: Didn't you ever wonder about all those meetings I attended?

VICTORIA: I'm a doctor, not a politician.

MAN: You never knew who I was.

VICTORIA: Don't brush me off. Like you never loved me. *(Short beat.)* You hurt me.

MAN: I didn't know you had time to be hurt.

VICTORIA: I had to study all those times. I wanted to be with you. You knew that.

MAN: You think some book's gonna give you the answers — some book's gonna give you the truth.

VICTORIA: I've found a lot of answers in books.

MAN: And I've found lots of answers in earth and air. That's the difference between you and me. *(Man turns, rejecting her.)*

VICTORIA: "Don't go to bed with a grudge." That's what the nuns in the barrio told us.

MAN: I'm surprised you remember anything about the barrio, Dr. Victoria.

VICTORIA: You know I left when I was a kid.

(He starts to leave.)

VICTORIA: Don't go. Don't leave while you're still angry.

MAN: That's how I leave. That's how I left this world. *(He leaves.)*

VICTORIA: Hey, I love you. *(Beat.)* Why do you always have to go away? *(Victoria breaks out of the moment. Paloma looks at the broken tree. Paloma turns. They leave the building.)*

VICTORIA: I hated that.

PALOMA: It's just a scroll.

VICTORIA: It doesn't mean anything.

PALOMA: Well, it does, but . . .

VICTORIA: I forgot. You're superstitious. You don't want to curse the ancients.

PALOMA: I suggest you be careful, too.

VICTORIA: You're right about my fiancé. He's sick.

PALOMA: With what?

VICTORIA: Sick of me. *(Beat.)* No, he's got pneumonia. He'll get over it.

PALOMA: *(She knows more than she is letting on.)* And you just left him in the hospital?

VICTORIA: He told me to go. See, we had to put off the wedding because of that. Just a temporary setback. We'll be back on track soon. *(Uncomfortable silence.)* You don't wear a ring. You never married, huh?

PALOMA: Once.

VICTORIA: Divorced? *(No answer.)* What was he like? *(No answer.)* It must have been miserable.

PALOMA: I'm still married to him.

VICTORIA: For a long time?

PALOMA: Longer than some people's lives.

VICTORIA: What's he like?

PALOMA: *(With a dismissive flick of her hand.)* I don't know. He's just a hus-
band. *(They exit.)*
*(Victoria with swim gear: a large beach umbrella, suntan oil, the works.
Paloma has on a wide-brimmed straw hat and a flowered cotton dress. Vic-
toria has put out two beach towels for them. Paloma moves awkwardly on
the towel. She seems unaccustomed to sunning. Victoria splashes herself with
suntan oil.)*
PALOMA: Why are you using that stuff? You're a Mexican.
(Victoria shrugs.)
PALOMA: Besides, it causes cancer.
VICTORIA: Well, you can cure that, so I guess, I'm okay.
PALOMA: Cancer can kill you.
VICTORIA: Would you stop saying that word? I'm trying to relax.
PALOMA: Your peace and quiet?
(Victoria stretches in the sun.)
VICTORIA: *(Beat.)* I'm glad you wanted to come to Acapulco.
PALOMA: That's what I always say. When I'm a viejita, I will wear floppy
hats and live on the beach.
VICTORIA: You're not an old lady.
PALOMA: My job makes me tired. Wrestling with the spirits.
VICTORIA: Whipping up potions in your cauldron.
PALOMA: *(Staring at Victoria.)* Picking up people that are on the brink of
suicide and giving them enough hope to keep living.
VICTORIA: *(A statement.)* That's what you do for other people.
PALOMA: Yes, other people.
VICTORIA: And yourself?
PALOMA: My life is not my own.
VICTORIA: *(Beat.)* Where's your husband?
PALOMA: He told me to come alone. He's not very traditional.
VICTORIA: Let's go in the water.
*(They come downstage and get their feet wet in the surf. Victoria becomes
mesmerized by something far away.)*
VICTORIA: What a cute little girl.
(Lights shift. Victoria wears a pained expression. It is a magical moment.)
VICTORIA: *(Beat; to herself.)* Oh, little girl, your parents don't love each other
anymore.
PALOMA: *(Beat.)* You saw inside her.
VICTORIA: I don't believe in all that.
PALOMA: *(Beat.)* That scroll we saw yesterday. It has awoken some things.

VICTORIA: Oh, yeah?

PALOMA: You looked inside that child and you saw the future of her heart.

VICTORIA: No.

PALOMA: You have the gift.

VICTORIA: The gift?

PALOMA: You know it's true.

VICTORIA: I don't know about that, but a spirit spoke to me. Today. If I'll only let myself believe it.

PALOMA: It's your journey. I feel it.

VICTORIA: And yours?

PALOMA: *(Beat.)* I did something very, very bad before I left home. Something you won't understand. *(Beat.)* I left. I took all the things I need to heal. It's the only thing I know how to do. *(Self-irony.)* But, you know, you can't always heal yourself. Your heart could be broken in two and there could be nothing you could do about it. That's the joke God plays on you when he gives you the gift. *(Beat.)* I bought that train ticket. I didn't tell my husband where I was going.

VICTORIA: You abandoned him?

(Paloma nods her head.)

PALOMA: I told you, you wouldn't approve.

VICTORIA: That's why there are so many problems in the world. People can't stick to their commitments.

PALOMA: I don't have to explain myself to you.

VICTORIA: Go call him right now.

PALOMA: I can't. I had to leave. He made me go.

VICTORIA: You have to at least let him know where you are.

PALOMA: I didn't even kiss my little boy goodbye.

VICTORIA: You have a little boy?

PALOMA: Four years old. We call him Angel. *(Beat.)* This whole thing's really stupid, but I can't go back.

VICTORIA: Why didn't you tell me? I asked you about your husband. I thought we were friends. You can't do that. You can't abandon your family like that.

PALOMA: I just need to be here — to be away.

VICTORIA: *(A statement.)* You just ran off to Mexico when someone needed you back home.

PALOMA: Aren't you running away, too? From Jesús with the pneumonia?

VICTORIA: I'm gonna call your husband.

PALOMA: *(Beat.)* I gave my husband my heart on a platter and he stuck a knife in it. *(Paloma gives Victoria a cool stare.)*

VICTORIA: *(Nervously.)* Your heart on a platter? Like an Aztec heart sacrifice?

PALOMA: My heart. That didn't need to be given away, I gave to him. And he did not hold it gently in his hands as he had promised.

VICTORIA: Your son's never gonna get over this, and the worst thing is, you don't care. *(Upset, Victoria, grabs her things.)*

PALOMA: I care.

VICTORIA: And your husband. Did you even think about him?

PALOMA: I thought about him. I thought about him all the time.

VICTORIA: What'd he ever do to you?

PALOMA: Nothing. He did nothing for a long time. Have you ever promised someone your whole life and he gave you nothing in return? Not a minute, not a thing. But nothing was okay. I'm strong. I never needed anyone. But then I saw he had something — something to give. But he didn't give that something to me. It's just so ridiculous.

(Woman enters as Aztec Woman. She watches Paloma. Victoria does not see or hear Woman.)

PALOMA: We had a party. For my parents. They'd been married 50 years. Not all of them happy. There were many years where they had nothing, but they had that. They had the marriage. So, I guess, they had something. And he, getting drunk, hanging out with my cousins and my brothers. Never me. *(Beat.)* And him. Well, you see, we had the party by the river, and there were lights hanging, and red and white lanterns from the Chinito store. We had it all made up real pretty for my mother. She'd always dreamed of a fancy 50th anniversary party with lots of lights and Mexican food. And he, laughing with my brothers, roughhousing with the men, and it's later, and there's music. Romantic music. And I don't care about him. I don't dream of dancing with him. My husband. Not anymore. I learned to run that love out of my heart long ago. And I turn, and out by the river. He's there. And he's not there with my brothers or my crazy cousins. He's there with my sister, giving her the sweetest kiss. And later, he says, he was drunk, he didn't know what he was doing, he thought she was me. And I'm supposed to believe him, like all those times, in the early days, when he'd tell me things, and I'd let him break my heart. *(Paloma rustles the air in front of her face, perhaps brushing away some internal tears. The tree changes hue.)*

WOMAN: If someone could put back together that three-hundred-year-old tree, the dead would dance in heaven with joy.

PALOMA: But it's already broken.

WOMAN: If you close your eyes, you will see inside its soul.

(Paloma resists closing her eyes.)

WOMAN: Close them. *(Woman brushes her hand down Paloma's face, closing her eyes.)*

WOMAN: In its veins runs a story, a story that only you and your husband know.

PALOMA: Nuestra historia.

WOMAN: It's worth saving.

PALOMA: I'd rather forget.

WOMAN: *(Softly.)* Don't lie. *(Beat.)* If you put back together that three-hundred-year-old tree, you will know to reach into somebody's body, how to peel open his chest until you hold, in your hands, his human heart. This is as our Aztec ancestors did before us, the curanderos of the past, the serpents of the clouds. *(Long beat. A spiritual phone call. On some level, Paloma has reached her husband's soul. Man enters as husband. He answers.)*

MAN: ¿Bueno?

(Paloma turns as if she has hung up. Victoria and Woman watch on.)

MAN: Paloma?

PALOMA: Not yet.

(Woman grabs Paloma's hand. She motions for Paloma to grab Victoria's hand. She does.)

PALOMA: Where are you taking us?

WOMAN: Far inside México. That country called the bellybutton of the moon.

(End of Act One.)

ACT TWO

Paloma and Woman stand behind the scrim. Victoria is gone.

PALOMA: Where's Victoria? What'd you do with her?

WOMAN: Like rings in a tree, Paloma. This bellybutton contains all. Past. Present. Future. Hell and heaven.

PALOMA: And the way out?

WOMAN: Go further in. Delve deeply into her core. And when she sees fit, México will spit you out.

(They exit. Lights shift. Victoria has found her way far inside the bellybutton of the moon to Mictlan — the realm of the ancient dead. Man enters as Jesús. They breathe heavily like they have been running.)

VICTORIA: *(Happy.)* See, I have this theory. About cancer. It's really a very simple solution. That's why no one's found it. Too easy. I'm right, Jesús. I'm right.

MAN: You can stop trying to save me.

VICTORIA: If I get this last bit of information, I'll have it.

MAN: I want my ring back.

VICTORIA: *(Beat.)* You want to break up?

MAN: You need to go back.

VICTORIA: Back where?

MAN: You aren't where you think you are.

VICTORIA: In my hotel?

MAN: You're not there. I mean, your soul isn't.

VICTORIA: Then where is it?

MAN: It followed me.

VICTORIA: To where?

MAN: To Mictlan. The realm of the ancient dead.

VICTORIA: *(Smiling; in disbelief.)* What kind of nightmare is this? My soul's not with the ancient dead.

MAN: It left your body in your grief. You cried it out through your tears, and then it found its way to me.

VICTORIA: *(To herself.)* Wake up, Victoria. Wake up.

MAN: *(As his urgency turns to sadness.)* Give me our ring.

VICTORIA: *(Saddened.)* I know you want me to, but I just can't. *(Victoria protects her left hand, afraid.)*

MAN: When you pass back through to the other side, you'll cross a valley of obsidian knives, slashing in the wind. Those knives will tear at your face, your arms, your lungs. You'll have to walk through there.

VICTORIA: I can do that. Knives don't scare me. Death doesn't.

MAN: I know. But your death scares me.

VICTORIA: *(Smiling.)* I won't die.

MAN: You're closer to death than you think.

VICTORIA: I'm gonna try something else first.

MAN: Please give me the ring and let me go.

VICTORIA: *(Harried.)* Just let me try one more thing.

MAN: *(Yells; he is fighting for her life.)* No.

(Victoria turns. Man disappears. Paloma appears in the bellybutton of the moon. Man transforms into husband.)

MAN: Paloma.

PALOMA: What you meant to say is that you wished you loved me — you would like to have loved me someday. What you meant to say is something different than what you said.

MAN: Where are you?

PALOMA: That place where my soul talks to yours. Will you listen?

MAN: Are you gonna come home?

PALOMA: I don't know. Do I have anything to come home to or are you still doing my sister?

MAN: It was just a kiss.

PALOMA: Yeah.

MAN: Hey, it was dark. I didn't realize what I was doing.

PALOMA: That's bullshit.

MAN: *(Sincere; he breaks.)* It is. *(Beat; sincere.)* Did I ever tell you that you're the most beautiful woman I've ever seen?

(Paloma fights the fact that he moves her.)

PALOMA: *(Covering.)* Don't try to sweeten me up.

MAN: It's how I feel.

PALOMA: I'm sure you don't lie to me anymore than you lie to yourself.

MAN: I'm not lying now.

PALOMA: You said you'd love me for all the days of your life. I suppose that was the truth, too. I suppose you can love many people at one time. I suppose there's so much love in your heart that there's no place to put it all.

MAN: *(Beat; the truth.)* Sometimes. Sometimes that's true. I don't know where to put it all.

PALOMA: You're pathetic.

MAN: Am I?

PALOMA: I just want your honest love.

MAN: I want yours.

PALOMA: You have mine.

MAN: How much love do you have left for me? When your life's so cluttered with sick people, seeking a cure, seeking your strength, grabbing your hand, kissing your cheek, falling down before you in adoration. Just to have you lift them up and say, "No, mijo. It's not me who heals, it's God." *(Beat; hurt.)* And here I am, broken inside, and you won't heal me.

PALOMA: Is that my job? To be your nurse? To take care of you?

MAN: You're right. It's not your job. It's my job.

PALOMA: It is.

MAN: *(Honest.)* I know it is. *(Beat.)* You hurt me. I know you never meant to but you did.

PALOMA: Don't switch this thing around on me.

MAN: Look, I'm just trying to tell you how I feel. Before you leave. *(Beat.)* Every day I wait for you. I sit there on the couch — okay, and sometimes I have a beer and watch the Cowboys. Is that so bad? I sit there while you disappear into your little room with the candles. You disappear in there. Away from me. The door opens and shuts all day long, but you never look out to see if I'm still there. *(Loud.)* Because you know I am.

MAN: They come from morning until night — the sick, the wounded, the brokenhearted. And they leave our house, content, and usually that makes me happy, but I still wait.

PALOMA: You're free to leave.

MAN: Healing makes you tired, you say, so your cousin cooks for us. Your cousin answers the phone. She even pays our bills. You have her watch our son. I'd like to cook for you sometime, write some checks, and God knows, I'd like you to trust me with our child, but you never think to let me. I don't suppose you think a man could cook or understand finances. And how could a man love a child? Is that what you think?

PALOMA: *(Lightly.)* I know you love him.

MAN: I love him so much. I love you both so much. Can't you all see this love burning inside me? *(Beat.)* Am I such a disappointment to you? *(Beat.)* That love scorched me from the inside out. I couldn't stand to keep it inside anymore. *(Strong.)* Sometimes, I drink, and bury it under my skin because you won't take it from me. But there's too much. Do you understand? There's still too much goddamn love. It has to go somewhere.

It has to catch something. Someone. *(Pained.)* 'Cause I am worth it, Paloma. *(Loud.)* I'm worth it.

That night, at your parents' anniversary party, I kept thinking about fifty years. Our fifty years. I asked myself if in fifty years you would still reject my love — my touch? I thought yes, you would. You would waste the one thing I know how to give. *(A hush.)* That's how you destroy me.

(Beat.) I looked to give it to you that night. Do you remember? When I tried to touch you during that song they played for our wedding? But you brushed me aside like I didn't matter. You ran over me with a glance, a brush of your hand, a flick of your finger. *(Stronger.)* I am your husband.

(Beat.) That night, there wasn't enough beer in the world to make me forget how I feel. *(Laughs.)* And the Cowboys lost. *(Real.)* And I was lost. *(Beat.)* I didn't love her. I don't even know how I convinced myself to do it.

Do you understand me? I've promised my life to you, but it seems you don't want it. I can't convince you to look my way with kindness in your heart, or to give me your affection in a kiss.

That affection I see you pour out onto the world all day long. Do you know what I settle for? *(Pain.)* I drink your love in through the eyes of strangers as they pass me when they leave.

(A moment where they just stand looking at each other, paralyzed by Man's revelation.)

PALOMA: *(Long beat.)* I'm sorry. *(Paloma turns her back to him.)*

MAN: Don't go.

PALOMA: *(Huge beat; sadly.)* I have to — I have to go. *(Paloma crosses to Victoria. They are in the hotel room. Victoria looks frazzled as if she has been up all night and she is losing it. She takes copious notes, writing furiously into a red notebook, surrounded by open books. Every once in awhile she underlines something in one of her books, and then writes it into her notebook. She moves quickly and erratically. Nothing makes sense.)*

PALOMA: What are you doing?

VICTORIA: Trying to find the cure for cancer.

(Paloma picks up one of the books. Victoria snatches the book out of Paloma's hand.)

VICTORIA: *(Shaky.)* The cure for cancer is not that hard.

(Paloma blesses Victoria on the forehead with holy water.)

VICTORIA: What's that?

PALOMA: You're shaky.

VICTORIA: Get that stuff away from me. *(Victoria intersects the water with her hand. She stops. She thinks, reconsiders her method.)* The answer's not in books. That's what he said. The answer's in earth and air. *(Frustrated.)* I don't remember. I've got to try something else. I've got to do something better.

PALOMA: Cálmate.

VICTORIA: *(Upset.)* No. I will not calm down. I will not just dull myself and forget about him. Like you all want me to. *(Quick beat.)* Haven't you ever been in love? *(Victoria hastily tries to find another solution. She finds her scalpel. She drains the blood out of her arm.)*

PALOMA: What're you doing?

VICTORIA: Giving him my blood.

PALOMA: Stop.

VICTORIA: *(Harried.)* See, the good blood can blot out the bad blood if you just say the right prayer, or do the right thing; it can make all the bad blood go away.

PALOMA: You misunderstand the meaning of a sacrifice. Your blood will not bring him back.

VICTORIA: What else is there for me to do? You told me the gods understand a sacrifice.

PALOMA: See, what a mess you've made.

VICTORIA: They listen to a sacrifice.

(Paloma lifts up Victoria's weak arm over Victoria's head to stop the bleeding.)

PALOMA: Your blood's everywhere.

VICTORIA: I'm just trying to make up my own thing because everything they try doesn't work.

PALOMA: Doctors don't know everything.

VICTORIA: They know a lot. I *believed* in them. But it's starting to feel like it's not going to work. And I don't know what happens to me if he dies in the end. *(Victoria pulls away from Paloma and pushes more blood out of her arm.)*

PALOMA: Stop.

VICTORIA: If I'm such a powerful curandera in training, the gods should take this from me.

PALOMA: Here, let me. *(Paloma tries to take Victoria's arm away; Victoria swings back.)*

VICTORIA: *(Getting irrational and vulnerable.)* See, I talked to him. On the phone. He wants to break up. I don't want to break up. I love him. *(Paloma takes Victoria's arm, holds it. She moves a crystal over the arm.)*

PALOMA: You have to concentrate for this to work.

VICTORIA: He wants his ring back. He wants me to let go of him, but I can't. Do you understand? I just can't.

PALOMA: You're bleeding all over the place.

VICTORIA: He wants things to be different.

PALOMA: You look white as a ghost.

VICTORIA: He's trying to change our agreement, but I won't let him.

PALOMA: You're bleeding all over the place.

VICTORIA: He can't do this to us.

PALOMA: You only have so much blood.

VICTORIA: You're frightening me.

PALOMA: *(A hush.)* You're frightening me.

VICTORIA: *(Frantic.)* Am I leaving this body? Did I already leave like he said? *(Really upset.)* Does anyone know where my soul went?

PALOMA: You've got to take your soul back to live.

VICTORIA: I won't die.

PALOMA: *(Almost crying.)* You know you will.

VICTORIA: *(Crying.)* He abandoned me. Just like your husband abandoned you when he did that thing.

PALOMA: Your love didn't abandon you.

VICTORIA: He's gone. Same thing.

PALOMA: *(Beat.)* I will heal you. Do you believe me?

VICTORIA: Yes.

(Paloma puts her arms around Victoria.)

PALOMA: Breathe. Think hard about your soul. You can't stay long on earth without it. And I promise you, this world would miss you if you were gone.

(Woman enters as Aztec Woman. She freezes Victoria who holds the knife.)

WOMAN: Are you going to heal her?

PALOMA: I feel it in my body now. I'm ready.

WOMAN: You can't this time.

PALOMA: *(A long beat.)* I have to heal myself and let myself love?

WOMAN: I've taught you well. *(Long beat.)* Her susto could lead to death.

PALOMA: I know.

WOMAN: *(Beat.)* I will keep her in this moment, but you must be willing to let yourself change. Are you?

(Paloma looks worried. This sounds hard to do.)

PALOMA: I don't know.

WOMAN: The spirits will lead. Like they have before. Ask us, Paloma, we will help you.

(Man enters as Paloma's husband. They are in the bellybutton of the moon.)

MAN: Hello, Paloma.

PALOMA: Hello, Husband.

MAN: I want to talk.

PALOMA: Yeah?

MAN: *(Gently.)* Tell me where you are.

PALOMA: *(Playful.)* It's a secret.

MAN: Forever?

PALOMA: For as long as I need it to be.

MAN: *(Sincerely.)* If I knew how to start over, I'd give you that.

PALOMA: You would? *(Paloma resists Man emotionally, but he moves her. He does not realize he has touched her.)*

MAN: *(Beat; hurt.)* You can heal anything, Paloma. Why don't you heal us?

PALOMA: I don't have the power.

MAN: *(Long beat; maybe grasping at his hair.)* It's too late, isn't it? I've done too much wrong and you can't forgive me. *(He touches her tenderly. She has her back to him. Beat.)* Shall I let you go? *(A moment where it seems like Paloma will leave. Long beat.)* They say when you love someone, you should be willing to do that.

(Paloma does not turn around. She starts to leave.)

MAN: Adiós, mi esposa. Te quiero.

(Paloma moves to another space.)

MAN: *(Broken.)* I love you with all my heart. *(Husband exits.)*

PALOMA: *(Beat.)* You talk about *your* heart, but my heart's missing in action. My heart just disappeared. Like my big brother who went to Viet
Nam and never came back. *(Beat.)* If it's true that you love me, my husband, the spirits will show me in a dream.

*(Woman enters as Dream Woman and induces Paloma into a dream from
which she quickly rises.)*

PALOMA: Help, I misplaced my heart. Someone did something with it.

WOMAN: Who stole it?

PALOMA: I don't know.

WOMAN: What does it look like?

PALOMA: I'm not sure. *(Remembering.)* It's got a knife in it.

WOMAN: Is it still beating?

PALOMA: Hurry. Someone send out a search party to look for my heart.

(Woman puts on her search party gear, a miner's hat with a light on it.)

WOMAN: I will. I'll head the search party. *(Woman flips the light on.)*

PALOMA: You gonna look?

WOMAN: Do you think it's buried somewhere?

PALOMA: Buried?

WOMAN: Deep in the ground where it can't be seen.

PALOMA: It's an emergency. I have to find it. Por favor.

WOMAN: Buried somewhere.

PALOMA: You mean buried alive?

WOMAN: *(Beat.)* If you search hard enough, you'll find it.

PALOMA: I will? *(Paloma looks up and down, nowhere near herself.)*

WOMAN: You know where it is.

(Paloma shakes her head as if she does not know where it is. Beat. Paloma peels some layers away from her chest. She takes in a deep breath and bravely scoops her hand as if to get her heart out of her chest.)

PALOMA: I found my heart.

WOMAN: You found it.

PALOMA: *(To her heart.)* Ay, Dios mío, I was worried about you. *(Beat.)* What happened to the knife?

WOMAN: It's gone. *(The Woman points to a place on the heart.)*

PALOMA: *(Emotional; still disbelieving.)* That's my heart?

WOMAN: It's yours.

(Paloma cradles her heart, relieved. She feels something underneath the heart.)

PALOMA: Mira, what's this back here? There's something stuck to it.

WOMAN: That's his heart. Your husband's.

(Paloma lifts it up to get a better look.)

PALOMA: *(With childlike awe.)* It's so large. I had no idea. *(Beat.)* And he loves me with this?

WOMAN: All of it. Like he said.

PALOMA: My husband. He has a beautiful heart. *(Paloma lifts both their hearts up, and then cradles them against her chest. Woman exits. Man enters as Paloma's husband.)*

MAN: You're a powerful woman.

PALOMA: And you're a powerful man.

MAN: *(Smiles.)* Don't steal my compliments.

PALOMA: Love is a very powerful thing. *(Paloma holds his heart.)* This is yours. *(Paloma presses Man's heart back into his chest where it belongs. He takes it in, inhaling, as if he were swallowing her love into himself. A beat. She begins to put her heart back into her own chest.)*

MAN: Wait.

(Paloma stops. She hesitates, covering her heart with her hand. He gazes at her. She removes her hand.)

MAN: Did I ever tell you? You have the most beautiful heart I've ever seen.

(Paloma smiles. She starts pressing her heart in again. He stops her hand. Man gives her heart the sweetest kiss. She lets him press it into her chest, inhaling as well. She sighs when he has completed putting it back. Man steps closer to her. They give each other a long, long embrace, heart against heart. They step back gazing at each other, holding hands.)

MAN: Your heart wants to heal somebody. I better let you go.

PALOMA: You understand my heart now?

MAN: When I touched it, I knew. Go ahead.

(Paloma steps away, looks back, lingers for a moment.)

MAN: Go.

(Paloma props Victoria up, sitting with her back to Victoria on the bed. Paloma links their arms together. Victoria begins speaking groggily, as if drugged, but comes out of it.)

PALOMA: Why did you start bleeding yourself?

VICTORIA: It's my fiancé.

PALOMA: With the pneumonia?

VICTORIA: Lung cancer.

PALOMA: Oh.

VICTORIA: The doctor said he had five months. He didn't have five months. He's dead.

PALOMA: *(Simultaneously.)* He's dead.

VICTORIA: I guess you already knew that. Dead and gone.

PALOMA: *(Beat.)* He loved you. He never tried to break up with you.

VICTORIA: I'd do anything to have any part of him now. That's why I keep this ring, but it's not enough. I want more. I want him. And last night. In my sleep. He came asking for my ring. Tell me. What's he gonna do with it in heaven?

(Paloma starts to turn toward Victoria to comfort her. Victoria keeps giving her her back.)

PALOMA: What do you want me to do?

VICTORIA: Bring him back. Conjure him up with a spell or something.

PALOMA: I thought you didn't believe in my magic.

VICTORIA: I do now.

PALOMA: And your own?

VICTORIA: Not without a prescription.

PALOMA: *(Beat.)* I can't bring him back. Nobody can.

VICTORIA: I don't think people should die young, do you?

PALOMA: I think they should die when they're supposed to die, and we shouldn't question it.

VICTORIA: I question it — I challenge it every day. I have saved people that were supposed to be dead. In the emergency room I did.

PALOMA: I believe you.

VICTORIA: And it felt great, and when he got sick, I thought, I'll save him, too. I know how to do this. I'm a doctor with a spanking new medical degree. Top of my class. I can lick this thing. *(Beat.)* He wasted away, did I tell you? Not a graceful death. Not a beautiful death. Not a death that was meant to be.

PALOMA: Let him go.

VICTORIA: How?

PALOMA: Let it burn. Walk into a fire and burn everything to the ground. Everything you are. Everything you were. Everything you thought you might become.

VICTORIA: Like his wife?

PALOMA: You burn it to the ground and let it become something new. The Aztecs taught us fire doesn't only destroy, it creates. Do this, and then you might be able to start living again.

VICTORIA: Do you know how to do all that?

PALOMA: I did something just like that today. And I found my heart again.

VICTORIA: I have to go.

PALOMA: *(Simultaneously.)* You have to go.

(Victoria does not even see Paloma exit as Man enters. He is Jesús.)

VICTORIA: Are you still angry with me?

MAN: It was never anger.

VICTORIA: I'm studying things. For you. *(Quick beat.)* In memory of you. Maybe I can save someone else. I just wanted to make you better.

MAN: I wanted to make the world better, but I didn't.

VICTORIA: *(Long beat; soft.)* How can you be dead when I still love you? *(They grasp hands.)*

MAN: *(Beat.)* I always thought you would come with me. I always dreamed you'd be my compañera.

VICTORIA: I wanted to come with you, I did. I want to come with you now.

MAN: *(A fantasy.)* We would negotiate jungles together with our machetes, our ponytails behind us, blowing in the wind. And every once in awhile, we'd forget who was chasing us, and wrap ourselves around each other like vines. And with the air so thick and wet in that tropical place, your sweat would meld with mine, and trickle down our bodies in a tiny stream.

(Laughs at himself.) Silly dreams. Stupid dreams. Dreams that don't amount to much.

VICTORIA: Please, let me come with you.

MAN: *(Beat.)* Love doesn't end with death. It's the only thing that doesn't.

VICTORIA: I'm going to cure cancer.

MAN: If anyone can, you will.

VICTORIA: You've got faith in me.

MAN: I've got faith. *(Man reaches into Victoria's backpack and pulls out a manila envelope. He hands it to Victoria.)*

VICTORIA: What's that?

MAN: I left these in your backpack for you.

VICTORIA: You did? I never found them. *(Ironically.)* I'm — a pendeja.

MAN: No, you're not. *(Beat.)* Pictures of my trip to México. Taped interviews with the people there. I want you just to hold these from time to time. And maybe when you're in your car — the tapes. You can hear my voice. If you want to listen. They're in Spanish, but . . .

VICTORIA: *(Firm.)* I'll learn. *(Victoria breaks into the envelope; shuffles through the pictures. Man looks over her shoulder as she looks at the pictures. It is intimate — close.)* They're wonderful. The colors. *(Victoria notices something in the pictures. She shuffles through them quickly, trying to confirm her suspicion.)*

VICTORIA: *(Realizing.)* These pictures are all of children, Jesús.

MAN: *(Beat.)* Something happened to me when I went far into México. *(Short beat.)* I went there looking for revolutionaries with Indian faces — but I found their children instead. *(Man gets sad. Perhaps, he wishes he could have done more.)*

VICTORIA: *(Short beat; slowly.)* You never wanted children. *(Quoting him; enjoying it.)* "The world is overpopulated, so I'm not having any." *(Laughs to herself.)*

MAN: I said that?

VICTORIA: You did.

MAN: *(A smile.)* I used to think I was pretty smart.

VICTORIA: *(Beat.)* That stuff I told you. About not wanting kids because of my career. That wasn't true. I only said that because I thought that's what you wanted.

(Man sighs.)

VICTORIA: *(Beat.)* I would like to have had —

MAN: *(Gently.)* Don't say it. *(Man puts his finger over Victoria's mouth, so she will not say a word. She breaks away.)*

VICTORIA: *(Finishing; slowly.)* Your children. *(Beat.)* I won't let your dreams die with you, Jesús. I'll learn the map — the roads — of México like the lines in my hand. I'll spread whatever truth I find in the world. No matter how hideous. I'll do that for you. *(Short beat.)* It's funny. All those times, watching you, admiring you from afar, I never dreamed there was part of you inside me.

(He touches her.)

MAN: I found my way inside there.

VICTORIA: You are — in me. You know. When you feel that way. When your feelings rustle inside you like leaves. That's how you always made me feel. Still do. *(Beat.)* You're not coming back, are you? *(Silence.)*

(Long beat; new urgency like she is trying to save him again.) If you really want something, and you're part of a certain people, part of a certain tribe, you give something up. I've been giving you blood.

MAN: But you've got to stop.

VICTORIA: I want to let it keep going, flow out of me, maybe find it's way through the ground into your ashes to give you life. *(Beat.)* I can see *you.* In a healed new body, breaking out of the earth like a fresh blade of grass. I whisk the dirt away from your face and kiss you. Your beard pricks my lip. You are my love.

(Man shakes his head no.)

VICTORIA: Are we saying good-bye?

MAN: You need to let yourself love a living person someday. Don't die with me. Promise. *(Beat.)* Will you let somebody heal you?

VICTORIA: *(A grin.)* Don't tell me you're a curandero, too. *(Victoria laughs. Tension breaks. Man takes her hand. Victoria starts to speak. He places one finger gently over her mouth.)* Just kiss me good-bye. That's all I ask. Just one kiss.

(Man shakes his head no. Man moves his hand up the ring finger of her left hand.)

VICTORIA: I'm not giving that to you. It was a gift.

(Man strokes her face. Beat as she tears up. Man moves his hand gently on hers as she lets him release the ring. He slowly releases her hand. Although we can still see Man, it seems Victoria no longer can. She does not seem to be able to see or hear Paloma either. Victoria wrings her hands. After a long silence, Man stops, looks back, watches her. Then, he slowly disappears. Victoria remains completely alone.)

VICTORIA: Paloma. Paloma!

(Paloma does not come. Victoria cannot see her. Victoria crumples to the

ground. It appears that she is dead. Paloma enters, carrying a white sheet, distraught to find Victoria in this condition. She hurriedly moves Victoria's limp arms until they make a cross in an outstretched position and tries to do her magic. She fluffs the sheet into the air and lays it down on Victoria's body, covering her completely. Paloma burns copal and herbs. Paloma sweeps Victoria, in the sign of a cross, using a large navel orange. As she sweeps, she recites her version of the Apostles' Creed.)

PALOMA: Creo en Dios, Padre Todopoderoso. I believe in God, the Father Almighty, Creator of heaven and earth.

WOMAN: We believe in the gods, the fathers and the mothers, the creators of the heavens and of the earth, of the rivers that run until they spill into the sea.

PALOMA: And the trees that live for hundreds of years and reach their arms up through the clouds, of the oceans that flow from the sun onto the beach to touch our feet, of all these things that have no end. We ask that you see our daughter, Victoria. We ask that you return her soul to her body, so she may stay here on earth.

WOMAN: *(Simultaneously.)* That you return her soul to her body, so she may stay here on earth.

PALOMA: Amén.

WOMAN: Amén. *(Woman lays her hand on Paloma. A transfer of power. Woman exits. A beat.)*

PALOMA: *(To Victoria.)* Vente. No te quedes allí. Come back. Don't stay over there. *(Paloma claps once loudly with arms outstretched and cupped hands. This calls Victoria's soul back to earth.)* Victoria! *(Paloma flips the sheet off Victoria's body as she rises up. A magical moment.)*

VICTORIA: Aquí vengo. Mi alma ha regresado a la tierra. *(Beat; Excited.)* I spoke Spanish. *(Short beat.)* I'm here. My soul came back to earth.

PALOMA: You are going to become a serpent. And you will slither through the clouds.
(Although Paloma has not exited, Victoria cannot see her. Victoria looks ahead, sees a vision. Victoria can clearly see into the spiritual realm.)
(The sound of romantic Mexican music.)

VICTORIA: You got back together with your husband.

PALOMA: You saw inside me.

VICTORIA: *(Excited.)* I can see right into both of you — through the spirit world into your hearts.

PALOMA: *(To Victoria.)* In this world there are many things that will rip us apart. Men and women. Healing comes when we come back together.

No matter how much it hurts. And I promise you, it will hurt. It will incinerate your hearts, but healing comes.

(Victoria touches her own heart. Paloma senses Victoria's pain.)

VICTORIA: *(Beat.)* He took his ring.

PALOMA: *(Short beat.)* Our dead are always with us, Victoria. *(Beat.)* Consider him a martyr to your heart.

VICTORIA: Jesús would have liked that. He would have liked to have died for something.

PALOMA: That would be you, mija. *(Beat.)* He died so that you could love. Your love will heal the world. *(Paloma looks at own hand, places it on Victoria's shoulder to give Victoria power. A serpent appears.)*

(Victoria traces the star on her hand with her finger. She raises her hand into the air. Victoria has el don, the gift of healing.)

END OF PLAY

Waiting to Be Invited

By S.M. Shephard-Massat

Based on a true situation taken from the life of my grandmother,
Mrs. Louise Sims, to whom this is dedicated.

To "Muddie,"
Much love always
And forever
From earth to heaven
Take care of the girls
"Your Oldest Gran',"

S.M. Shephard-Massat
1995

ORIGINAL PRODUCTION

Originally staged in reader's theatre format by Karamu Performing Arts Theatre, Cleveland, OH, 1996

Originally produced at the Denver Center Theatre Company, a division of the Denver Center for the Performing Arts, A U.S. West World Premiere.
ORIGINAL CAST:

MS. LOUISE . . . . Lynette Dupree
MS. ODESSA . . . . Ebony JoAnn
MS. DELORES . . . . Candi Brown
MS. RUTH . . . . Michelle Shay
MS. GRAYSON . . . . Jane Welsh
PALMEROY BATEMAN . . . . Keith Hatten

ABOUT THE AUTHOR

S.M. Shephard-Massat *(playwright)* attended New York University's Tisch School for the Arts as a dramatic writing major, and spent a year in London interning at the Royal Court Theatre. She has worked with several small American film and theater companies. Her play, *Waiting to be Invited* first became an ARENAFEST finalist at Karamu House in Cleveland, OH. On the strength of this play, Shephard-Massat was chosen to receive the Young Dramatist's Award from the Adrienne Kennedy Society, the Connections Award for Best Original Play/1997 from the Delaware Theatre Company in Dover, DE, became a Roger L. Stevens Award recipient/1999 given by the John F. Kennedy Center in Washington, DC, received the Westword Best of Denver 2000 Award for Best New Play/Denver, CO., and received the Osborn Award from the American Theatre Critics Association for 2001. *Someplace Soft to Fall* received the Francesca Primus award for 2001 presented by Ms. Sylvie Drake, editor of Applause Magazine/Denver, CO., and the Denver Center Theatre Company.

Ms. Shephard-Massat has also been an invited guest at many theater festivals, including: US West Theatre Fest/Denver Theatre Company, Denver, CO (1999 and 2001); Winter Festival/GeVa Theatre Company, Rochester, NY (2001); and Taking It To The River series/Ensemble Studio Theatre, New York, NY (2001). She has had work featured in staged readings for the New Federal Theatre, New York, NY; Theatre In The Square, Marietta, GA; and Urban Stages Theatre Company, New York.

CHARACTERS

MS. LOUISE: late thirties to early forties; short in stature, black
MS. ODESSA: early to late fifties, black
MS. DELORES: middle to late thirties, black
MS. RUTH: late thirties to early forties; light-complexioned black
PALMEROY BATEMAN: bus driver; middle to late forties, black
MS. GRAYSON: early to late seventies, white

SETTING
Atlanta, Georgia

TIME
Summer 1964

WAITING TO BE INVITED

ACT ONE

Setting: The women's dressing room of the Hornsby Toy Company. The décor has not been changed or attended to since the forties. A good-sized table stands center stage with three chairs surrounding it. Two of the chairs hold cumbersome shopping bags. A fan whirls downstage/left. Ms. Delores and Ms. Louise are changing into their summer white ensembles from their work uniforms now lying on table in front of them. Ms. Louise checks herself in mirror before putting on hat. Ms. Odessa rushes in, carrying two good-sized shopping.

MS. ODESSA: Damn tha' woman! Hot damn 'er time, tha' woman! *(Odessa slams her bags down on table; begins laying out her change of clothing including shoes, hat, etc.)*

MS. ODESSA: She made me mad, tha' woman. Sssshhhooottt, Mizz Hornsby come in 'ere tellin' e'rybody tha' don' wanna listen, talkin' two miles a minute, 'bout 'er ole "choo-choo" train trip to New Orleans. Like we s'-posed to care, right? Like e'rybody's s'posed to jus' laugh, n' carry on wit' 'er about it. She didn't bring me nothin' back. Thought we wann't gon' never git' outta there. *(Odessa begins removing work clothes and shoes.)* *(Louise and Delores zip each other up.)*

MS. ODESSA: *(Mimics.)* Conductor say, anybody tha' can spell Kudzu gets a free lunch. Say she didn't even know how to spell Kudzu. Well, I laughed at tha'. I sho' did. Wha' dummie don't know is wha' I wannit to say.

MS. LOUISE: So, why didn' cha'?

MS. ODESSA: An' wha' the hell do I care 'bout she dun' met some bare-mouth, hunnert n' fifty-year ole goat geezer, in a two-hunnert n'fifty-year ole tweed suit, in three-hunnert degree weather, wunderin' up n' down "choo-choo" train aisles like a ghost, she say, lookin' fo' the res' room, huh? If you made such good friends wit' 'im, you shoulda showed tha' ole man where to go pee. Tha's wha' I said to 'er. *(Stands in front of whirling fan in her slip.)*

MS. DELORES: Tha's wha' chu' tole 'er?

MS. ODESSA: Damn right.

MS. LOUISE: You tole Mizz Hornsby tha'? To 'er face?

MS. ODESSA: I jus' said I did, didn' I? She oughta be ashamed. She ain't but two-three seconds younger n' dirt 'erself.

MS. LOUISE: Fo' somebody tha' wann't innerested, you sho' was pickin' up on a lot a' details 'bout tha' trip.

(*Ms. Odessa begins to dress.*)

MS. ODESSA: Shoot, e'rytime she say somethin' you gotta nod n' smile, nod n' smile, but tha' ole lady don' rang my bell. You can b'lieve tha'. Never has, never will.

MS. LOUISE: She might not rang yo' bell, but she sho' pay yo' sal'ry e'ry week though, don' she?

MS. ODESSA: Awh, Louise, I know wha' cho' problem is. You been sweatin' fo' tha' woman an' 'er fam'ly fo' fifteen years.

MS. LOUISE: So? You were here foe' I was, Dessa.

MS. ODESSA: So, I ain't tryin' ta' like them people. Only job you ever had, though. Bet cha'. I cain't say tha'.

MS. LOUISE: Matter of fact, Dee, this where I met 'er but I guess she dun' fo'got about tha' too, huh?

(*Delores begins gathering her things into shopping bag.*)

MS. ODESSA: I ain't fo'got nothin'. Grits ain't groceries, Louise.

MS. LOUISE: Wha' tha' mean?

MS. ODESSA: I don' choose to owe them crackers crap is wha' tha' mean. They ain't doin' nothin' special fo' me in 'ere. You the one dun' raised one chile into College offa this doll factory, an two mo' on the git'-ready. All my chirruns was raised n' grown when I come in tha' doe.

MS. LOUISE: Don' mean nothin', an' I did so have a job foe' I came to Hornsby, fo' yo' info'mation. (*Places Odessa's hat correctly on her head.*) I wrote the numbers.

MS. DELORES: (*Looks at watch.*) Come on, y'all. Les' go. (*Delores straightens Odessa's dress.*)

(*Ladies gather up their things into shopping bags and exit.*)

(*Set Changes.*)

(*Ladies begin rooting through their purses for change.*)

MS. ODESSA: (*To Delores.*) You sho' Ruth gon' be out there?

MS. DELORES: Yeah, she said she would.

MS. ODESSA: 'Cause I don' intend to wait on nobody.

MS. DELORES: You mean, you don' intend to wait on her. You jus' don' like 'er.

MS. ODESSA: She awright sometimes. She jus' let 'erself git' all hincty. Like 'er stuff don' stink like e'rybody elses' jus' 'cause her husband preach at tha' big ole church y'all go to, an' 'er chirrun sang on Gospel Jubilee Radio e'ry Sunday. You know how she got sta' goin' on . . . *(Mimics.)* "Brotha Peterson said this, n' Brotha Peterson said tha', n' Brotha Peterson said my chirrun got the prettiest voices. Bet tha' ain't how them chirrun got on Gospel Jubilee Radio. Wha' chu' thank?

MS. DELORES: Is tha' nice to say?

MS. ODESSA: I ain't talkin' 'bout chu'.

MS. DELORES: It don' matter. You gon' try to hurt tha' girl's feelins.

MS. ODESSA: Ssshhhooottt, she ain't no girl. Them days is 'way behind 'er, honey. She been 'round the moon twice foe' she got religion. She know wha' time it is an' I ain't talkin' 'bout wha's on a wristwatch neither.

MS. DELORES: You don' know nothin' 'bout Ruth. Ruth is nice. *(Walks away as though spotting something coming.)*
(Stage becomes red surrounding the inside of an express city bus, including the entrance, doorway and steps.)
(Palmeroy Bateman, in bus driver's uniform, is at wheel.)
(Delores flags bus.)
(We hear the usual noontime street noices and the whirling of a small fan located behind Palmeroy's head.)

MS. ODESSA: I know'd Ruth from when she was a teenager hangin' 'roun the ole Eighty-One Club wit' grown men, Dee. She don' want me to speak on wha' I know; truly. Nawh, she don' remember me but I seen 'er in action plenty times. Oh yeah, Mizz Ruth can take care a' 'erself, though.

PALMEROY: Well, well, this mus' be the day, then. I ain't never got ch'all on a Friday afternoon befo'. Awright now.
(Odessa struggles a bit with bags, breathless; picks through change for fare.)

MS. ODESSA: This mus' be yo' lucky day, then.

PALMEROY: Yes, ma'am, my lucky day indeed, Mizz Odessa. Step right up. Step right on up.
(Ms. Odessa boards bus.)

MS. ODESSA: Awright there, Mr. Bateman.

PALMEROY: Limme help ya some. *(Raises up from driver's seat.)*

MS. ODESSA: I got it. *(Puts money in fare slot.)*

PALMEROY: Oh, you ain't got ta put nothin' in tha' slot, Mizz Dessa.

MS. ODESSA: Say I ain't?

PALMEROY: Nawh. . .

MS. ODESSA: Well, the transit folk say I do. *(Odessa sits on long seat facing audience directly behind Palmeroy.)*

PALMEROY: Jus' fo' y'all lookin' so good, gon' be e'rybody's good luck day. Let e'rybody on free jus' 'cause a' y'all.

(Delores begins boarding while struggling with her extra bag and fare.)

MS. ODESSA: Uh-huh, you let e'rybody on 'ere fo' free n' yo' job gon' be free too. Good n' free to the next application.

PALMEROY: Awh, they cain't even beg nobody take a bus job on a hot day like this. *(Wipes his face and neck with a pocket-handkerchief.)*

MS. ODESSA: Plenty people. Hush, now. Too hot fo' all tha' conversatin'. *(Takes handkerchief from purse; dabs herself.)*

PALMEROY: How you, Mizz Dee, on this day so hot chu' could cook a' egg right out there on the sidewalk?

(Delores puts money in slot.)

MS. DELORES: Don' make me no nevermind.

PALMEROY: An' look at chu' all dressed up in the hot heat.

MS. DELORES: Thank you, Palmeroy. I was raised up in the hot heat myself. *(Turns to proceed to seat; stumbles.)*

PALMEROY: Awright, Mizz Dee, don' hurt my bus, now. Watch yo'self.

MS. DELORES: I'm watchin'. *(Takes seat next to Odessa facing her.)*

PALMEROY: Well awright, then. Today mus' be the day n' why not?

(Louise puts her fare into slot; sits directly behind Palmeroy next to Ms. Odessa on long seat.)

PALMEROY: My my, look at chu', Miss Lou. E'rybody gathered up so calm, cool n' crisp. Jus' like a lil' ole bag a' brand new potato chips.

MS. ODESSA: Palmeroy, don' nobody look noway like no bag a' potato chips.

PALMEROY: Yeah, y'all do. I mean, you look fresh. All three of ya.

MS. ODESSA: We jus' changed clothes. Cain't go in 'ere lookin' like any ole thang now, can we?

PALMEROY: You sho' cain't, Mizz Dessa.

MS. LOUISE: How you today, Palmeroy?

PALMEROY: Oh, I do fine so far, Mizz Louise. *(Mops his head with handkerchief; checks rearview.)* Hot enuff fo' ya? *(Prepares to depart.)*

MS. LOUISE: Ooh, it's scorchin' me, Palmeroy. It ain't teasin' out 'ere. *(Fumbles through her bag.)*

PALMEROY: It ain't teasin' out 'ere. I second tha' motion. *(Pulls into traffic; begins to hum.)*

MS. ODESSA: Ooh, ain't it scorchin', Louise? *(Fumbles through her bag.)*

MS. LOUISE: Ummm-hmmm, I'm tellin' you the truth. Glad we didn't have ta wait on you no time, Palmeroy. Did, we'd be three, drippin, black spots fo' sho'.

MS. ODESSA: Yes, Lawd.

(All ladies pull out similar church fans from bags; begin fanning themselves vigorously.)

ALL LADIES/PALMEROY: Yes, Lawd.

MS. ODESSA: An' tha' lil', ole, bitty, piece a' fan thang you got goin', makin' all tha' noise. Cain't nobody feel it but chu', Palmeroy. Tha' ain't fair.

PALMEROY: Ain't doin' me no good neither, Mizz Dessa. Ain't no blessin'.

MS. ODESSA: These ole buses stay broke though, don' they?

MS. LOUISE: Don' they, though?

PALMEROY: Yes, ma'am, they sho' do.

MS. ODESSA: The heat don' hardly work in the winter, an' the cool don' do nothin' in the summertime but blow hot air on ya. Somebody white oughta fall out in the flo' wit' a stroke, or catch the double-pneumonia n' sue the bus com'pny. Tha'd git' tha' fixed up in a hurry . . .

PALMEROY: I call myself openin'. . .

MS. DELORES: Nip it mighty quick.

MS. LOUISE: Ummm-hmmm.

PALMEROY: Up all the windows n' vents foe' I started my route to git' some kinda circulation ciculatin' but, sshhooottt, the cool, it's hot too. Comin' from all the exhaust from all the cars on the road you see, Mizz Dessa. Ole Palmeroy cain't do nothin' 'bout tha', I'm afraid.

MS. ODESSA: I see. I still say, one a' them white folks oughta fall out so *they'll* see.

(Bus stops for black passenger.)

(Palmeroy nods politely.)

PALMEROY: How you? *(Bus pulls off again.)* So, today is it then huh, ladies?

MS. ODESSA: Sho' is.

MS. LOUISE: 'S got to be.

MS. DELORES: 'S now or never, y'all.

MS. ODESSA: Ssshhoottt, one a' them crackers in Marsh's hit me in my head, I'm mad enuff n' bad enuff to take 'em all on today.

PALMEROY: *(Laughs.)* Awright now, Mizz Dessa. *(Checks rearview.)*

MS. ODESSA: Tha's how come I say it like tha'. 'Cause I'm ready.

PALMEROY: Ready. Yes, ma'am, Mizz Dessa. I hear too them at Marsh's, they make a special salad outta lettuce, tomato an' my'naise on Fridays.

MS. LOUISE: Me too.

PALMEROY: You heard tha' too, Mizz Louise?

MS. LOUISE: Ummm-hmmm. From Macy. She cleans up down 'ere some nights.

PALMEROY: Uh-huh, from Mizz Macy. She got the inside scoop, ain't she?

MS. LOUISE: Oh-huh. Don't she, though?

PALMEROY: Awright now, lettuce, tomato n' my'naise salad. Y'all gon' be eatin' good today. *(Laughs.)*

MS. ODESSA: I eat good e'ryday.

MS. LOUISE: We see tha', Ms. Healthy-As-A-Mule Hand.

MS. ODESSA: Dawggone right. I don't need they stink.

MS. LOUISE: *(To Palmeroy.)* Tha' salad to go wit' these 'ere thangs called, Fish Sticks, they serve, Bateman. Fish in sticks, I guess. And they puttin' some kinda dressing on it. She say it's French.

(Dee clutches her chest.)

MS. DELORES: (Sighs deeply.) Ooohhhh . . . French . . .

PALMEROY: *(Nods.)* Um-humph. Um-humph.

MS. DELORES: Mmmmmm, sounds right tasty to me. I luv French seafood.

PALMEROY: All the fish I ever come in contact wit' had a head n' tail attached, Mizz Dee, but say theirs come in sticks. You b'lieve tha'?

MS. DELORES: If they say it, it mus' be so. Les' they be dupin' the public.

MS. LOUISE: Yeah, don' b'lieve e'rything somebody say, Dee.

PALMEROY: Awright now, dupin' the public.

MS. ODESSA: Palmeroy, shut up repeatin' stuff.

PALMEROY: I cain't help it, Mizz Dessa. Y'all 'bout to crack me up.

MS. DELORES: But, how they do it though, I wunder? How they git' reg'lar ole fish to be like a stick, y'all?

MS. LOUISE: I'm sho' I cain't say, myself.

PALMEROY: Me neither, Mizz Dee.

MS. ODESSA: Do it matter?

MS. DELORES: Well, how they eat it, number one?

MS. ODESSA: Knife n' fork, chile. Eatin' is eatin'. Pro'bly ain't nothin' but ole Salmon Croquette anyway. Bet cha'.

MS. DELORES: Dessa, is it finger food is wha' I'm askin'. I jus' don' wanna look like no dummie. Tha's all.

MS. ODESSA: Wha'ever they doin' to the po' fish, it cain't be too hard.

PALMEROY: Listen at chu', Mizz Dessa.

MS. LOUISE: Long as don' taste like some sticks I'll be satisfied.

PALMEROY: I bet cho' bottom dollar might can find 'em in somebody's curb market you look hard enuff. Maybe not cho' corner A & P but somewhere. Pro'bly could fix 'em up jus' as nicely if you tried; an' cheaper too. Wha' chu' thank, Mizz Dessa?

MS. ODESSA: Don' say nothin' ta me.

MS. DELORES: Awh, we jus' goin' in 'ere to exercise our right to be, Palmeroy. I wouldn' care if I didn' eat nothin' at all.

MS. LOUISE: You better care 'cause ain't nobody goin' 'ere to jus' sit now. Tha' ain't the game plan.

MS. ODESSA: They ain't got ta' gimme nothin' but bread n' water. Sssshhhooottt, they can gimme the tablecloth to chew on. I'll sprinkle a lil' salt over it an' pick my teeth afterwards.

MS. LOUISE: Now, tha's the spirit, Dessa.

PALMEROY: *(Laughs.)* Go 'head on, Mizz Odessa.

MS. ODESSA: I sho'ly will. Like I dun' had a seven-course meal.

PALMEROY: They ain't givin' away nothin', tho'. They spit on ya, it'll cost twenty cent apiece.

MS. LOUISE: Dee, you got ta' either eat somethin' or drink somethin'. Nawh, change tha'. You haf'ta' eat somethin' *an'* drink somethin' this day.

PALMEROY: Yeah, but wha'?

MS. DELORES: I know, Louise. I know.

MS. ODESSA: *(Sucks teeth.)* Wha' indeed. They bet' not try no funny stuff. An' I need to git' by tha' bank foe' they close too. Don' ch'all let me fo'git', please.

MS. LOUISE: We all do, if Friday gon' continue to be grocery night.

PALMEROY: Well, this trip jus' might break into yo' reg'lar bank time, ladies. So, I hope you financially prepared right now. I hope you ain't gon' be fiddlin' 'roun in yo' pocketbook fo' loose change after the fact. They li'ble ta' thank y'alls nuts.

MS. ODESSA: Wha' is your talkin' 'bout? Tha' ain't none a' yo' look-out n' I dun' tole' chu' to stop this conversatin', Palmeroy. I got stuff on my mind.

PALMEROY: I wouldn't want 'em thankin' y'alls out cho' minds, goin' in 'ere wit'out no money. Tha's all.

MS. ODESSA: Number one, you don't know what' we got. Out my mind. Hell, I ain't never been mo' in my mind.

PALMEROY: *(Laughs.)* I see.

MS. DELORES: Said the blind man.

MS. LOUISE: Now, wait a minute, now. You do have some money don' cha', Dessa?

PALMEROY: Wha's wrong, Mizz Dessa?

MS. LOUISE: 'Cause they might try to charge us double or somethin' we ain't careful.

MS. ODESSA: Yeah, I got money, Louise. An' wha' chu' mean wha's wrong, man?

PALMEROY: Well, now, seems to me . . .

MS. ODESSA: *(To Louise.)* Enuff ta do wha' I got to wit' it.

MS. DELORES: I didn't thank about tha'.

MS. LOUISE: You ain't got no money neither, Dee? Oh, Lawd. . .

PALMEROY: If you gon' already be mad . . .

MS. DELORES: Yes, but cha' thank we should go to the bank first, Louise?

MS. LOUISE: We do tha' we ain't gon' never git' this show on the road.

PALMEROY: You might as well not sta' go . . .

MS. LOUISE: We keep it simple, we'll be awight.

(Delores thinks; nods.)

PALMEROY: You lookin' fo' trouble.

MS. ODESSA: Ain't chu' never been jus' sick n' tired?

PALMEROY: Well . . .

MS. ODESSA: Awright . . .

PALMEROY: We all tha', one way or another.

MS. ODESSA: You know wha' I'm talkin' 'bout, then. Ain't got to say no mo'. Ain't got ta' paint pictures fo' all the ignoramus bus drivers in the world named Palmeroy Bateman.

MS. LOUISE: Odessa, tha's not necessary.

(Pause.)

PALMEROY: *(Laughs.)* Too hot to talk anyway though, ain't it?

(Delores and Louise laugh.)

MS. ODESSA: Who he laughin' at? He the one tryin' to act like he don' know.

PALMEROY: Mus' be two-hunnert degrees.

MS. ODESSA: Like he need schoolin'. You ain't no youngsta.

PALMEROY: Yes, ma'am. I'm mo' cook me somethin' ta eat right out there on the sidewalk soon as I git' lunch.

MS. ODESSA: Humph, you hear me. You ain't as simple as you playin' like.

MS. LOUISE: Odessa, cool it. You suckin' up all the fresh air.

MS. ODESSA: Wha' fresh air?

(Palmeroy picks up another black passenger.)

PALMEROY: How you? *(Checks rearview, hums again; pulls off.)* Say y'all gon' do this e'ry Friday, huh?

MR. LOUISE: We'll see how this one go first.

PALMEROY: I hear ya, Mizz Lou. Well, other peoples is doin' it, or thankin' 'bout doin' it too so, y'all ladies gon' be awright.

MS. LOUISE: We know we is.

PALMEROY: Tha's right, don' ch'all let cho'selves go feelin' like no Lone Rangers, okay? If it's real, go deal. Awright now!

MS. LOUISE: Well, then, when is you n' Missus Bateman goin' in 'ere?

PALMEROY: Who n' how 'bout never? Both a' us can cook better n' them at Marsh's, I bet cha'.

MS. LOUISE: But, it ain't about the food.

PALMEROY: An' ain't nothin' in 'ere I wanna taste neither, Mizz Lou. I promise you tha'. Palmeroy Bateman don' buy nobody's cooked food nowhere where I got to git' it hot in one place, then go eat it cold in they basement. The Colored Lounge, they wanna call it. Ssshhhoott, by the time you sit down to it, you got ice sicles hangin' all off yo' stuff. Nawh, I made up my mind n' stopped tha' years ago. Plus the fact, I ain't got no point to prove. Any place I ever wannit to go, I been; straight up n' upright. Walked, not ran, right thu' the front doe' like a man oughta do e'rytime . . .

MS. LOUISE: Uh-huh . . .

PALMEROY: If he a man.

MS. ODESSA: Well . . .

MS. LOUISE: Where at? Where you been?

MS. ODESSA: Tha's goody-good fo' you.

MS. DELORES: He ain't been nowhere.

PALMEROY: Awright now . . .

MS. LOUISE: Or, he mus' be talkin' 'bout Church.

MS.DELORES: I bet cha'.

PALMEROY: I been enuff to know.

MS. LOUISE: Nowhere 'round 'here, noway . . .

MS. DELORES: Nowhere wo'th goin' . . .

MS. ODESSA: Some juke joint.

PALMEROY: Who?

MS. LOUISE: Where you say you been, Palmeroy?

MS. DELORES: Dessa say, some juke joint, Louise.

PALMEROY: Who?

MS. DELORES: You, tha's who. You ole hoot owl.

PALMEROY: Nawh, nawh . . .

MS. LOUISE: 'Cause you ain't been nowhere 'roun 'ere. Tha's fo' sho'.

PALMEROY: I don' juke no joint, Mizz Dee. Not no mo'.

MS. LOUISE: Even the hospital got a back doe' say, *Colored n' Garbage Pick-Up Here.*

MS. ODESSA: He mus' be talkin' 'bout Church, then.

PALMEROY: N' I goes to Church too. My own church.

MS. DELORES: Yo' church? Don' chu' tell me you dun' built a church somewhere now, Palmeroy. *(Ladies laugh.)*

PALMEROY: Darn near. Twenty-five years wo'th a dues I dun' paid.

MS. DELORES: I'm mo' have ta see tha' one fo' myself, though, if you don't mind, Rev'rend Palmeroy.

PALMEROY: Glad to have you, Mizz Dee; anytime. Ssshhooott, I'll give you the address. Remind me.

MS. DELORES: Fo' sho' I will.

(Another black passenger boards bus).

(Palmeroy nods again politely.)

(Delores continues laughing.)

MS. DELORES: Say he got a church. Y'all hear tha'? Let me see the church then, Mista Bateman.

(Palmeroy checks rearview.)

PALMEROY: Leastways, lemme put it to you ladies like this: Anybody don' want my money, I don' give it to 'em. Anybody don' want me, don' want my money . . .

MS. DELORES: Well awright, then.

PALMEROY: An' tha's how tha' go.

MS. LOUISE: A-man, Rev'rend Palmeroy.

PALMEROY: I can keep it in my pocket, though. Ain't tha' right?

MS. LOUISE: Ain't nothin' wrong wit' tha'.

MS. DELORES: Ain't a thang wrong wit' it.

PALMEROY: Plus the fact, I got twenty fo' hours in my day, n' seven days in my week jus' like e'rybody else do . . .

MS. DELORES: A-man. A-man, Brother Palmeroy.

PALMEROY: So, tha's how come I say I ain't got no points ta prove to no-body white nor black. 'Cause tha' part is all up to me.

MS. LOUISE: But, this ain't about chu' by yo'self though, Brother.

MS. ODESSA: Tha's right. Tha's jus' like a man, y'all. Thankin' it's all the time all about him . . .

PALMEROY: Awh now . . .

MS. ODESSA: Him by himself.

PALMEROY: Yeah, wha' cho' husband thankin' 'bout all this, then?

MS. ODESSA: Who husband?

PALMEROY: Yo's.

MS. ODESSA: Chollie Brown don' run me.

PALMEROY: But, he the first somebody they gon' call to come down to the police station to pick y'all up if they ever let ch'all go.

MS. ODESSA: I say, he don' run me.

PALMEROY: The police can run you, though, Mizz Dessa. . .

MS. ODESSA: Don' no man run me.

PALMEROY: All up n' down Peachtree Street wit' a stick . . .

MS. DELORES: Do you mind, Mista Bateman?

PALMEROY: Wit' a big, ole billy stick; a club. Crack a skull wide open. Tha', I dun' seen.

MS. DELORES: I don' thank them in the back wanna know all our bi'niss.

PALMEROY: I jus' don' wanna see one a' y'all, or alla y'all, knocked upside the head one too many times. You my bes' customers. I look fo'ward to seein' some folk e'ryday. I like y'all. I don' need ch'all all punch-drunk. Y'all ain't no prize-fighters. Y'alls ladies.

(Another black passenger gets on bus.) (Palmeroy nods.)

MS. DELORES: Awh, Palmeroy, ain't nobody gon' git' knocked nowhere up-side nothin'. I'm sho' we ain't even gon' be the first ones in 'ere.

(Bus stops for red light.)

PALMEROY: You countin' on tha' is ya'?

MS. DELORES: Pro'bly have a whole line a' folk.

PALMEROY: So, you might not be the last ones to git' cho' heads knocked neither.

MS. DELORES: No need to mumble, Mista Bateman. I hear ya an' so do them in the back. I dun' told chu' one time.

PALMEROY: Awright now, I'm lookin' out fo' you. You might not thank so but, I am. Nawh, though, he ain't nothin' but a' ole Palmeroy, ole Bate-man, tha' ole bus driver. He don' know nothin' 'bout us. Wha' he care 'bout wha' we do? Well, you all know I'm not educated. Do the bes' I can, an' I don' always know wha's exactly right, but killin' people n' hurtin' 'em jus' 'cause they wanna do fo' themselves the right way is wrong. Pun-ishin' people jus' 'cause they wanna live is wrong. I do know tha'.

MS. ODESSA: Palmeroy?

PALMEROY: Punch-drunk or no punch drunk.

MS. ODESSA: Say, looka-here, man, is you the bus driver?

PALMEROY: Ma'am? Yes, ma'am.

MS. ODESSA: 'Cause I thought you was the bus driver or, is you finished? You dun' retired fo' the afternoon?

PALMEROY: No, ma'am, I'm still the bus driver.

MS. ODESSA: Then drive the bus, then. Gon' leave us standin' out 'ere in the middle a' the street, I guess.

PALMEROY: Yes, ma'am. No, ma'am.

MS. ODESSA: Tha' light dun' changed foe' years ago.

(Palmeroy starts bus.)

PALMEROY: Awright now . . .

MS. ODESSA: He so busy runnin' off at the lip into my personal bi'niss.

PALMEROY: I'm sorry, Mizz Odessa. I'm sorry, ladies.

MS. ODESSA: Come askin' me wha' Chollie thank.

MS. DELORES: Don' worry 'bout it, Dessa . . .

MS. ODESSA: Like he my daddy . . .

MS. DELORES: Those who can do . . .

MS. LOUISE: Ain't nobody botherin' you, Dessa. He jus' teasin'.

MS. DELORES: Those who cain't, run off at the lip. Don' mind 'im.

PALMEROY: Tha's right, Mizz Dessa. Forgimme, Mizz Dessa.

MS. ODESSA: Chollie Elwood Brown ain't my daddy. Ssshhooott, you ain't never even seen Chollie anyway. Never even met 'im. Don' know nothin' 'bout Chollie Brown.

MS. DELORES: He jus' jealous.

MS. LOUISE: Awh hush, both a' y'all.

MS. ODESSA: Don' even know 'em on the street, Dee.

PALMEROY: Oh, yeah, I do. He a big man. I seen 'em last month pick y'all up at the bus stop tha' day it rained so hard. Yeah, he a real big man. Had big ole arms n' hands.

MS. ODESSA: Well, wha'? Now, tha' gon' make two horrays fo' you, then? 'Cause you dun' seen Chollie Elwood one time.

MS. DELORES: One time.

PALMEROY: Big ole mountain man. Why, he so big . . .

MS. ODESSA: Awright, chu' watch it now . . .

PALMEROY: He look like he mus' haul Frigidaires fo' a livin' e'ryday . . . by 'imself. Do he?

(Ladies chuckle.)

MS. ODESSA: Nawh, he don'.

PALMEROY: Awh, you know I didn't mean no harm.

MS. LOUISE: It's awright, Palmeroy. She know.

PALMEROY: Like I say, I'm on yo' side.

MS. LOUISE: We know.

MS. ODESSA: I know I bet I'm mo' call yo' boss up n' tell 'em 'bout how you out on yo' route flirtin' n' tryin' to give away free rides. Tha's wha' all I know.

PALMEROY: Nawh, Mizz Dessa. Don' do tha' to me, now. I needs ma' job.

MS. ODESSA: Okay then, straighten up this piece a' bus n' fly it right on downtown quick. We got stuff to 'tend to. We dun' tole' chu'.

MS. DELORES: Yeah, an' read yo' paper too, Palmeroy, hear? 'Cause ain't nobody goin' to the police station no mo' neither. The United States Congress dun' said so now.

PALMEROY: Awh, Ms. Dee . . .

MS. DELORES: Highest court in the land . . .

PALMEROY: I mean, do you read cho' newspaper? I mean e'ry day?

MS. DELORES: An' so tha' stuff is over wit'. I don' care wha' nobody say.

PALMEROY: No mo' sep'rate facilities. Tha's wha' cho' paper say, huh?

MS. DELORES: Tha's right.

PALMEROY: Uh-huh, you thank so? "Cause Lil' Rock was in the paper too seems like yesterday. Y'all remember tha', don' cha'?

MS. LOUISE: Remember it? Nineteen n'fifty-seven. Was yesterday.

PALMEROY: We strollin' up Memory Lane it ain't far is it, Mizz Louise?

MS. LOUISE: No, sir.

PALMEROY: Wha' was it, now? Six girls n' three boys.

MS. LOUISE: The Lil' Rock Nine. Tryin' ta go to tha' high school.

MS. ODESSA: Well, one monkey don' stop no show. Them nine from Lil' Rock proved it, didn't they?

MS. DELORES: Tha's right. So, you jus' need to buck up then, Bateman. You need to put cho' good suit on n' hit it down to Marsh's, or any one a' them other places an' make 'em serve you.

PALMEROY: Well, I'll tell you, Mizz Dee . . .

MS. DELORES: Tha's wha' chu' need to do.

PALMEROY: I'm about as bucked up as I ever wish to be. Nawh, I can put my good suit on n' hit it over to The Livin' Inn or The Suzie Q fo' a good meal, an' pleasant com'pny to boot, if an' when tha's wha' I need. Not only do Mizz Q know how to stomp-down pee on 'erself some smoked turkey, n' sauce up some candy yams out this world, she can lay hands on some chessnut n' cranberry dressin' an' macaroni n' cheese cassarole tha's sayin' somethin' e'ry day a' the week an' twice on Sunday!

MS. ODESSA: E'ryday ain't Thanksgivin'. Why would I wanna eat somebody's ole dried-out turkey n' dressin' e'ryday?

PALMEROY: It beats tha' tablecloth-eatin' scheme by a mile I'm sho' *(Laughs.)* *(Delores and Louise laugh.)*

MS. ODESSA: Don' play wit' me, Palmeroy.

PALMEROY: Awh, you know how I do. I don' need tha' other aggravation is all. I jus' don' need the aggravation.

MS. ODESSA: You go tell tha' to Emmet Till's mama an' them others tha's been done outta they lives n' they chirruns; to the Scottsboro boys.

PALMEROY: You goin' back a ways now.

MS. ODESSA: You got cho' strollin' shoes on, remember tha'. Hell, they wan-n't doin' nothin' but lookin' fo' work. Teenage boys, barely off they mamas. Two white girls come along, say they raped 'em an' boom, off they all go to chain gang. Young boys when they went in 'ere. Ole men now, if they still alive, all bent over n' shriveled up, still bustin' rocks somewhere on somebody's chain gang fo' somethin' they didn' even do thirty years ago.

PALMEROY: So, the kids dun' already took all them licks, though. Ain't they?

MS. ODESSA: You know, I'm on the verge a' not even likin' you no mo'. Wha' the hell tha's s'posed to mean? Ain't nothin' else ta do? Ain't nobody else got ta try?

PALMEROY: I'm jus' tryin' to be agreeable, Mizz Dessa.

MS. LOUISE: It is a shame, though. It's a dawggone shame how they do them babies; them young people.
(Sound of traffic.)
(Bus Stops.)

PALMEROY: *(Announces.)* Downtown Express. *(Opens door; stands.)*
(Ms. Grayson, also wearing summer white, carrying sizeable shopping bag and purse, begins to board.)

PALMEROY: Afternoon, Mizz Grayson. *(Gets off bus; helps her.)* How you? Wha' chu' doin' out 'ere today?

MS. GRAYSON: Jus' fine, Palmeroy, thank you. Jus' fine. How you?

PALMEROY: Jus' fine.

MS. GRAYSON: Yeah, but it's sho' hot, though; yessir.

PALMEROY: Yes, ma'am, but wha' chu' doin' out in this fo' by yo'self? You gon' mess aroun' n' have a heat stroke.

MS. GRAYSON: Well, you in it. Why come I cain't be out in it?

PALMEROY: 'Cause I got 'sta be out in it. I cain't pick n' choose my work time by wha' the weatherman say.

MS. GRAYSON: By God but not by the weatherman. *(Laughs.)* You could sho' cook an egg on tha' sidewalk, though, cain't cha', Bateman?

PALMEROY: I was jus' sayin' tha' myself, Mizz Grayson. You should have yo' chirruns or somebody to take you aroun'.
(They board bus.)

MS. GRAYSON: Umm-hmm . . .

PALMEROY: Tha's wha' chirruns fo'.
(Ms. Grayson gives Palmeroy her fare.)

MS. GRAYSON: If I was 'sta wait on my children ta do fo' me the way I wan-nit dun' when I wannit dun', I'd be lookin' square in the face a' Jesus n' still waitin'. I'd be dead, Palmeroy, I would.

(Palmeroy puts fare in slot, changes bus sign; sits back in driver's seat.)

PALMEROY: You gon' be tha' anyway, you play aroun' in this humid'ty.

MS. GRAYSON: Who's playin'? I'm on a mission. *(Stands in front of Louise.)*

(Palmeroy checks rearview.)

PALMEROY: Uh, we got plenty a' seats, Mizz Grayson. Folks mus' be stayin' in much as they can.

(Louise slowly moves over.)

PALMEROY: News say you ought to.

MS. GRAYSON: Excuse me . . . *(Sits between Louise and Odessa.)* Thank you. I always sit 'ere. I'm an ole lady. Too ole to change my ways, I'm afraid. Hot today, innit? *(Looks at Louise.)*

(Buss pulls off.)

MS. LOUISE: Yes, ma'am, it is.

(Ms. Grayson adjusts herself; points out of window.)

MS. GRAYSON: Look at the steam. Look, look at the steam risin' up off the pavement. Look at the steam.

(All three ladies look hesitantly.)

MS. GRAYSON: You could put cho' face down there an', if you ain't stomped ta death, you'd get a mighty fine steam bath facial. *(Takes out her fan and handkerchief; wipes her brow.)* I know I don' have no bi'niss bein' out 'ere like this but, I jus' had ta get up n' go, Palmeroy. You see, Mizz Grier called me early this mornin'.

PALMEROY: Mizz Grier?

MS. GRAYSON: Uh-huh, bless 'er heart.

PALMEROY: She ain't been aroun' much lately.

MS. GRAYSON: Tha's 'cause she cain't get 'roun hardly. She been sick, poor doll. Called me up talkin' nonsense this mornin'. Talkin' 'bout nothin'. Remember how she dotes on them birds so? Them pesky, noisy parakeets she keeps like they was babies?

PALMEROY: Well, I ain't never seen 'em, myself.

MS. GRAYSON: Trust me, though. She got 'em. Anyway, she said somethin' ta me along in the conversation 'bout puttin' them birds to bed last night. Hear me, Palmeroy? Puttin' 'em to bed, I say.

PALMEROY: Yes, ma'am, I hear ya.

MS. GRAYSON: Like she act'ally put them in a bed. Now, I been to yo' house befo', I says to myself 'cause I've known Grier over fo'ty years. Lawd knows I don' wanna hurt 'er feelins. An' I know they got a special cage. I helped 'er pick it out n' order it from a special farm stoe' out in Tucson, Arizona fo' them pesky thangs to stay in but, you ain't never called it no bed so, in my mind, I'm wunderin', wha' bed is they in? Her bed?

(Ladies cover up their giggles.)

MS. GRAYSON: Poor thang. Dear heart. She's slippin', Palmeroy. Right offa the hill an' into the valley. An', she's got so over-weight 'til she cain't even clean 'erself prop'ly. I mean, it has gotten so it's jus' as well she don' come out no more. I mean, on a day like this so hot, she'd have this whole bus smellin' like ole, sour buttermilk. I'm sorry to say it.

PALMEROY: Nawh, now. Awh . . .

MS. GRAYSON: It's a shame, Palmeroy. It's a dawggone shame when you jus' do not have anyone to see 'bout cha'; none a' yo' folk. Lawd have mercy on us all. There but fo' the grace a' God walk I.

PALMEROY: Well, where 'er chirruns at to help 'her? I thought she had some.

MS. GRAYSON: She did. She had twins once; twin boys. I helped deliver them boys; beautiful. Both lost in Korea, though; both of 'em. Can you imagine? She truly did give 'er all, I mean. An' Mister Grier, Rev'rend Grier, her husband, he was assistant pastor at my husband's church while he lived . . .

PALMEROY: Uh-huh, I remember somebody tellin' me somethin' like tha'.

MS. GRAYSON: Wann't never much of a position, though, tell you the truth. A lil' piece a' nothin' parish up in the woods a' Forsythe County. We was country folk; still are. We didn't know nothin' ta know. We thought we was awright back then. I feel, though, like it's my sisterly duty to carry on; to be as helpful as I can to 'er. Afterall, you never know who'll have to bring you a bowl a' chicken soup sometime, an' we both alone, with-out our men now. My-my, 'er beautiful boys. I never knew which one I was talkin' to an' I helped bring 'em into this world; this world a' trou-ble. They were as close to the right Rev'rend Grayson n' me as our own children were. But, there again, fo' the grace a' God. *(Opens her shopping bag; shows ladies and Palmeroy contents.)* So, I'm takin' Grier over some few bath salts an' alil' air freshener. Inn' tha' nice a' me? Palmeroy?

PALMEROY: Yes, ma'am, mighty nice. I agree.

MS. GRAYSON: I'm after my blessins ya see, Palmeroy. I'm gon' get 'em too. Praise God I will. You jus' watch my steam. When my day is done, an' my race is run, I wanna be in tha' number. Yessir, I'm gon' be able to look King Jesus eyeball ta eyeball, an' I'm gonna say to 'em, 'How you, King Jesus? I got my mind right. I know you do. *Hot Dawg!*

PALMEROY: You gon' say all tha' to 'em, Mizz Grayson?

MS. GRAYSON: Sho' am.

PALMEROY: To King Jesus? You gon' say, 'hot dawg'?

MS. GRAYSON: Yessir, he gon' take me into his unchangin' hand n' lead me on to the promised land. *Hot Dawg!*

PALMEROY: Awright, now. *Hot Dawg!*

MS. GRAYSON: *Hot Dawg n' halleluyah!*

PALMEROY: Halleluyah, then.

MS. GRAYSON: *(To Ms. Louise.)* Ain't tha' right?

MS. LOUISE: Yes, ma'am, I s'pose.

MS. GRAYSON: Halleluyah! You know wha' I mean.

MS. LOUISE: We all oughta have it tha' good.

MS. ODESSA: We sho' oughta.

MS. GRAYSON: If we can. Listen to this . . . *(Sings.)* Swing low, sweet chariot, comin' for to carry me home . . . *(Speaks to ladies.)* You all know tha' song, don' cha'?

MS. LOUISE: Yes . . .

MS. ODESSA: Too hot to sing it, though.

MS. DELORES: Heat don' bother me. *(Joins in.)*
(Odessa gives a stern glance.)

MS. GRAYSON: *(Still sings.)* Swing low, sweet chariot, comin' for to carry me home hmmm . . .

PALMEROY: An' speakin' a' King Jesus . . .
(Ms. Grayson continues humming.)

PALMEROY: 'Scuse me, Mizz Grayson . . .
(Ms. Grayson stops mid-hum.)

MS. GRAYSON: Humph?

PALMEROY: But, ch'all hear 'bout tha' woman out there in Califo'nia somewhere say she dun' seen Jesus on 'er Frigidaire?

MS. LOUISE: Say wha'?

MS. GRAYSON: Could you repeat tha' please, Palmeroy?

PALMEROY: I say, she say she dun' seen Jesus on 'er Frigidaire.

MS. GRAYSON: In 'er Frigidaire?

PALMEROY: No, ma'am, not in 'er Frigidaire. On 'er Frigidaire. In 'er kitchen, Ms. Grayson. Out in Califo'nia.

MS. GRAYSON: You makin' this up, Palmeroy?

PALMEROY: Oh no, ma'am, I'm not makin' it up. Go check yesterday's Constitution. Page three, I thank it was.

MS. GRAYSON: Tha' mus' be the comic strip section, then. There betwix Dick Tracy n' The Misadventures a' Barney Google n' Snuffy Smith, it mus' be huh, Palmeroy?

PALMEROY: No ma'am. Aroun' page three, though.

MS. GRAYSON: Hmmmm, surprised my grandsons didn' run 'cross of it. They'da showed it to be lickity-split.

PALMEROY: It's in 'ere.

MS. GRAYSON: Uh-huh. So, wha's so wonderful 'bout 'er Frigidaire? Righteous fruit? Tell me, since chances are my daughter-in-law has already used up yesterday's paper fo' linin' all the trash buckets in the house.

PALMEROY: Well, accordin' to the paper, the lady say . . .

MS. GRAYSON: Hold on. White woman?

PALMEROY: Yeah, I don' thank it woulda made the paper if she'da been Colored, Mizz Grayson. She'da jus' been crazy. Anyway, this woman, this white woman, she say she dun' took a picture a' Jesus on 'er Frigerator back 'roun Easter time. Wha' chu' think about tha'?

MS. GRAYSON: You say she jus' seen it tho, Bateman. You didn't say she took no pictures.

PALMEROY: Well, she seen it then, she took the picture, Mizz Grayson. Anywho, then afterwards, the Lawd tole' 'er, she say, to call up some other dead folk an' take they pictures.

MS. GRAYSON: Like wha' other dead folk? Like who?

PALMEROY: Oh, I forgit now . . .

MS. GRAYSON: Well, if it was jus' yesterday . . .

PALMEROY: Limme thank . . .

MS. GRAYSON: 'Cause first off, Jesus is not dead; is not in tha' number . . .

PALMEROY: Yes, ma'am . . .

MS. GRAYSON: Anybody's a true church-goer would know tha'.

PALMEROY: It was somebody like a George Washington or a Abraham Lincoln.

MS. GRAYSON: You sho' 'bout tha'?

MS. ODESSA: You is makin' this up, Palmeroy.

PALMEROY: No, ma'am.

MS. GRAYSON: Not a Rudolph Valentino, nor a John Garfield? Not some movie personality?

PALMEROY: I don' do the Lawd nor none a' his folk like tha'; bad luck. They the last ones you wanna make stuff up on.

MS. DELORES: Listen 'ere Palmeroy. Wha' she s'posed to gon' call these dead folk up on? Telephone?

MS. GRAYSON: If the Lawd wannit' to speak with you, he'd call ya up 'imself, honey. In yo' heart, in yo' mind, in yo' soul. He sho' wouldn' need no long distance operator woman out a' Califo'nia 'cause he *is* the operator. Long distance *an'* such n' such. Hear me, y'all?

PALMEROY: A-man.

MS. GRAYSON: A-man, an' if the Lawd had meant for' tha' woman to get a picture a' King Jesus fo' posterity, to published in a newspaper tha's gon' do nothin' but get to line somebody's trash can dispenser, he'da put Miss Missy in a robe, n' a pair a' sandals, an' stuck 'er on the scene, at the foot a' the cross, wit' a Brownie camera. Tha's wha' I know.

PALMEROY: Uh-oh, I dun' started somethin' else . . . *(To Ms. Grayson.)* Better . . .

MS. GRAYSON: Tha' woman's evil.

PALMEROY: Better save yo' strength, Mizz Grayson.

MS. GRAYSON: I can tell tha' right now. Folks, how they lie on the Lawd all the time.

MS. ODESSA: A-man to tha'.

MS. GRAYSON: Don' no blessins come from tha'. Don' they know? Tha' woman needs to get 'erself a proper Bible n' read it. Joshua-Chapter One/Verse Eight: 'This book of law shall not depart out of thy mouth; but thou shalt meditate therein day an' night, tha' thou mayest observe to do accordin' to all tha' is written therein: for then, thou shalt make thy way prosperous, an' then thou shalt have good success.' Tha' woman's a mystic, an' ain't gon' come to no good. She pro'bly gon' eat a piece a bad fruit outta tha' mystical Frigidaire a' hers an' go like tha' . . . Dead. Then, somebody can take 'er picture.

PALMEROY: It is a shame, though, how peoples use the Lawd an' the Bible fo' they own taste n' discretion.

MS. ODESSA: Sho' is.

MS. LOUISE: Well, you acted like you b'lieved tha' woman, Palmeroy.

MS. GRAYSON: The Bible teaches specifically against mysticism, an' card-readin' an' fortune-tellin' . . .

PALMEROY: I ain't never said I b'lieved 'er.

MS. GRAYSON: You bet' not b'lieve 'er. Psalm One Hundred n' Nineteen/Verse Eleven: 'Thy word have I hid in mine heart, tha' I might not sin against thee.'

MS. ODESSA: An' ye shall know the truth . . .

MS. GRAYSON: John-Eight/Verse Thirty-Two.

MS. ODESSA: An' the truth shall set chu' free.

MS. GRAYSON: A-man.

MS. ODESSA: A-man.

PALMEROY: The truth shall set chu' free. I'm fo' tha'. Tha's like when I first got this job. They started lettin' Colored drive. Tha' foreman, he didn' wanna give it to us, ya know. Says to me an' a couple-three other Colored fellas, to us he say, "Colored boys cain't drive no bus." Says we cain't even learn how. He say, the Lawd say Colored cain't drive no bus.

MS. GRAYSON: Well, there goes another somebody wrong wann't 'e, Palmeroy?

PALMEROY: Yes, ma'am, but tha's sho' wha' he say to us, tho' . . .

MS. GRAYSON: 'Cause if you cain't drive a bus . . .

PALMEROY: He say the Lawd say we cain't. Too many gears to shift.

MS. GRAYSON: Then, I wunder wha' it is you doin' up there in tha' driver's chair, wit' the stirrin' column in yo' clutches, an' yo' foot workin' the gas pedal like it is. Tha's wha' all I wunder. I jus' wunder wha'.

PALMEROY: Say, wha' church you brought up in , Mizz Grayson? I been meanin' to ask.

MS. GRAYSON: Methodist. An' you?

PALMEROY: Me? I'm Baptist.

MS. GRAYSON: Baptized?

PALMEROY: Yes, ma'am. Since the age a' three.

MS. GRAYSON: Good. Well Baptist, tha' jus' one step below *(To ladies.)* My-my, everybody looks so nice n' crisp. I wish I could keep it up such as you-all. *(Dabs herself with handkerchief.)* I jus' cain't keep it up. I jus' cannot do it. Sometimes I sweat like it's goin' outta style. I used ta' could take the strain, tho'. When I was young pastor's wife, sittin' in the church three, foe' nights a week an' all day Sunday, rain or shine, in the cold, no heat, in darn near wha' felt like one-thousand degree temperatures, an' no air-conditionin' nor nothin' else modern. But now, I jus' sweat like a P-I-G hog. *(Ms. Grayson looks at Louise.)*

MS. LOUISE: Yes, ma'am, me too sometimes. *(Dabs herself.)*

MS. GRAYSON: Well, not today. Age s' wha' does tha' to ya', anyway. You-all real young yet. An' you look so nice n' cool. You know each other? *(Louise nods.)*

MS. GRAYSON: Today mus' be a extra special day fo' y'all.

MS. LOUISE: We . . .

MS. ODESSA: We goin' downtown to Marsh's, if you don' mind. *(Palmeroy pauses.)*

MS. GRAYSON: Marsh's Department Store? Oh, bet' not go there. Haven't chu' heard? Don' ch'all read? They've had more n' alil' bit a' trouble lately at tha' place an' lots others 'roun town. Oh, don' ch'all . . .

MS. ODESSA: Yes, ma'am, an' we goin' down there to have lunch in the restaurant.

MS. GRAYSON: Oh . . .

MS. ODESSA: An, if it go well, we gon' be there this time e'ry Friday.

MS. GRAYSON: I see.

MS. ODESSA: Even if it don' go well. Yes, ma'am.

(Sound of bus and traffic.)

MS. GRAYSON: When I was a small girl, I had an ole, hateful, boy cousin named Synn wit' Y n' two Ns. Mean-spirited he was too; awful mean. He used to terrorize folks behind his mama n' daddy's backs. Or, maybe they knew, seein' as how they named 'im tha' awful thang: Synn. Folks he bothered couldn't do nothin' 'bout it themselves. Colored children on their way back n' fo'th to school e'ryday. Ugly, ugly creature. Anyway, they musta tole' their big sister or somebody, an' she figured she could do somethin' if they couldn' 'cause one day, while he was pickin' on 'er fam'ly, she come along. I thank she was act'ally waitin' on him. Caught 'im redhanded, so to speak. Busted him so hard upside his skull wit' a baseball bat 'til he went into a coma an' never come out again. I mean to tell you tha' tha' demon chile never regained consciousness; never. I was the one half run fo' the doctor. I saw the whole thang but I never even opened by mouth about it. To nobody. Told e'rybody I didn't know nothin'. Told 'em I found 'im on the road. Know why? 'Cause in the back a' my mind, an' at tha' young age, I had sense enuff ta recognize when a body asks fo' wha' it gets, it surely gets wha' it asks fo'. An' he was a hateful boy. Used to try to make me do all kinds a' . . . *(Looks out window; rings bell.)* This my stop, Palmeroy. Stop the bus.

PALMEROY: Yes, ma'am.

(Ms. Grayson gathers her bags; stands to depart.)

MS. GRAYSON: I believe tha' anybody with the price of a ticket, or a dress, or a lunch ought to be able to go, an' to buy, an' to eat, an' to work anywhere they want to. I'd like to go on record havin' said tha'.

MS. LOUISE: Ma'am, where did you say tha' story hap'ned?

MS. GRAYSON: Oh, tha's no story. Tha's real life, honey. Hap'ned in Senoia, Georgia where I'm born n' raised.

MS. LOUISE: *(Stands.)* Would you happen to remember tha' Colored fam'ly's surname?

MS. GRAYSON: Why sorry, I sho' don'. *(Ms. Grayson drops one of her bags as bus comes to full stop.)*

(Louise stands, picks it up; hands it gently.)

(Ms. Grayson looks from Louise to Odessa.)

MS. GRAYSON: *(to Louise.)* Why are you doin' this?

MS. LOUISE: Ma'am?

MS. GRAYSON: Why are *you* doin' this? Seems to me, you should be crystal clear on tha' or it won' be no use. Goin' down there to git' cho'self hurt. *(Gestures towards Odessa and Delores.)* Enjoy yo' meal, ladies. *(Palmeroy takes her arm as she departs bus.)*

PALMEROY: Awright, now, catch cha' next time.

MS. GRAYSON: Thank you, Palmeroy. I'll see ya, hear? *(Exits stage.)*

MS. DELORES: Louise . . . Lou . . .

PALMEROY: *(In driver's seat.)* Awright now, we pullin' off.

(Bus jerks forward.)

MS. DELORES: Louise, ain't cho' folk from down Senoia way?

MS. LOUISE: Who is tha', Palmeroy?

PALMEROY: Tha's ole Mizz Grayson. Stay up 'ere wit' 'er son n' daughter-in-law. Was married to a pastor fo' fo'ty years or somethin' like tha'.

MS. DELORES: I can b'lieve it, myself.

PALMEROY: She a good lady.

MS. ODESSA: An' I bet chu' cain't stand ta hear nobody say nothin' 'bout cho' good lady Grayson neither, can ya'? *(Mimics.)* Enjoy yo' meal, ladies . . .

PALMEROY: I couldn't stand to hear nobody say nothin' 'bout chu', Mizz Odessa.

MS. ODESSA: Louise, sit down foe' you fall.

MS. LOUISE: *(Sits.)* She kinda reminds me a' Mizz Hornsby, tha's all.

MS. ODESSA: Ssssshhhooootttt, in ole lady Grayson's day, she was prob'ly whoppin', n' hollerin', n' lynchin' wit' the best of 'em. She jus' dun' lost 'er strength. Lost 'er full taste fo' it . . . maybe.

MS. DELORES: She look pretty strong to me.

MS. LOUISE: Sound pretty strong too. Palmeroy got tha' ole lady all cranked up.

MS. ODESSA: Them ole crackers stay all cranked up like tha'. How many times we been strung up by them country-ass, holy-rollers, huh? A pastor's wife my ass; a Methodist. One step below. A holy-roller. Hell, to hear them tell it, they all b'lieve in God. Recitin' Bible verses all the time they stretchin' yo' neck. They pro'bly let'er hold the rope an' she was thankful. Don' b'lieve e'rythang somebody say to *you*, Louise. Ssshhhooott, I got cho' cousin Synn wit' a Y n' two Ns.

PALMEROY: Calm down, Mizz Dessa. We all friends 'ere, ain't we?

MS. ODESSA: Why? I ain't tryin' ta be friends wit' them people. You let 'er scream up n' thu' the bus quotin' chapter n' verse. Wha's wrong wit me?

I'll stand up n' say mine. She jus' too ole to care 'bout it the same now. Tha's all the dif'rence. "Er strength's gone. Ain't got the same strength no mo'. Hear how she tryin' to go to heaven? On somebody else's back.

PALMEROY: Mizz Dessa, please sit down. You gon' have a stroke. You the one said it too hot fo' all this conversatin' . . .

MS. ODESSA: Mizz Dessa please hell. The hell you say. I put money in tha' slot e'ryday jus' like she do; mo' times, in fact, 'cause I still punch a clock. Wha' she do? Runnin' 'roun the streets totin' bath salts.

PALMEROY: Yes, ma'am.

MS. LOUISE: Dessa, sit down. You worryin' e'rybody.

MS. ODESSA: I ain't finished yet. An' speakin' a Mizz Hornsby, I told y'all 'bout how my chirrun come to pick me up last week. Hey, Palmeroy, my chirrun come to pick me up last week, the security man say he didn' recognize 'em. My chirrun say he sicked the dawgs on 'em. Thought they was protestors, he said. How they gon' be protestin' standin' still, waitin' on me by my car, I say.

MS. LOUISE: Tha' wann't Mizz Hornsby's fault.

MS. ODESSA: Whose was it, then? She own the comp'ny. She make the rules. Tha' to me say Mizz Hornsby; she responsible. She shoulda fired 'im. Bet he got a raise instead. I see he ain't gone nowhere. Still on the job.

MS. LOUISE: Awh, you jus' wanna thank tha' way.

MS. ODESSA: An' hope I don' stop thankin' tha' way. *(Sits.)*

MS. LOUISE: Listen, how is one security man gon' keep up . . .

MS. ODESSA: I know wha' I'm goin' downtown fo'.

MS. LOUISE: Wit' the faces a' e'ry chile a' e'ry person tha' work fo' Hornsby Toy Comp'ny?

MS. ODESSA: Do they sick the dawgs on any white chirrun?

MS. LOUISE: Did chu' ask 'im?

MS. ODESSA: Nawh, I didn' have to. Damn, Lou, Mizz Hornsby jus' wanna git' tha' work out. Don' chu' unnerstand yet ole as you is? Tha's 'er claim to fame, if she so good to you. She know if she don' treat us half-way decent, the merchandise won' leave out right an' there go 'er pocketbook.

MS. LOUISE: An' we jus' be fired too . . .

MS. ODESSA: I tell ya, I ain't lickin' between no white woman's toes.

MS. LOUISE: An' she can get somebody in 'ere tha' will do it right. She ain't got to keep none a' us, an' wha' chu' mean, ole as I'm is?

MS. ODESSA: Keep me? I ain't no slave.

MR. LOUISE: I mean, on the job. You know wha' I mean.

MS. ODESSA: She don' keep me. Don' nobody keep Odessa Mae Brown, honey. I work hard fo' my money an' you do too, last time I looked over at chu' on yo' sewin' machine.

MS. LOUISE: Looka-here, is you finished? You thank you dun' made cho' point?

MS. ODESSA: Awh, Louise . . .

MS. LOUISE: Awh shut up, Odessa. Pickin' on people.

MS. DELORES: Come on, y'all. We here.

PALMEROY: *(Announces.)* Downtown Atlanta. Marsh's Department Stoe'.

MS. DELORES: Straighten up, now.

(Ladies gather bags; begin to depart.)

PALMEROY: Awright, y'all be careful. I'm prayin' fo' ya'. Remember tha'.

MS. LOUISE: We'll see ya', Palmeroy.

MS. DELORES: Thank you, Palmeroy. You too. We'll see ya Monday, hear?

PALMEROY: Yes, ma'am.

MS. ODESSA: Thought we wann't never gon' git 'ere. This raggedy piece a' thang took all day. . .

(Lights dim on Palmeroy and bus setting.)

(Ladies stand, huddled together.)

(Street sounds.)

(Huge white sign reads Marsh's.)

(Blackout. End of Act One.)

ACT TWO

Setting: A continuation of previous scene ending; a raising of lights finds ladies in same positions. Street sounds still encircle them.

MS. DELORES: Well . . . *(Looks around.)*

MS. ODESSA: Well is fo' water n' I need me some. I'm goin' over 'ere to the Tastey Freeze in a minute.

MS. DELORES: Wait, now wait. I told Ruth to meet us right near the bus stop. Les' not get sep'rated.

MS. ODESSA: *(Looking.)* Well, where she at, then?

MS. DELORES: In my pocketbook, I guess, Dessa. I don' know. How I'm s'posed to know? I got' 'ere same time you did.

MS. ODESSA: We better see 'er quick, or we gon' have ta go in wit'out 'er. I never did feel good about chu' askin' 'er anyway.

MS. LOUISE: There she is. *(Calls towards bench.)* Sistah Waldon!
(Lights up on Ruth, wearing sun glasses, sitting on bench down/right.)

MS. ODESSA: Tha' ain't Ruth.

MS. DELORES: Tha' is Ruth. I know Ruth better n' y'all. She my friend.

MS. LOUISE: She my pastor's wife.

MS. DELORES: Mine too.

MS. LOUISE: *(Calls again.)* Sistah Waldon!

MS. ODESSA: Ruth mo' yella than tha' woman; got mo' hair.

MS. DELORES: Maybe she dun' cooked some, an' 'er hair dun' shrunk while she been waitin'.

MS. ODESSA: Tha's the bus fault.

MS. LOUISE: I'm mo' go check the stoe'.

MS. ODESSA: Yeah, see wha's goin' on, Lou. Be careful. *(Calls.)* Ruth . . .
(Louise exits towards Marsh's sign.)
(Delores and Odessa approach Ruth.)

MS. DELORES: Hey, Ruthie girl, you ready?

MS. ODESSA: Come on, Ruth. How you?
(Ruth doesn't move.)

MS. ODESSA: Ruth . . .

MS. DELORES: She lookin' alil' heat-stroked.

MS. ODESSA: You gon' be awright, Ruth?

MS. RUTH: *(Looks ladies over.)* You dressed fine but . . .

MS. ODESSA: She awight.

MS. RUTH: All those bags.

MS. ODESSA: All wha' bags?

MS. RUTH: Wha's all those bags fo'?

MS. ODESSA: All wha' bags?

MS. RUTH: They gon' thank we in 'ere tryin' to shop-lift wit' all them bags you all's carryin'.

MS. DELORES: Ain't nothin' in 'em but our dirty, ole work smocks an' some extra sewin' crap off the job.

MS. RUTH: Nevertheless . . .

MS. DELORES: Don' nothin' in here look like nothin' they got in there.

MS. RUTH: Nevertheless, they gon' be watchin' us.

MS. ODESSA: Let 'em. Hell, they do tha' anyway.

MS. RUTH: I didn' even wanna bring this pocketbook. Brought the smallest one I could find. I made a point a' comin' as free-handed as possible. You see? Comin' in peace.

MS. ODESSA: Oh, Lorrrr . . . *(Sits on bench.)*

MS. RUTH: I thought chu'da caught on to tha'.

MS. DELORES: *(Opens bag.)* They jus' work uniforms, Ruth. Now, you know we wann't goin' in 'ere in our work stuff. You n' me did talk about wha' e'rybody was gon' wear today, didn' we? *(Takes smock out.)* An' you see they got our names on 'em now, don' they? So, how anybody gon' say we stealin' anythang? *(Puts smock back in bag.)*

MS. RUTH: I don' know. They'll find a way.

MS. ODESSA: *(Stands.)* Les' go now, Ruth.

MS. RUTH: Well . . . I been thankin' . . .

MS. ODESSA: Hey, it's too hot fo' this. If you had some thankin' ta do, you shoulda dun' thunk on it befo' you got 'ere. Don' say you didn' have time.

MS. RUTH: Wha' if they don' let us in is wha' I been thankin'. S'pose they got a quota?

MS. ODESSA: A wha'?

MS. DELORES: A quota?

MS. RUTH: S'pose they let in five or six fo' the day, fo' instance.

MS. DELORES: I know wha' a quota is.

MS. RUTH: An' they tell the rest to go 'way somewhere or worse.

MS. DELORES: No.

MS. ODESSA: Wha' chu' mean is wha' if they jus' let me, Louise n' Dee in an' tell you to go 'way somewhere or worse. She worried it might git physical.

MS. DELORES: It's not gon' work like tha'.

MS. RUTH: Well, how you know how it's gon' work? You never been inte-
grated befoe'.

MS. ODESSA: You seen some trouble today, Ruth?

MS. RUTH: It's gon' work the way they tell it to work, I guarantee you tha'.

MS. ODESSA: You seen some trouble?

MS. RUTH: No, Odessa, it's been pretty quiet so far.

MS. DELORES: How long you been sittin' 'ere?

MS. RUTH: Wha' difference does it make?

MS. ODESSA: You dun' stood out 'ere long enuff . . .

MS. RUTH: Not long.

MS. ODESSA: To git cho' stomach all rolled up in knots.

MS. DELORES: They gon' let us in, Ruth. You hear me?

MS. ODESSA: They tho' us out, it's 'cause you dun' tho'ed up on e'rythang.

MS. DELORES: Don' worry, okay? Law say they got to let us all in now.

MS. RUTH: Honey, you n' me both know we not talkin' tha' kinda law.

MS. DELORES: No quota, no loopholes.

(Odessa sits again on bench; fans herself and hums.)

MS. RUTH: We not necessarily talkin' 'bout wha's s'posed to be legal.

MS. DELORES: Then, we'll sue 'em.

MS. RUTH: Sue who?

MS. DELORES: Sue Mr. Marsh.

MS. ODESSA: Tha's right.

MS. RUTH: Excuse me? Wha' Twilight Zone episode this s'posed to be from,
Dee?

MS. DELORES: We can do tha' they don' treat us right. Cain't we, Dessa?

MS. ODESSA: Sho' can.

MS. DELORES: 'Cause Justice William O. Douglas of the Supreme Court
declared, Negroes are as much a part of the public as are white and . . .

MS. RUTH: Marsh's is prob'ly a big comp'ny a' folk.

MS. DELORES: Well, I don' know all they names. We'll jus' sue the place,
tha's all. It's been done befoe'.

MS. RUTH: When n' where, Dee?

MS. DELORES: Somewhere I know.

MS. ODESSA: Leave 'er alone, Dee.

MS. RUTH: Sue a whole, big comp'ny a' rich, white folk, huh?

MS. DELORES: Uh-huh.

MS. RUTH: Tell me about the last time foe, poe Colored women sued a rich,
white comp'ny n' won. They prob'ly got a whole ball park full a' ole-time,
crook lawyers. The kind that'll crush ya under they boots n' won' even

stop to clean off the carcus. Uh-uh, I'm Reverend Waldon's wife. I cannot be involved in anything like tha'.

MS. DELORES: Why not? Doctor King's a minister an' his wife does 'er duty. Coretta marches right 'long side of 'im.

MS. ODESSA: An' so wha', Ruth?

MS. DELORES: Both of 'em leadin'.

MS. ODESSA: Coretta don' know how ta act? Tha's wha' all you tryin' to say?

MS. RUTH: I'm not Coretta.

MS. ODESSA: Dawggone right she not.

MS. DELORES: Then, I don' know who you are. What hap'ned to you?

MS. ODESSA: I'm 'bout to burn up. Tha's who I am.

MS. DELORES: We all know it's hot, dammit! You jus' makin' it hotter.

MS. ODESSA: Me? She the one got cho' pressure up, girl.

MS. RUTH: I'd appreciate you stop talkin' at me like I'm not here, Ms. Odessa.

MS. ODESSA: I thought chu' wished you wann't 'ere, or is my hearin' off?

MS. DELORES: I thought chu' was goin' to the Tastey Freeze.

MS. ODESSA: Soon as I find me some change . . . *(Opens purse.)* Is you got some?

MS. DELORES: You know we ain't been to the bank yet. Got jus' enuff fo' this.

MS. RUTH: An' we don't even know how much this is gon' cost fo' sure. Might jack the prices up two, three hunnert percent on us while we sittin' 'ere.

MS. ODESSA: They can jack it up a thousand, two-hunnert percent. So wha'? They say fifty dollars fo' foe' cups a' dirty dishwater an' a loaf a' penicillin an' we s'posed to jus' hand it over? No.

MS. DELORES: They cain't do tha'.

MS. ODESSA: We wastin' our time n' breath.

MS. RUTH: They can do wha' they wanna and will do wha' they wanna. They been in tha' bi'niss fo' a very, very long time, I'm afraid.

MS. ODESSA: Now, tha's the bottom line tho', ain't it? You not jus' worried, you downright scared. I need me somethin' to drank, Dee.

MS. DELORES: Wha' I look like? A soda fountain? If you ain't got no spare money then, why you keep cryin' 'bout Tastey Freeze, Tastey Freeze?

MS. ODESSA: So, why you jumpin' on me, all of a sudden?

MS. DELORES: I told you I don' have no money.

MS. ODESSA: You n' Louise both. All a' y'all tryin' me, in fact.

MS. DELORES: 'Cause you talkin' mo' trash today tha's why.

MS. ODESSA: Wha' trash? She the one. Yo' friend. *(Points to Ruth.)*

MS. DELORES: I ain't never heard mo' stuff come outta yo' face.

MS. ODESSA: I can say the same fo' you n' feel awright about it.

MS. DELORES: Shut up talkin' to me while I'm tryin' to thank. Please.

MS. ODESSA: Look how you got Dee's bloomers all bunched up, Ruth. Po' girl's 'bout to cry.

MS. DELORES: I'm not cryin'.

MS. ODESSA: Now she too nervous to function. You satisfied?

MS. RUTH: Talkin' 'bout suin'.

MS. DELORES: Ruth, Louise gon' be back soon. Wha' chu' gon' do?

MS. ODESSA: Yeah, wha'? 'Cause I'm not gon' stand out 'ere turnin' navy blue fo' you.

MS. RUTH: Wha' if they don't let us in?

MS. ODESSA: Listen fo' the last time. Can you do tha'?

MS. RUTH: I hear y'all loud n' clear.

MS. ODESSA: They gon' at least let us in this lobby fo' we melt.

MS. RUTH: Wha' they care 'bout us meltin'? They care less about tha'. Goin' in the lobby an' shoppin' in 'ere never has been the issue. They'd let a stray cat in they lobby long as he got spendin' money in his paws.

MS. DELORES: It ain't just' about wha' they wanna do no mo'. Tha's wha' we sayin' to ya.

MS. RUTH: But innit', though?

MS. DELORES: I truly thought chu' unnerstood wha' we wannit' to do today, Ruth.

MS. RUTH: I do understand.

MS. DELORES: I really did.

MS. RUTH: Do *you*? Jus' 'cause the Supreme Court say it's okay don' mean a thang. They can still spit in our food. They can put rat poison innit', cain't they?

MS. ODESSA: So's we can tell the papers n' whoever else we ate at Marsh's n' got rat-poisoned.

MS. RUTH: Presumin' we survived it.

MS. DELORES: Tha'd be 'way bad fo' they bi'niss.

MS. ODESSA: It sho' would. See, Dee? Yo' friend dun' had half the day to whip 'erself up to this frenzy.

MS. RUTH: E'rybody'll know they don' poison people; jus' us.
(Louise returns.)

MS. ODESSA: She scared of alil' rat-poisonin'.

MS. LOUISE: Who?

MS. ODESSA: Wha' took you so long?

MS. LOUISE: Who got rat-poisoned?

MS. ODESSA: Say it's quiet in 'ere, Lou?

MS. LOUISE: Who got rat-poisoned?

MS. DELORES: Nobody.

MS. LOUISE: Yeah, it's quiet. They kept a good eye on me, tho'. Some lil, bitty cock-eyed woman in a pair a' too-tight pumps kept tippin' roun' askin', "Can I help you?" Tryin' to be nice, I thank. Lookt like she was 'bout to cry. Kept shiftin' from one foot to the other. Standin' on one leg like tha' bird. I thought she was jus' as nervous as I was 'til I finally lookt down myself. Chile's corns lookt like they was tryin' to sprout grapefruits in them too-tight shoes. But they watched me leave, though. 'Bout the whole stoe' did. They made sho' I came on outta there.

MS. ODESSA: Anybody in the restaurant at all?

MS.LOUISE: Looks like we gon' be the first today.

(Ladies freeze at the thought.)

MS. ODESSA: You got a quarter, Lou? I want me a Tastey Freeze somethin' ter'ible.

MS. LOUISE: They got dranks in Marsh's.

MS. ODESSA: If I'm 'bout ta be rat-poisoned in Marsh's, I'd rather have somethin' cool on my stomach first.

MS. DELORES: Maybe we should jus' go on n' do the bank, then, All the time we spent out 'ere we coulda gone to the bank five times. Maybe we shoulda jus' dun' tha' first.

MS. LOUISE: Wha' ch'all been talkin' 'bout?

MS. DELORES: Why don' chu' go on home, Ruth, foe' you spoil it.

MS. ODESSA: Yeah, go on home.

MS. LOUISE: Ain't nobody goin' home. Wha's wrong wit' ch'all?

MS. RUTH: They still don't want chu' in 'ere . . .

MS. DELORES: I know tha' 'cause, if they did . . .

MS. RUTH: Whether I'm with you or not.

MS. DELORES: If they did, we wouldn' be out 'ere goin' thu' this bakin' like foe' potatoes.

MS. ODESSA: Ain't tha' the truth. *(Points to Ruth.)* This girl is terrified. Look at 'er, y'all. Shakin' in 'er shoes.

MS. RUTH: Stuff is still hap'nin'. It hasn't stopped.

MS. DELORES: Stuff was still hap'nin' last night when you said you'd meet us too.

(Louise hands Odessa some change.)

MS. ODESSA: *(To Louise.)* Thank you. *(To Delores.)* Thank you. You want somethin', Lou?

MS. LOUISE: I mo' git' mine in 'ere.

MS. DELORES: Wha's ya' holdup, then? Go on n' do it, Ruthie. Go on home. You git' this next bus tha's comin'. I'm sorry I even called you.

MS. RUTH: An' somethin' else too. Wha' if they give us some, ole, crazy, white folk's germs in our water, in our dranks? Germ warfare. Somethin' we could take home to give to our fam'lies like TB; contagious TB. Spread it all aroun' the neighborhoods.

MS. LOUISE: Wha' kinda sense do tha' make, Sistah Waldon?

MS. RUTH: Plenty sense. My great uncle Kidd n' his fam'ly all caught contagious TB when I was a lil' girl. Him, his wife n' all six of their chirrun. Whenever they'd come visit cha', mama said e'rythang they used had to be steamed, sterilized an' otherwise tho'ed away. They finally died; all of 'em. All skinny an' diseased from contagious TB. Don' ask me why they wanted ta be visitin' people, loved ones, spreadin' killer germs 'cause I do not know but, I didn' git' it then an' I don' want it now. I do not.

MS. ODESSA: Dee, don' most a' the people we know do work in white folks homes, in they kitchens, aroun' they food? Huh? Don' they? They give us somethin', we give it right back to 'em n' they unnerstan' tha'. They ain't stone fools now.

MS. RUTH: They are gon' feed us offa dirty dishes too, you know. They ain't gon' hardly serve us on the same silverware as they do the white customers.

MS. DELORES: If it's dirty, we'll send it back.

MS. RUTH: Bet' not do tha' too many times, tho'.

MS. DELORES: Then, we don' pay, Ruth. We jus' won' pay.

MS. RUTH: Don' pay? Won' pay? They could bring the rat 'imself out on a platter. You thank them white folks gon' let us walk outta there wit'out payin'? After we had the nerve to put our body heat on they precious seats? I don' care wha' chu' eat nor how many times you send it back. Y'all better look out in 'ere. This law stuff is still new.

MS. DELORES: Listen 'ere, you embarrassin' me. The Supreme Court says we are within our rights.

MS. RUTH: The Supreme Court?

MS. DELORES: The Supreme Court says . . .

MS. RUTH: You jus' cain't stop believin' like a child huh, Dee? Jus' cain't let it go. You talk about it like you got a personal relationship with them people. The Supreme Court don' luv you. Don' even know yo' name, girl. Don' chu' git' it yet? It might not be blunt on a piece a' paper, *Kill The Nigga* per se but, it's still on people's hearts n' in they minds. An' deep down, we all know tha'. You cain't put a gun to a dawg's head an' make 'im stop eatin' jus' 'cause you say, hold it, nor make 'im follow you jus' by tuggin' at his leech an' sayin' Come on, dawgie, come on.

MS. DELORES: Oh, I wouldn't let nothin' happen to ya, Ruth. Look y'all, I'll eat first. I'll eat first, okay? Okay? I don' have chirrun dependin' on me, an' some man waitin' somewhere so, I wouln't be missed the way y'all would. I can git' sick. I can go to jail. You all got peoples, see? But, I'm alone an' I can do this wit' out puttin' loved ones livelihoods in jeopardy. No ole folks, no mama n' daddy to look after. I ain't got nobody but myself. Nobody gon' miss me. They can poison me, awright? Ssshhoottt, they poison me, I'll jus' fall right over, sittin' right there on tha' chair, at tha' table, or wha'ever they got, an be glad ta go so's y'all can bring the newspapers, n' cameras right on in 'ere to take pictures a' me droolin' at the mouth. An I'm mo' drool too. I don' mind. So, I mean, I'm mo' put on the Delores Bradley Show, y'all. E'rybody gon' thank I got rabies if I live.

MS. RUTH: You talk a great game, Dee honey. *(She finally realizes the weight of the situation.)* Les' jus' hope it doesn't come down to tha' kinda personal sacrifice.

MS. ODESSA: I tell y'all wha's clear as crystal. It's clear you ain't 'bout ta go in 'ere wit' us. We all see you shakin' in yo' shoes. So, don' chu' worry 'bout it no mo', Lil' Ruthie. We big girls know wha' we doin'. I'm mo' git' me a big drank befo' I go in 'cause I wanna be calm, cool an' collected when they come at me.

MS. DELORES: Remember how we talked, Ruthie-girl? You was right in 'ere wit' it, wann't ya? Jus' as gung-ho.

MS. RUTH: Look, I didn' show up 'ere to be nobody's drum major.

MS. DELORES: Jus' go on home.

MS. ODESSA: Yeah, git'.

MS. RUTH: You thank tha' the world has opened up it's doors to you jus' 'cause you imagine some men in robes dun' patted chu' on the head n' said, "Go on, baby, get chu' somethin' ta' eat. Anywhere you want to. Sit where you want. Go buy wha' chu' want wherever it is you want it from." I didn' spoil nothin' fo' you, did I? If y'all so brave, you got all this umph worked up so's you can go in 'ere n' start chewin' this whole community a new behind then, go ahead, sistahs. Go right ahead. Please don' let me stop none of ya'. We tell our congregation to right back . . .

MS. ODESSA: You ain't no Rev'rend Waldon, woman. You jus' a' ole wife.

MS. RUTH: But, If you cain't . . .

MS. ODESSA: *You* ain't got no congregation.

MS. RUTH: If you not all as big, an' as sassy as you thought you was, then don' blame me. If you came down 'ere believin' so hard in the good, white decision of the good white gentlemen of the Supreme Court but, now you scared off by a few, lil' ole wha'-ifs, then do not fix yo' face, to screw yo' mouth, to open up yo' lungs, to blow one breath out behind a word to blame me.

MS. LOUISE: Who's blamin' you, Ruth?

MS. RUTH: I won' let chu' blame me.

MS. LOUISE: Why would anybody try to blame you? See? This is wha' happens when folks git' scared n' confused, tha's all. You git' unfocused, n' turn on each other which is jus' wha' they want. Now, we jus' need to git' back organized right, Dee?

MS. DELORES: Right. Right.

MS. LOUISE: Tha's right; organized. Organization.

MS. RUTH: Odessa, honey.

MS. LOUISE: Now, ain't nothin' gon' be fancy 'bout this meal, Ruth.

MS. ODESSA: I ain't cho' honey.

MS. RUTH: Ms. Lady wha' swears she got 'er finger on e'rybody's pulse, got e'rybody's number . . .

MS. ODESSA: I know I got cho's.

MS. RUTH: Ummm-hmmm, if you wanna drank so bad, darlin' . . .

MS. ODESSA: An' I ain't cho' darlin', darlin.

MS. RUTH: Forget tha' Tastey Freeze, why don' cha'? Go on in Marsh's n' get cha' one. Afterall, tha's where you was bound fo' wannit?

MS. ODESSA: You thank I'm scared to?

MS. RUTH: Limme' see ya' do it, then.

MS. LOUISE: Stop this. Y'all ain't no kids.

MS. DELORES: Y'all gon' git' us in trouble fo' real. I got too much goin' today.

MS. RUTH: I'm not gon' argue wit' chu' out 'ere like a common street woman.

MS. ODESSA: Tha' used ta be yo' turf.

MS. LOUISE: Ain't nothin' to argue about.

MS. RUTH: I have a good reputation to uphold.

MS. ODESSA: A good reputation? I know 'bout chu', Miss Eighty-One Club.

MS. RUTH: What?

MS. ODESSA: Goin' wit' married men at age fifteen, tha's you. You got lucky, got cleaned up alil' n' now you s'posed to be somebody to e'rybody but still a dish rag to me. Had spunk back then, tho'. Wha' did hap'n to you? Wha' was it? Religion? Yeah. Religion dun' tore you up. Ain't even got half a' wha' chu' used ta have do ya? Pretty lil' yella gal wit' all tha' slan-gin' hair in men's faces. Them fallin' at cho' feet.

MS. RUTH: My reputation is in the church.

MS. ODESSA: In the church, under the pew . . .

MS. DELORES: Awright! Awright!

MS. ODESSA: Remember A Chollie Elwood Brown? Huh, pretty Ruthie?

MS. RUTH: No.

MS. ODESSA: A pretty, dark-chocolate man. Big as a bear but gentle . . .

MS. RUTH: I said, no.

MS. ODESSA: An' sweet he was. Right off a' Alabama farm an married . . . to me.

MS. RUTH: *(Covers ears.)* I don' hear you. I don' hear you.

MS. ODESSA: Nawh, you wouldn' remember 'cause he was jus' one a' yo' many. She was a tramp, Louise. Dee, yo' buddy, yo' good pastor's wife. She'd take a man, baby right outta it's mama's arms if she wanted it. You used to could pull some low-down, dirty stunts n' let the bullet shoot where it might. I'mma witness.

MS. DELORES: Odessa, tha' was a million years ago. A whole other life. Ruth is my friend, an' w're not talkin' 'bout tha' anymo'.

MS. RUTH: Wait a minute, Dee. No need fo' you n' Louise to git' this sec-ond-hand. No, I didn't write the book, but I put a few chapters in 'ere; yeah. Any son-of-a-seacook tha' looked at me n' didn' see heaven was deaf, dumb n' blind, but tha' didn' even matter 'cause if he had somethin' in his pocket, it was mine if I wannit it. I didn' give a cryin' dime if he was a Chollie who, Chollie wha, Chollie when, where n' how. Didn' make me no dif'rence whether he was fresh off a farm, jus' stepped outta Al-abama, or jus' stepped off the top a' yo' weddin' cake. Married to you? He coulda been married to my mama. But chu' cain't keep doin' certain kinds a' thangs wit'out 'em comin' back on you through people you love, an' mean-spirited types who like to keep stuff goin' so, I stopped. An' I found God through my husband an' my chirrun. I am grateful to the Lawd fo' bringin' peace to my soul by puttin' me in the path of someone tha' finally saw me fo' me an' found tha' worthy enough. I drop to me knees e'ry night an' praise his holy name fo' the health n' strength of my babies who don' see me as nothin' but love no matter wha' I was, an' I say thank you over n' over fo' a bountiful life in Christ Jesus. But the next time a big, corn-fed, barefoot, cow-milkin' cow-breedin' heffa talks ta me any kind a' way, she ain't gon' need a Tastety Freeze 'cause you ain't fixin' to make history. You gon' *be* history right now!

MS. ODESSA: Now, tha's the heffa I know!

MS. RUTH: Fo' God git' the news! Damn straight!

MS. DELORES: Stop all this yellin!

MS. RUTH: Look-ere, my chirrun, my husband n' I are pillars in the community.

MS. ODESSA: Pillars!?

MS. RUTH: Tha' means we are leaders.

MS. ODESSA: Well, lead some people.

MS. RUTH: When was the last protest march you were on, Odessa?

MS. ODESSA: When was the last time you did somethin' wit' out' yo' husband tellin' you exactly wha' to do? Tha's it, innit? Y'all s'posed to be leaders but ch'all make 'em too scared to move. Tha's wha' chu' do. Tha's wha' chu' do best. Too scared to take a step. You dun' pratic'ly reduced this chile to nothin'. Hell, people like you cain't even step fo'ward they own selves 'til a white man come along an' tell you wha' side yo' bread buttered on. Here we is. We people. Me, Louise n' Dee. We live in the community. We b'lieve in the Lawd. So take us by the hands, you so proud; yo' rep is all tha'. Lead us!

MS. DELORES: *(Gathers herself.)* Wha' we gettin' ready to do, then . . .

MS. ODESSA: You ain't supposed to be scared. . .

MS. DELORES: Huh? Wha' ch'all wanna do? Leave? *(Downstage.)* Tell me now 'cause my bus is comin'.

MS. LOUISE: Ain't nobody leavin', Dee. Dee, ain't nobody goin' nowhere. *(Louise takes her arm.)* Come on, come on back.

MS. DELORES: *(Shakes head.)* Ah-ah, Louise. This too much loudness, fo' me . . .

MS. LOUISE: Come on, y'all. Come on.

MS. DELORES: They gon' come out 'ere an' git' us wit' all this noise.

MS. LOUISE: Stop this!

MS. DELORES: I cain't be bothered with these people! I gotta hit tha' bank foe' it close. I got ta' buy groceries fo' next week . . .

MS. LOUISE: Come on now, Dee! Please don' go!

MS. DELORES: Ah-ah, Louise, let me go! My bus is comin'! My bus is comin'! *(Sound of bus passing.)* *(Delores collapses on bench.)*

MS. RUTH: I want to be a Coretta or one a' those other brave women marchin' arm n' arm with their men into the shadow a' death simply because it is right.

MS. ODESSA: Then, you better stand up to it.

MS. RUTH: You askin' me to put my home, my future an' my reputation on the line.

MS. ODESSA: If you cain't do it then all you'll ever have is a reputation.

MS. RUTH: You want me to defy my husband, my family, and my faith over here, to look in the faces a' those who'd wanna cut me up over there.

MS. ODESSA: If you cain't do this then you won't be worth the spit offa the lip of the lowest cracker . . .

MS. RUTH: I don' know how to do it.

MS. ODESSA: In the lowest kitchens a' Marsh's or any other stoe'.

MS. RUTH: Wha' will my chirrun do if I'm in jail or worse?

MS. ODESSA: Ruth!

MS. RUTH: The Lord hates a coward. I am afraid and so ashamed.

MS. ODESSA: If you wanna lead somebody, lead somebody.

MS. LOUISE: My oldest daughter, Doom, the one go to Morris Brown, she say, when the kids come back to school from boycottin', or bein' in somewhere, they have food all over theyselves, bruises all over 'em, clothes torn off 'em, spit on 'em. An' she say, they come back to school like tha' on purpose, an' sit in class all day jus' to let e'rybody know where they been an' wha's goin' on. My girl is smart, Ruth. My girl's in college but, wha' fo' when they still say she cain't count change? An' my son, he my middle chile. He caught the pneumonia when he was three years old goin' up all them back steps to the Fox Theatre 'cause he wanna see a movie, *Song of the South*. I took 'im wit' all them dancin' n' singin' slaves in it. He was jus' a baby. He didn' know. But, my baby boy almost froze goin' up n' down them back steps to n' from the Colored Section, seem near 'bout five or six stories up, instead a ' jus' in the front doe' like all the other chirrun, jus' 'cause he wannit to see a movie. We all scared, Ruthie. We all goin' against e'rythang we ever been taught. Scared but, we goin' in 'ere. Okay? To say, "No More." We gon' be dif'rent when we come out too. Life gon' look dif'rent to us, if we make it so. Life n' God. You'll see. An' one day, won' nobody care. Won' even remember. This'll be ole news. Ole hat. But, fo' today, now, it's about wha' we were an' wha' we will become. Wha' our grand chirrun will be. So, we goin'. An' we gon' order our salad. An' we gon' eat our fish sticks. Hear me? We goin'. *(To ladies.)* We are goin'. For our babies. The ones we got an' the ones we gon' have.

MS. ODESSA: I come out from work las' Friday. 'Bout the last one to leave. My son lookin' half scared to death. My daughter cryin' hysterical when

I got to 'em. My car all scratched up. Dawg marks on both sides. Ruth,
they sicked the dawgs on my chirrun.

(Ruth looks upward.)

MS. RUTH: The Lawd is my shepherd, I shall not want.

He maketh me to lie down in green pastures:

(Delores gathers her bags; joins in.)

MS. RUTH/MS. DELORES: He leadeth me beside the still waters.

He restoreth my soul:

(Louise gathers her bags; joins in.)

MS. RUTH/MS. DELORES/MS. LOUISE:

He leadeth me in the path of righteousness for his namesake.

Yea, though I walk through the valley of the shadow of death,

(Odessa gathers her bags; joins in.)

ALL LADIES:

I will fear no evil:

Fo' thou art with me;

Thy rod n' thy staff

They comfort me.

Thou preparest the table befo' me

In the pre sense of mine enemies:

Thou anointeth my head with oil;

My cup runneth over.

Surely, goodness an' mercy shall follow me

All the days of my life:

And I will dwell in the house of the Lawd forever.

(Stand facing Marsh's, holding hands.)

(Spotlight on Palmeroy looking at the first page of newspaper.)

(Spotlight on Ms. Grayson stage left standing; also looking at newspaper.)

PALMEROY: Lawd, ladies. Hot dawg.

MS. GRAYSON: *Hot Dawg!*

LADIES: A-man.

(Move toward store together.)

(Lights dim.)

(Blackout.)

END OF PLAY

GLOSSARY

a' – of
ain't – isn't
an' – and
awright – all right
befo' – before
bes' – best
bet' – better
bi'niss – business
cain't – can't
ch'all – y'all/you all
cho'self – yourself
chu' – you
doe' – door
don' – don't
dun' – have
enuff – enough
'ere – here
e'rybody – everybody
e'ry time – every time
fo' – for
foe' – before/four
forgimme – forgive me
git' – get
gon' – going to
gon'ta' – going to
hunnert – hundred
'imself – himself
I'm mo' – I'm going to
inn't – isn't
jus' – just

Lawd – Lord
lil' – little
limme – let me
ma' – my
mo' – more
mus' – must
n' – and
nawh – no
nothin' – nothing
otha' – other
'roun – around
's – is – it's
sho' – sure
'sta – to
'ta – to
tha' – that
thang – thing
thankin' – thinking
tho'd – throwed
thu' – through
tole' – told
wannit – wanted
wann't – wasn't
wha' – what
wha's – what's
wit' – with
wo'th – worth
ya – you
yo' – your